THE LITERATURE MACHINE

Italo Calvino was born in Cuba in 1923, and grew up in Italy. He was an essayist and journalist and a member of the editorial staff of Einaudi in Turin. His books include *Marcovaldo*, *Invisible Cities*, *The Castle of Crossed Destinies*, *If on a winter's night a traveller* and *Mr Palomar*. In 1973 he won the prestigious Premio Feltrinelli. He died in 1985.

BY ITALO CALVINO

The Path to the Nest of Spiders
Adam, One Afternoon
Our Ancestors
Difficult Loves
Marcovaldo
Cosmicomics
t zero
The Watcher and Other Stories
Italian Folktales
Invisible Cities
The Castle of Crossed Destinies
If on a winter's night a traveller
Mr Palomar
The Literature Machine
Six Memos for the Next Millennium
Under the Jaguar Sun
The Road to San Giovanni
Numbers in the Dark

Italo Calvino

THE LITERATURE MACHINE

Essays

TRANSLATED FROM THE ITALIAN BY
Patrick Creagh

VINTAGE

Published by Vintage 1997

1 3 5 7 9 10 8 6 4 2

First published in Great Britain
by Secker & Warburg Ltd, 1987

Vintage
Random House, 20 Vauxhall Bridge Road,
London SW1V 2SA

Random House Australia (Pty) Limited
20 Alfred Street, Milsons Point, Sydney,
New South Wales 2061, Australia

Random House New Zealand Limited
18 Poland Road, Glenfield,
Auckland 10, New Zealand

Random House (Pty) Limited
Endulini, 5A Jubilee Road, Parktown 2193,
South Africa

The Random House Group Limited Reg. No. 954009
www.randomhouse.co.uk

A CIP catalogue record for this book
is available from the British Library

ISBN 0 09 943085 1

Papers used by Random House are natural, recyclable
products made from wood grown in sustainable forests.
The manufacturing processes conform to the environ-
mental regulations of the country of origin.

Printed and bound in Great Britain by
Cox & Wyman Ltd, Reading, Berkshire

Contents

I

Cybernetics and Ghosts   3

Two Interviews on Science and Literature   28

Philosophy and Literature   39

Literature as Projection of Desire   50

Definitions of Territories: Comedy   62

Definitions of Territories: Eroticism   65

Definitions of Territories: Fantasy   71

Cinema and the Novel: Problems of Narrative   74

Whom Do We Write For? or
      The Hypothetical Bookshelf   81

Right and Wrong Political Uses of Literature   89

Levels of Reality in Literature   101

2

Why Read the Classics? 125

The Odysseys Within the Odyssey 135

Ovid and Universal Contiguity 146

The Structure of *Orlando Furioso* 162

Candide: An Essay in Velocity 175

The City as Protagonist in Balzac 182

The Novel as Spectacle 190

Manzoni's *The Betrothed*:
    The Novel of Ratios of Power 196

On Fourier, I: Brief Introduction to
    the Society of Love 213

On Fourier, II: The Controller of Desires 219

On Fourier, III: Envoi: A Utopia of Fine Dust 245

Guide to *The Charterhouse of Parma*
    for the Use of New Readers 256

Stendhal's Knowledge of the "Milky Way" 266

Montale's Rock 284

The Pen in the First Person 291

In Memory of Roland Barthes 300

The Bestiary of Marianne Moore 307

Man, the Sky, and the Elephant 315

Cyrano on the Moon 331

By Way of an Autobiography 339

I

Cybernetics and Ghosts

Lecture delivered in Turin and other Italian cities, November 1967.

I

It all began with the first storyteller of the tribe. Men were already exchanging articulate sounds, referring to the practical needs of their daily lives. Dialogue was already in existence, and so were the rules that it was forced to follow. This was the life of the tribe, a very complex set of rules on which every action and every situation had to be based. The number of words was limited, and, faced with the multiform world and its countless things, men defended themselves by inventing a finite number of sounds combined in various ways. Modes of behavior, customs, and gestures too were what they were and none other, constantly re-

3

peated while harvesting coconuts or scavenging for wild roots, while hunting lions or buffalo, marrying in order to create new bonds of relationship outside the clan, or at the first moments of life, or at death. And the more limited were the choices of phrase or behavior, the more complex the rules of language or custom were forced to become in order to master an ever-increasing variety of situations. The extreme poverty of ideas about the world then available to man was matched by a detailed, all-embracing code of rules.

The storyteller began to put forth words, not because he thought others might reply with other, predictable words, but to test the extent to which words could fit with one another, could give birth to one another, in order to extract an explanation of the world from the thread of every possible spoken narrative, and from the arabesque that nouns and verbs, subjects and predicates performed as they unfolded from one another. The figures available to the storyteller were very few: the jaguar, the coyote, the toucan, the piranha; or else father and son, brother-in-law and uncle, wife and mother and sister and mother-in-law. The actions these figures could perform were likewise rather limited: they could be born, die, copulate, sleep, fish, hunt, climb trees, dig burrows, eat and defecate, smoke vegetable fibers, make prohibitions, transgress them, steal or give away fruit or other things—things that were also classified in a limited catalogue. The storyteller explored the possibilities implied in his own language by combining and changing the permutations of the figures and the actions, and of the objects on which these actions could be brought to bear. What emerged were stories, straightforward constructions that always contained correspondences or contraries—the sky and the earth, fire and water, animals that flew and those that dug burrows—and each term had its array of attributes and a repertoire of its own. The telling of stories allowed certain relationships among the various elements and not others, and things could happen in a certain order and not in others: prohibition had to come before transgression, punishment after transgression, the gift of magic objects before the trial of courage. The immobile world that surrounded tribal man, strewn with signs of the fleeting correspondences between words and things, came to life in the voice of the storyteller, spun out into the flow of a spoken narrative within which each word acquired new values and transmitted them to the ideas and images they defined. Every animal, every object, every relationship took on beneficial or malign powers that came to be called magical powers but should, rather, have been called narrative powers, potentialities contained in the word, in its ability to link itself to other words on the plane of discourse.

Primitive oral narrative, like the folk tale that has been handed down almost to the present day, is modeled on fixed structures, on, we might almost say, prefabricated elements—elements, however, that allow of an enormous number of combinations. Vladimir Propp, in the course of his studies of Russian folk tales, came to the conclusion that all such tales were like variants of a single tale, and could be broken down into a limited number of narrative functions. Forty years later Claude Lévi-Strauss, working on the myths of the Indians of Brazil, saw these as a system of logical operations between permutable terms, so that they could be studied according to the mathematical processes of combinatorial analysis.

Even if the folk imagination is therefore not boundless like the ocean, there is no reason to think of it as being like a water tank of small capacity. On an equal level of civilization, the operations of narrative, like those of mathematics, cannot differ all that much from one people to another, but what can be constructed on the basis of these elementary processes can present unlimited combinations, permutations, and transformations.

Is this true only of oral narrative traditions? Or can it be maintained of literature in all its variety of forms and complexities? As early as the 1920s, the Russian Formalists began to make modern stories and novels the object of their analysis, breaking down their complex structures into functional segments. In France today the semiological school of Roland Barthes, having sharpened its knives on the structures of advertising or of women's fashion magazines, is at last turning its attention to literature; the eighth issue of the magazine *Communications* was devoted to the structural analysis of the short story. Naturally enough, the material that lends itself best to this kind of treatment is still to be found in the various forms of popular fiction. If the Russians studied the Sherlock Holmes stories, today it is James Bond who provides the structuralists with their most apt exemplars.

But this is merely the first step in the grammar and syntax of narrative fiction. The combinatorial play of narrative possibilities soon passes beyond the level of content to touch upon the relationship of the narrator to the material related and to the reader: and this brings us to the toughest set of problems facing contemporary fiction. It is no coincidence that the researches of the French structuralists go hand in hand (and sometimes coexist in the same person) with the creative work of the "Tel Quel" group. For the latter—and here I am paraphrasing statements by one of their authorized interpreters—writing consists no longer in narrating but in saying that one is narrating, and what one says becomes identified with the very act of saying. The psychological person is replaced by a linguistic or even a grammatical person, defined solely by his place in the discourse. These formal repercussions of a literature at the second or third degree, such as occurred in France with the *nouveau roman* of ten years ago, for which another of its exponents suggested the word "scripturalism," can be traced back to combinations of a certain number of logico-linguistic (or better, syntactical-rhetorical) operations, in such a way as to be reducible to formulas that are the more general as they become less complex.

I will not go into technical details on which I could only be an unauthorized and rather unreliable commentator. My intention here is merely to sum up the situation, to make connections between a number of books I have recently read, and to put these in the context of a few general reflections. In the particular way today's culture looks at the world, one tendency is emerging from several directions at once. The world in its various aspects is increasingly looked upon as *discrete* rather than *continuous*. I am using the term "discrete" in the sense it bears in mathematics, a discrete quantity being one made up of separate parts. Thought, which until the other day appeared to us as something fluid, evoking linear images such as a flowing river or an unwinding thread, or else gaseous images such as a kind of vaporous cloud—to the point where it was sometimes called "spirit" (in the sense of "breath")—we now tend to think of as a series of discontinuous states, of combinations of impulses acting on a finite (though enormous) number of sensory and motor organs. Electronic brains, even if they are still far from producing all the functions of the human brain, are nonetheless capable of providing us with a convincing theoretical model for the most complex processes of our memory, our mental associations, our imagination, our conscience. Shannon, Weiner, von Neumann, and Turing have radically altered our image of our mental processes. In the place of the ever-changing cloud that we carried in our heads until the other day, the condensing and dispersal of which we attempted to understand by describing impalpable psychological states and shadowy landscapes of the soul— in the place of all this we now feel the rapid passage of signals on the intricate circuits that connect the relays, the diodes, the transistors with which our skulls are crammed. Just as no chess player will ever live long enough to exhaust all the combinations of possible moves for the thirty-two pieces on the chessboard, so we know (given the fact that our minds are chessboards with hundreds of billions of pieces) that not even in a lifetime lasting as long as the universe would one ever manage to make all possible plays. But we also know that all these are implicit in the overall code of mental plays, according to the rules by which each of us, from one moment to the next, formulates his thoughts, swift or sluggish, cloudy or crystalline as they may be.

I might also say that what is finite and numerically calculable is superseding the indeterminateness of ideas that cannot be subjected to measurement and delimitation; but this formulation runs the risk of giving an oversimplified notion of how things stand. In fact, the very opposite is true: every analytical process, every division into parts, tends to provide an image of the world that is ever more complicated, just as Zeno of Elea, by refusing to accept space as continuous, ended up by separating Achilles from the tortoise by an infinite number of intermediate points. But mathematical complexity can be digested instantly by electronic brains. Their abacus of only two numerals permits them to make instantaneous calculations of a complexity unthinkable for human brains. They have only to count on two fingers to bring into play incredibly rapid matrices of astronomical sums. One of the most arduous intellectual efforts of the Middle Ages has only now become entirely real: I refer to the Catalan monk Raymond Lully and his *ars combinatoria*.

The process going on today is the triumph of discontinuity, divisibility, and combination over all that is flux, or a series of minute nuances following one upon the other. The nineteenth century, from Hegel to Darwin, saw the triumph of historical continuity and biological continuity as they healed all the fractures of dialectical antitheses and genetic mutations. Today this perspective is radically altered. In history we no longer follow the course of a spirit immanent in the events of the world, but the curves of statistical diagrams, and historical research is leaning more and more toward mathematics. And as for biology, Watson and Crick have shown us how the transmision of the characteristics of the species consists in the duplication of a certain number of spiral-shaped molecules formed from a certain number of acids and bases. In other words, the endless variety of living forms can be reduced to the combination of certain finite quantities. Here again, it is information theory that imposes its patterns. The processes that appeared most resistant to a formulation in terms of number, to a quantitative description, are not translated into mathematical patterns.

Born and raised on quite different terrain, structural linguistics tends to appear in terms of a play of contraries every bit as simple as information theory. And linguists, too, have begun to talk in terms of codes and messages, to attempt to establish the entropy of language on all levels, including that of literature.

Mankind is beginning to understand how to dismantle and reassemble the most complex and unpredictable of all its machines: language. Today's world is far richer in words and concepts and signs than the world that surrounded primitive man, and the uses of the various levels of language are a great deal more complex. Using transformational mathematical patterns, the

American school led by Chomsky is exploring the deep structure of language, lying at the roots of the logical processes that may constitute no longer a historical characteristic of man, but a biological one. And extreme simplification of logical formulas, on the other hand, is used by the French school of structural semantics headed by A. J. Greimas. This school analyzes the narrative quality of all discourse, which may be reduced to a ratio between what they call *actants*.

After a gap of almost thirty years, a "Neo-Formalist" school has been reborn in the Soviet Union, employing the results of cybernetic research and structural semiology for the analysis of literature. Headed by a mathematician, Kholmogorov, this school carries out studies of a highly academic scientific nature based on the calculation of probabilities and the quantity of information contained in poems.

A further encounter between mathematics and literature is taking place in France, under the banner of hoaxing and practical joking. This is the Ouvroir de Littérature Potentielle (Oulipo), founded by Raymond Queneau and a number of his mathematician friends. This almost clandestine group of ten people is an offshoot of the Collège de Pataphysique, the literary society founded in memory of Alfred Jarry as a kind of academy of intellectual scorn. Meanwhile, the researches of Oulipo into the mathematical structure of the sestina in the work of the Provençal troubadours and of Dante are no less austere than the studies of the Soviet cyberneticists. It should not be forgotten that Queneau is the author of a book called *Cent Mille Milliards de poèmes*, which purports to be not so much a book as the rudimentary model of a machine for making sonnets, each one different from the last.

Having laid down these procedures and entrusted a computer with the task of carrying out these operations, will we have a machine capable of replacing the poet and the author? Just as we already have machines that can read, machines that perform a linguistic analysis of literary texts, machines that make translations and summaries, will we also have machines capable of conceiving and composing poems and novels?

The interesting thing is not so much the question whether this problem is soluble in practice—because in any case it would not be worth the trouble of constructing such a complicated machine—as the theoretical possibility of it, which would give rise to a series of unusual conjectures. And I am not now thinking of a machine capable merely of "assembly-line" literary production, which would already be mechanical in itself. I am thinking of a writing machine that would bring to the page all those things that we are accustomed to consider as the most jealously guarded attributes of our psychological life, of our daily experience, our unpredictable changes of mood and inner elations, despairs and moments of illumination. What are these if not so many linguistic "fields," for which we might well succeed in establishing the vocabulary, grammar, syntax, and properties of permutation?

What would be the style of a literary automaton? I believe that its true vocation would be for classicism.

The test of a poetic-electronic machine would be its ability to produce traditional works, poems with closed metrical forms, novels that follow all the rules. In this sense the use so far made of machines by the literary avant-garde is still too human. Especially in Italy, the machine used in these experiments is an instrument of chance, of the destructuralization of form, of protest against every habitual logical connection. I would therefore say that it is still an entirely lyrical instrument, serving a typical human need: the production of disorder. The true literature machine will be one that itself feels the need to produce disorder, as a reaction against its preceding production of order: a machine that will produce avant-garde work to free its circuits when they are choked by too long a production of classicism. In fact, given that developments in cybernetics lean toward machines capable of learning, of changing their own programs, of developing their own sensibilities and their own needs, nothing prevents us from foreseeing a literature machine that at a certain point feels unsatisfied with its own traditionalism and starts to propose new ways of writing, turning its own codes completely upside down. To gratify critics who look for similarities between things literary and things historical, sociological, or economic, the machine could correlate its own changes of style to the variations in certain statistical indices of production, or income, or military expenditure, or the distribution of decision-making powers. That indeed will be the literature that corresponds perfectly to a theoretical hypothesis: it will, at last, be *the* literature.

II

Now, some of you may wonder why I so gaily announce prospects that in most men of letters arouse tearful laments punctuated by cries of execration. The reason is that I have always known, more or less obscurely, that things stood this way, not the way they were commonly said to stand. Various aesthetic theories maintained that poetry was a matter of inspiration descending from I know not what lofty place, or welling up from I know not what great depths, or else pure intuition, or an otherwise not identified moment in the life of the spirit, or the Voice of the Times with which the Spirit of the World chooses to speak to the poet, or a reflection of social structures that by means of some unknown optical phenomenon is projected on the page, or a direct grasp on the psychology of the depths that enables us to ladle out images of the unconscious, both individual and collective; or at any rate something intuitive, immediate, authentic, and all-embracing that springs up who knows how, something equivalent and homologous to something else, and symbolic of it. But in these theories there always remained a void that no one knew how to fill, a zone of darkness between cause and effect: how does one arrive at the written page? By what route is the soul or history or society or the subconscious transformed into a series of black lines on a white page? Even the most outstanding theories of aesthetics were silent on this point. I felt like someone who, due to some misunderstanding, finds himself among people who are discussing business that is no business of his. Literature as I knew it was a constant series of attempts to make one word stay put after another by following certain definite rules; or, more often, rules that were neither definite nor definable, but that might be extracted from a series of examples, or rules made up for the occasion—that is to say, derived from the rules followed by other writers. And in these operations the person "I," whether explicit or implicit, splits into a number of different figures: into an "I" who is writing and an "I" who is written, into an empirical "I" who looks over the shoulder of the "I" who is writing and into a mythical "I" who serves as a model for the "I" who is written. The "I" of the author is dissolved in the writing. The so-called personality of the writer exists within the very act of writing: it is the product and the instrument of the writing process. A writing machine that has been fed an instruction appropriate to the case could also devise an exact and unmistakable "personality" of an author, or else it could be adjusted in such a way as to evolve or change "personality" with each work it composes. Writers, as they have always been up to now, are already writing machines; or at least they are when things are going well. What Romantic terminology called genius or talent or inspiration or intuition is nothing other than finding the right road empirically, following one's nose, taking short cuts, whereas the machine would follow a systematic and conscientious route while being extremely rapid and multiple at the same time.

Once we have dismantled and reassembled the process of literary composition, the decisive moment of literary life will be that of reading. In this sense, even though entrusted to machines, literature will continue to be a "place" of privilege within the human consciousness, a way of exercising the potentialities contained in the system of signs belonging to all societies at all times. The work will continue to be born, to be judged, to be destroyed or constantly renewed on contact with the eye of the reader. What will vanish is the figure of the author, that personage to whom we persist in attributing functions that do not belong to him, the author as an exhibitor of his own soul in the permanent Exhibition of Souls, the author as the exploiter of sensory and interpretive organs more receptive than the average. . . . The author: that anachronistic personage, the bearer of messages, the director of consciences, the giver of lectures to cultural bodies. The rite we are celebrating at this moment would be absurd if we were unable to give it the sense of a funeral service, seeing the author off to the Nether Regions and celebrating the constant resurrection of the work of literature; if we were unable to introduce into this meeting of ours something of the gaiety of those funeral feasts at which the ancients re-established their contact with living things.

And so the author vanishes—that spoiled child of ignorance—to give place to a more thoughtful person, a person who will know that the author is a machine, and will know how this machine works.

III

At this point I think I have done enough to explain why it is with a clear conscience and without regrets that I state that my place could perfectly well be occupied by a mechanical device. But I am sure that many of you will remain rather unconvinced by my explanation, finding that my attitude of oft-repeated abnegation, of renunciation of the writer's prerogatives out of the love of truth, must surely be wrong; and that under all this something else must be lurking. I already feel that you are searching for less flattering motives for my attitude. I have nothing against this sort of inquiry. Behind every idealistic position that we adopt we can find the nitty-gritty of practical interest, or, even more often, of some basic psychological motivation. Let us see what my psychological reaction is when I learn that writing is purely and simply a process of combination among given elements. Well, then, what I instinctively feel is a sense of relief, of security. The same sort of relief and sense of security that I feel every time I discover that a mess of vague and indeterminate lines turns out to be a precise geometric form; or every time I succeed in discerning a series of facts, and choices to be made out of a finite number of possibilities, in the otherwise shapeless avalanche of events. Faced with the vertigo of what is countless, unclassifiable, in a state of flux, I feel reassured by what is finite, "discrete," and reduced to a system. Why is this? Does my attitude contain a hidden element of fear of the unknown, of the wish to set limits to my world and crawl back into my shell? Thus my stance, which was intended to be provocative and even profane, allows of the suspicion that, on the contrary, it is dictated by some kind of intellectual agoraphobia, almost a form of exorcism to defend me from the whirlwinds that literature so constantly has to face.

Let us attempt a thesis contrary to the one I have

developed so far (this is always the best way to avoid getting trapped in the spiral of one's own thoughts). Did we say that literature is entirely involved with language, is merely the permutation of a restricted number of elements and functions? But is the tension in literature not continually striving to escape from this finite number? Does it not continually attempt to say something it cannot say, something that it does not know, and that no one could ever know? A thing cannot be known when the words and concepts used to say it and think it have not yet been used in that position, not yet arranged in that order, with that meaning. The struggle of literature is in fact a struggle to escape from the confines of language; it stretches out from the utmost limits of what can be said; what stirs literature is the call and attraction of what is not in the dictionary.

The storyteller of the tribe puts together phrases and images: the younger son gets lost in the forest, he sees a light in the distance, he walks and walks; the fable unwinds from sentence to sentence, and where is it leading? To the point at which something not yet said, something as yet only darkly felt by presentiment, suddenly appears and seizes us and tears us to pieces, like the fangs of a man-eating witch. Through the forest of fairy tale the vibrancy of myth passes like a shudder of wind.

Myth is the hidden part of every story, the buried part, the region that is still unexplored because there are as yet no words to enable us to get there. The narrator's voice in the daily tribal assemblies is not enough to relate the myth. One needs special times and places, exclusive meetings; the words alone are not enough, and we need a whole series of signs with many meanings, which is to say a rite. Myth is nourished by silence as well as by words. A silent myth makes its presence felt in secular narrative and everyday words; it is a language vacuum that draws words up into its vortex and bestows a form on fable.

But what is a language vacuum if not a vestige of taboo, of a ban on mentioning something, on pronouncing certain names, of a prohibition either present or ancient? Literature follows paths that flank and cross the barriers of prohibition, that lead to saying what could not be said, to an invention that is always a reinvention of words and stories that have been banished from the individual or collective memory. Therefore myth acts on fable as a repetitive force, obliging it to go back on its tracks even when it has set off in directions that appear to lead somewhere completely different.

The unconscious is the ocean of the unsayable, of what has been expelled from the land of language, removed as a result of ancient prohibitions. The unconscious speaks—in dreams, in verbal slips, in sudden associations—with borrowed words, stolen symbols, linguistic contraband, until literature redeems these territories and annexes them to the language of the waking world.

The power of modern literature lies in its willingness to give a voice to what has remained unexpressed in the social or individual unconscious: this is the gauntlet it throws down time and again. The more enlightened our houses are, the more their walls ooze ghosts. Dreams of progress and reason are haunted by nightmares. Shakespeare warns us that the triumph of the Renaissance did not lay the ghosts of the medieval world who appear on the ramparts at Dunsinane or Elsinore. At the height of the Enlightenment, Sade and the Gothic novel appear. At one stroke Edgar Allan Poe initiates the literature of aestheticism and the literature of the masses, naming and liberating the ghosts that Puritan America trails in its wake. Lautréamont explodes the syntax of the imagination, expanding the visionary world of the Gothic novel to the proportions of a Last Judgment. In automatic associations of words and images the Surrealists discover an objective rationale totally opposed to that of our intellectual logic. Is this the triumph of the irrational? Or is it the refusal to believe that the irrational exists, that anything in the world can be considered extraneous to the reason of things, even if something eludes the reasons determined by our historical condition, and also eludes limited and defensive so-called rationalism?

So here we are, carried off into an ideological landscape quite different from the one we thought we had decided to live in, there with the relays of diodes of electronic computers. But are we really all that far away?

IV

The relationship between combinatorial play and the unconscious in artistic activity lies at the heart of one of the most convincing aesthetic theories currently in circulation, a formula that draws upon both psychoanalysis and the practical experience of art and letters. We all know that in matters of literature and the arts Freud was a man of traditional tastes, and that in his writings connected with aesthetics he did not give us any pointers worthy of his genius. It was a Freudian art historian, Ernst Kris, who first put forward Freud's study of word-play as the key to a possible aesthetics of psychoanalysis. Another gifted art historian, Ernst Gombrich, developed this notion in his essay on Freud and the psychology of art.

The pleasure of puns and feeble jokes is obtained by following the possibilities of permutation and transformation implicit in language. We start from the particular pleasure given by any combinatorial play, and at a certain point, out of the countless combinations of words with similar sounds, one becomes charged with special significance, causing laughter. What has happened is that the juxtaposition of concepts that we have stumbled across by chance unexpectedly unleashes a preconscious idea, an idea, that is, half buried in or erased from our consciousness, or maybe only held at arm's length or pushed aside, but powerful enough to appear in the consciousness if suggested not by any intention on our part, but by an objective process.

The processes of poetry and art, says Gombrich, are analogous to those of a play on words. It is the childish pleasure of the combinatorial game that leads the painter to try out arrangements of lines and colors, the poet to experiment with juxtapositions of words. At a certain moment things click into place, and one of the combinations obtained—through the combinatorial mechanism itself, independently of any search for meaning or effect on any other level—becomes charged with an unexpected meaning or unforeseen effect which the conscious mind would not have arrived at deliberately:

an unconscious meaning, in fact, or at least the premonition of an unconscious meaning.

So we see that the two routes followed by my argument have here come together. Literature is a combinatorial game that pursues the possibilities implicit in its own material, independent of the personality of the poet, but it is a game that at a certain point is invested with an unexpected meaning, a meaning that is not patent on the linguistic plane on which we were working but has slipped in from another level, activating something that on that second level is of great concern to the author or his society. The literature machine can perform all the permutations possible on a given material, but the poetic result will be the particular effect of one of these permutations on a man endowed with a consciousness and an unconscious, that is, an empirical and historical man. It will be the shock that occurs only if the writing machine is surrounded by the hidden ghosts of the individual and of his society.

To return to the storyteller of the tribe, he continues imperturbably to make his permutations of jaguars and toucans until the moment comes when one of his innocent little tales explodes into a terrible revelation: a myth, which must be recited in secret, and in a secret place.

V

I am aware that this conclusion of mine contradicts the most authoritative theories about the relationship between myth and fable.

Until now it has generally been said that the fable is a "profane" story, something that comes after myth, a corruption or vulgarization or secularization of it, or that fable and myth coexist and counterbalance each other as different functions of a single culture. The logic of my argument, however—until some more convincing new demonstration comes along to blow it sky-high—leads to the conclusion that the making of fables precedes the making of myths. Mythic significance is something one comes across only if one persists in playing around with narrative functions.

Myth tends to crystallize instantly, to fall into set patterns, to pass from the phase of myth-making into that of ritual, and hence out of the hands of the narrator into those of the tribal institutions responsible for the preservation and celebration of myths. The tribal system of signs is arranged in relation to myth; a certain number of signs become taboo, and the "secular" storyteller can make no direct use of them. He goes on circling around them, inventing new developments in composition, until in the course of this methodical and objective labor he suddenly gets another flash of enlightenment from the unconscious and the forbidden. And this forces the tribe to change its set of signs once more.

Within this general context, the function of literature varies according to the situation. For long periods of time literature appears to work in favor of consecration, the confirmation of values, the acceptance of authority. But at a certain moment, something in the mechanism is triggered, and literature gives birth to a movement in the opposite direction, refusing to see things and say things the way they have been seen and said until now.

This is the main theme of a book called *Le due tensioni* (*The Two Tensions*), which comprises the previously unpublished notes of Elio Vittorini (Milan: Il Saggiatore, 1967). According to Vittorini, literature until now has been too much the "accomplice of nature," that is, of the mistaken notion of an immutable nature, a Mother Nature, whereas its true value emerges only when it becomes a critic of the world and our way of looking at the world. In one chapter that may well state his definitive position, Vittorini seems to be starting from scratch on a study of the place of literature in human history. As soon as writing and books are born, he says, the human race is divided into a civilized part—the part of the race that long ago took the step into the Neolithic Age—and another part (called savage) that got stuck in the Paleolithic, and in which the Neolithics could not even recognize their ancestors: a part of humanity that thinks that things have always been the way they are, just as they think that masters and servants have always existed. Written literature is born already laden with the task of consecration, of supporting the established order of things. This is a load that it discards extremely slowly, in the course of millennia, becoming in the process a private thing, enabling poets and writers to express their own personal troubles and raise them to the level of consciousness. Literature gets to this point, I would add, by means of combinatorial games that at a certain moment become charged with preconscious subject matter, and at last find a voice for these. And it is by this road to freedom opened up by literature that men achieved the critical spirit, and transmitted it to collective thought and culture.

VI

Concerning this double aspect of literature, here, toward the end of my little talk, it is relevant to mention an essay by the German poet and critic Hans Magnus Enzensberger, "Topological Structures in Modern Literature," which I read in the Buenos Aires magazine *Sur* (May–June 1966). He reviews the numerous instances of labyrinthine narratives from ancient times up to Borges and Robbe-Grillet, or of narratives one inside another like Chinese boxes, and he asks himself the meaning of modern literature's insistence on these themes. He evokes the image of a world in which it is easy to lose oneself, to get disoriented—a world in which the effort of regaining one's orientation acquires a particular value, almost that of a training for survival. "Every orientation," he writes, "presupposes a disorientation. Only someone who has experienced bewilderment can free himself of it. But these games of orientation are in turn games of disorientation. Therein lies their fascination and their risk. The labyrinth is made so that whoever enters it will stray and get lost. But the labyrinth also poses the visitor a challenge: that he reconstruct the plan of it and dissolve its power. If he succeeds, he will have destroyed the labyrinth; for one who has passed through it, no labyrinth exists." And Enzensberger concludes: "The moment a topological structure appears as a metaphysical structure the game loses its dialectical balance, and literature turns into a means of demonstrating that the world is essentially impenetrable, that any communication is impossible. The labyrinth thus ceases to be a challenge to human intelligence and establishes itself as a facsimile of the world and of society."

Enzensberger's thesis can be applied to everything in literature and culture that today—after von Neumann—we see as a combinatorial mathematical game. The game can work as a challenge to understand the world or as a dissuasion from understanding it. Literature can work in a critical vein or to confirm things as they are and as we know them to be. The boundary is not always clearly marked, and I would say that on this score the spirit in which one reads is decisive: it is up to the reader to see to it that literature exerts its critical force, and this can occur independently of the author's intentions.

I think this is the meaning one might give to my most recent story, which comes at the end of my book *t zero*. In this story we see Alexandre Dumas taking his novel *The Count of Monte Cristo* from a supernovel that contains all possible variants of the life story of Edmond Dantès. In their dungeon Edmond Dantès and the Abbot Faria go over the plans for their escape and wonder which of the possible variants is the right one. The Abbot Faria digs tunnels to escape from the castle, but he always goes wrong and ends up in ever-deeper cells. On the basis of Faria's mistakes Dantès tries to draw a map of the castle. While Faria, by the sheer number of his attempts, comes close to achieving the perfect escape, Dantès moves toward imagining the perfect prison—

the one from which no escape is possible. His reasons are explained in the passage I shall now quote:

If I succeed in mentally constructing a fortress from which it is impossible to escape, this imagined fortress either will be the same as the real one—and in this case it is certain we shall never escape from here, but at least we will achieve the serenity of knowing we are here because we could be nowhere else—or it will be a fortress from which escape is even more impossible than from here—which would be a sign that here an opportunity of escape exists: we have only to identify the point where the imagined fortress does not coincide with the real one and then find it.

And that is the most optimistic finale that I have managed to give to my story, to my book, and also to this essay.

Two Interviews on
Science and Literature

I. *L'Approdo Letterario* (Rome), January–March 1968; based on television interviews.
II. Interview for *Kolo* (Zagreb), October 1968. Topics were: (1) the term "Neo-Enlightenment"; (2) science and morals: "does substituting science for morals call into question all existing ethics, as in your story "The Pursuit"? (3) the need (as it might emerge from your *t zero*) for the avant-garde writer to become a scientist.

I

In your opinion, what is the relationship today between science and literature?

I recently read an article by Roland Barthes called "Literature versus Science." Barthes tends to think of literature as the awareness that language has of being language, of having a density of its own, and its own independent existence. For literature, language is never *transparent*, and is never merely an instrument to convey a "meaning" or a "fact" or a "thought" or a "truth"; that is, it cannot mean anything but itself. Whereas, on the other hand, the idea of language given by science is that of a neutral utensil that is used to say something else, to mean something foreign to it. This different concept of language is what distinguishes science from literature. Proceeding along these lines, Barthes gets to the point of maintaining that literature is more scientific than science, because literature knows that language is never naïve, and knows that in writing one cannot say anything extraneous to writing, or express any truth that is not a truth having to do with the art of writing. The science of language, according to Barthes, if it wishes to remain a science, is destined to be transformed into literature, total writing, and will also lay claim to the pleasures of language, which are at present the exclusive prerogative of literature.

But can the science of today really be defined by such trust in an absolute code of references, or is it not in itself by this time a continual questioning of its own linguistic conventions? In his polemic against science Barthes appears to envisage a kind of science far more compact and sure of itself than it really is. And—as far as mathematics is concerned—rather than claiming to base an argument on a truth beyond itself, we find a science not guiltless of tinkering with its own formulative processes.

The above-mentioned article by Barthes is included in an issue of the *Times Literary Supplement* from a few months ago that was devoted to continental European literature, and in particular to the relations between literature and other fields of research. In the same issue another French writer, Raymond Queneau, older than Barthes and belonging to quite another cultural background, talks about science in a very different way. Queneau is a writer whose hobby is mathematics, and he has more friends among mathematicians than among men of letters. In his article he stresses the place that mathematical thought, through the increasing "mathematicization" of the human sciences, is now acquiring in humanistic culture, and therefore in literature as well. Along with a mathematician friend of his, Queneau founded the Ouvroir de Littérature Potentielle, Oulipo for short, a group of ten people who carry out mathematico-literary research. Here we are in a totally different climate from the austere and rarefied atmosphere of the analyses of Barthes and the writings of the Tel Quel group of authors. The dominant feature here is play, and the acrobatics of the intellect and the imagination. It is no coincidence that Oulipo is an offshoot of the Collège de Pataphysique, that "academy" of mockery and practical joking founded in memory of Alfred Jarry. It is the (semiclandestine) magazine of the Collège de Pataphysique, *Subsidia Pataphysica*, that publishes the work of Oulipo, as for example a study of the mathematical problems posed by the series of rhymes in the metrical form of the sestina in the work of the Provençal poets (and in Dante), a series that can be represented as a spiral. I think that the two positions I have described define the situation pretty well: they are the two poles between which we find ourselves oscillating, or at least I find myself oscillating, feeling the attraction and being aware of the limitations of each of them. On the one side is Barthes with his followers, "enemies" of science, who think and talk with scientific precision; on the other is Queneau with his, friends of science, who think and talk in terms of caprice and somersaults of language and thought.

You recently said that the greatest Italian writer is Galileo. Why?

In the *Zibaldone* (*Miscellany*), Leopardi admires Galileo's prose for being elegant and precise at one and the same time. And we have only to look at the choice of passages from Galileo that Leopardi includes in his *Crestomazia* (*Anthology*) of Italian prose to realize how much the language of Leopardi—even Leopardi as a poet—owes to Galileo. But, to get back to what I was saying a moment ago, Galileo uses language not as a neutral utensil, but with literary awareness, with a continuous commitment that is expressive, imaginative, and even lyrical. When I read Galileo I like to seek out the passages in which he speaks of the moon. It is the first time that the moon becomes a real object for mankind, and is minutely described as a tangible thing, yet as soon as the moon appears one feels a kind of rarefaction, almost of levitation, in Galileo's language. One rises with it into an enchanted state of suspension. It was no coincidence that Galileo admired and annotated Ariosto, cosmic and lunary poet that he was. (Galileo also commented on Tasso, and in that case he was not a good critic, for the very reason that his downright partisan enthusiasm for Ariosto led him to criticize Tasso for the most part with unfair severity.) The ideal way in which Galileo regarded the world, even as a scientist, is nourished by literary culture. So much so that we can draw a line from Ariosto to Galileo to Leopardi and call it one of the mainstreams of our literature.

When I said that Galileo is still the greatest Italian writer, Carlo Cassola leaped to his feet and said, "What? I thought it was Dante!" Well, thanks a lot for telling us. In the first place, what I meant to say was "prose writer," in which case the question boils down to Machiavelli or Galileo, and this puts me on the spot, because I also love Machiavelli very much. What I can say is that in the particular direction my work is taking at the moment I find more nourishment in Galileo, in his precision of language, his scientific-poetic imagination, his posing of conjectures. But Galileo, says Cassola, was a scientist, not a writer. I think we can dispose of this argument pretty easily. In the same way, though in a different cultural context, Dante created an encyclopedic and cosmological work, and he, too, tried to construct an image of the universe by means of the written word. This is a deep-rooted vocation in Italian literature, handed on from Dante to Galileo: the notion of the literary work as a map of the world and of the knowable, of writing driven on by a thirst for knowledge that may by turns be theological, speculative, magical, encyclopedic, or may be concerned with natural philosophy or with transfiguring, visionary observation. It is a tradition that exists in all European literatures, but I would say that in Italian literature it has been dominant in every shape and form, making our literature very different from others, very difficult but at the same time perfectly unique. In the last few centuries this vein has emerged less frequently, and since that time, certainly, our literature has diminished in importance. Maybe now is the time to find that vein again. I must say that recently, perhaps because of the kind of thing I have begun to write, Italian literature has become more indispensable to me than it was before. From time to time I get the feeling that the road I am taking is leading me back to the true but forgotten source of the Italian tradition.

From your latest books it appears that your sympathies are directed more toward the cell than toward mankind, more toward mathematical calculation than the reasons of the heart, and mental impulses rather than ideas. Why is this?

The cell rather than man—is that really the case? Because my cosmicomic stories might easily be reproached for exactly the opposite; that is, for making cells talk as if they were people, for inventing human figures and language in the primeval void, and, in short, of playing the old game of anthropomorphism. We remember that years ago Robbe-Grillet came out with a bitter attack on anthropomorphism, against the writer who still humanized the landscape and said that the sky "smiled" or that the sea "was angry."

I, on the other hand, have fully accepted and vindicated this anthropomorphism as an absolutely basic literary procedure, and one that even before being literary was mythical, linked to one of primitive man's earliest explanations of the world: animism. It is not that Robbe-Grillet's argument didn't convince me. It is just that in the course of writing I have come to take the opposite route in stories that are a positive delirium of anthropomorphism, of the impossibility of thinking about the world except in terms of human figures—or, more precisely, of human grimaces and human babblings. Of course, this, too, is a way of putting the laziest, most obvious, and most vainglorious image of man to the test: by multiplying his eyes and his nose in every direction until he no longer knows who he is.

Writers like me, who are not attracted to psychology, to the analysis of feelings, or to introspection, are greeted by horizons certainly no less broad than those dominated by characters with clear-cut personalities, or those revealed to people who explore the depths of the human mind. What interests me is the whole mosaic in which man is set, the interplay of relationships, the design that emerges from the squiggles on the carpet. Anyway, I know that there is no way that I can escape from what is human, even if I do not strain myself to sweat humanity from every pore. The stories I write come into being within a human brain, by means of a combination of signs worked out by the human cultures that have gone before me. And so, in the recent stories with which I end the volume *t zero*, I have tried to make narrative out of a mere process of deductive reasoning, and perhaps—in this case, yes—I have departed from anthropomorphism. Or, rather, from a certain kind of anthropomorphism, since these human presences defined only by a system of relationships, by a function, are the very ones that populate the world around us in our everyday lives, good or bad as this situation might appear to us.

II

(1) The term "Enlightenment" is rather unpopular at the moment. The Enlightenment is accused of being at the root of the technocratic ideology that wields power in the industrialized nations, against which youth is rebelling all over the world. The original text upon which this criticism is based is a book by Horkheimer and Adorno, *Dialectic of Enlightenment*, published in the United States some thirty years ago and in Germany some fifteen years ago. The authors go so far as to start with the *Odyssey* as the first manifesto of the enlightened, technocratic, bourgeois ideology. I am not very convinced by this thesis. I have always had a soft spot for Ulysses, but I don't care, just like that, to accept the label of an exponent of the Neo-Enlightenment, which is one that a number of critics have attached to me, some in a positive sense and others in a critical one. Certainly the eighteenth century remains one of the historical periods that fascinate me most, but this is because I find it increasingly rich and many-faceted and full of contradictory ferments that are still going on today. I still very much feel the spirit in which, eleven years ago, I wrote *Il barone rampante* (*The Baron in the Trees*) about a kind of Don Quixote of the "Philosophy of the Enlightenment."

(2) I do not think that modern science—and the theory of relativity in particular—provides us with any justification for moral relativity. On the contrary, our age is marked by a clear division between talk about

science and talk about values. This means that moral responsibility cannot hide behind self-interested justifications. On the other hand, I believe that, even in the past, what has really counted, more than the weight of well-defined moralities, has been a process of ethical seeking, forever problematical and forever risky. A Christian too sure of himself about what is right and wrong has never, I believe, been a good Christian. And the most rational and all-embracing ethical construction ever attempted—that of Kant—demands that in every situation we should start again from scratch. For Marxists this problematical aspect of ethics is taken to its extreme consequences: a Marxist is a man who knows that in the process of history every value can be denied (or confirmed) by an antithetical value. Much of the work of Bertolt Brecht is based on these pitiless reversals.

However, moral problems reside not in the field of literature, but in that of practical behavior. Literature creates autonomous figures that may be used as terms of comparison with experience or with other constructions of the mind. It is only by means of such reflection on the part of the reader that literature can be linked to some ethical activity; that is, only by means of a comparison of the values the reader is looking for with those the work of literature seems to suggest or imply. But this has to be a *critical* reflection, which is why "moralizing," "edifying," or "educative" literature has never been any good as a moral stimulus, except for the reader who strips it of the hoax and discovers the falsity and hypocrisy of it.

If in my story "The Pursuit" I say that, in a system of pursuer and pursued, everyone pursued is also a pursuer (or must change into a pursuer), I am above all following a *formal* logic—almost geometric, I would say—and one that is implicit in my story. But I also say something that might stir the reader into some ethical activity. The reader may accept or reject this metaphor, but if he rejects it he will have a better knowledge of what it is he wants to reject, whereas if he accepts it he will be forced into a critical examination of such an intolerable situation. The important thing is that the story provide the reader with imaginative materials that chime in with his own particular language, that provoke reactions and objections in him.

(3) Scientific writing tends toward a purely formal and mathematical language based on an abstract logic indifferent to its content. Literary writing tends to construct a system of values in which every word, every sign, is a value for the sole reason that it has been chosen and fixed on the page. There could never be any meeting between the two languages, but (on account of their extreme disparity) there can be a challenge, a kind of wager between them. In certain situations it is literature that can work indirectly as a spring to propel the scientist along, providing an example of imaginative courage in taking a hypothesis to its ultimate consequences, and so on. Similarly, in other situations it can work the other way around. At the moment the language of mathematics, of formal logic, can save the writer from the disrepair that words and images have fallen into as a result of being misused. Even so, the writer should not

think that he has found anything valid absolutely. Here, too, the example of science can be of use to him, and teach him the patient modesty of considering each and every result as being part of a possibly infinite series of approximations.

Philosophy and Literature

Times Literary Supplement, September 28, 1967 (a special issue entitled "Crosscurrents," containing short articles commissioned from a number of European authors).

Philosophy and literature are embattled adversaries. The eyes of philosophers see through the opaqueness of the world, eliminate the flesh of it, reduce the variety of existing things to a spider's web of relationships between general ideas, and fix the rules according to which a finite number of pawns moving on a chessboard exhaust a number of combinations that may even be infinite. Along come the writers and replace the abstract chessmen with kings and queens, knights and castles, all with a name, a particular shape, and a series of attributes royal, equine, or ecclesiastical; instead of a chessboard they roll out great dusty battlefields or stormy seas. So at this point the rules of the game are turned topsy-turvy, revealing an order of things quite different from that of the philosophers. Or, rather, the people who discover these new rules of the game are once again the philosophers, who dash back to demonstrate that this operation wrought by the writers can be reduced to the terms of one of their own operations, and that the particular castles and bishops were nothing but general ideas in disguise.

And so the wrangle goes on, with each side confident of having taken a step ahead in the conquest of truth, or at least of *a* truth, and at the same time perfectly well aware that the raw material of its own constructions is the same as that of the opposition: words. But words, like crystals, have facets and axes of rotation with different properties, and light is refracted differently according to how these word crystals are placed, and how the polarizing surfaces are cut and superimposed. The clash between philosophy and literature does not need to be resolved. On the contrary, only if we think of it as permanent but ever new does it guarantee us that the sclerosis of words will not close over us like a sheet of ice.

This is a war in which the two contestants must never take their eyes off each other, but must never come to close quarters either. The writer who wishes to compete with the philosopher by launching his characters into very profound dissertations ends up in the best of cases by rendering the dizzy spells of thought habitable, persuasive, and everyday, without ever letting us breathe the pure air of the heights. In any event, this type of writer belongs to the first decades of our century, to the era of the rationalizing theatre of Pirandello and all those intellectual conversations in Huxley's novels; and to us today he seems rather a distant figure. The intellectual novel itself, the discussion novel, is a thing of the past. Anyone today who sat down to write a new *Magic Mountain* or *Man without Qualities* would not write a novel at all, but an essay on the history of ideas or on the sociology of culture.

In the same way, philosophy, when it is too fully clothed in human flesh, too sensitive to immediate, lived experience, is for literature a less exciting challenge than is the abstraction of metaphysics or of pure logic. Phenomenology and existentialism border on literature along frontiers that are not always very clearly marked. Can the writer-philosopher cast a fresh philosophic look upon the world, a look that at the same time is also fresh for literature? For a moment, when the protagonist of *La Nausée* looks at his face in the mirror, this might be possible; but throughout a large part of his work the writer-philosopher appears as a philosopher who has at his command a writer who is versatile to the point of eclecticism. The literature of existentialism fell by the wayside because it did not succeed in acquiring a literary stringency of its own. It is only when the writer writes *before* the philosopher who interprets him that literary stringency can serve as a model for philosophic stringency, even if the writer and the philosopher happen to dwell together in the same person. This holds good not only for Dostoyevsky and Kafka, but also for Camus and Genêt.

The names of Dostoyevsky and Kafka remind us of the two supreme examples in which the authority of the writer—that is, the power to transmit an unmistakable message by means of a special intonation of language and a special distortion of the human figure and of situations—coincides with the authority of the thinker on the highest level. This also means that "the Dostoyevsky man" and "the Kafka man" have altered the image of man, even for those who have no particular inclination toward the philosophy that lies more or less explicitly behind such representations. On this level of authority, the writer of our times who might be placed alongside those two is Samuel Beckett. The image we have of man today cannot fail to take into account the negative absoluteness of "the Beckett man."

We are bound to say that the game of giving philosophical labels to writers (What is Hemingway? A behaviorist. What is Robbe-Grillet? An analytical philosopher) is a societal pastime that would be excusable only if it were very witty, which it is not. How many times has the name of Wittgenstein been invoked in discussing writers who have nothing in common except the fact that they have nothing in common with Wittgenstein! To decide who is the writer of logical positivism would be a perfect theme for an international conference of the PEN Club. As for structuralism—after the brilliant results it has attained in various fields, it would be as well to wait until it has given rise to both a philosophy and a literature of its own.

The terrain on which philosophy and literature traditionally meet is ethics. Or, rather, ethics has always provided an excuse for philosophy and literature not to look each other directly in the face, being certain and confident of being able to reach easy agreement about their task of teaching virtue to mankind. This has been the sad literary fate of all practical philosophies, and above all of Marxism: to drag along a literature of explanation and exhortation that tends to make the philosophic vision of the world seem natural and akin to spontaneous feelings. And thus we lose the real revolutionary value of a philosophy, which consists in its being all snags and thorns, in its power to upset common sense and sentiments and to outrage every "natural" manner of thinking.

The definition of "Marxist writer" perhaps applies only to Brecht, who, in contrast to the official ethics of communism, looked not at the surface of "realism" but, rather, at the logic of the inner mechanism of human relations, at the overturning of values, while at the same time flaunting a doctrine opposed to virtue. In Germany today, in Italy, and to some extent also in France, there is in the literature of the "New Left" (which claims descent from Marxism while rejecting the "realistic" and pedagogical explication of it) a tendency that still hails Brecht as a master because he was didactic in a paradoxical and provocative way. For another trend of opinion, on the other hand, Marxism is and has to be purely and simply the awareness of the hell we live in, and anyone who tries to suggest ways out is sapping this awareness of its vital force. For these people, revolutionary literature is nothing but the literature of total negation.

At the same time, it is clear by now that if it is true that when philosophers have interpreted the world they have to change it, it is equally true that if they stop interpreting it for a single instant they do not manage to change a single thing. Dogmatism has lost ground, and the expectation of finding some hidden truth in opposing ideologies now unites ex-sectarians and neo-extremists.

From the point of maximum resistance this situation radiates out on all sides. That literature is once again becoming interested in philosophy is only the sign of a voracious eclecticism. We find writers of a traditional stamp drawing inspiration from reading the latest philosophical works, without causing the least crack to appear in the monochromatic, uniform surface of their world. The philosophical literature of the globe may serve both to confirm and to question what we already know, quite independently of the philosophy that inspired it. It all depends on how the writer penetrates below the surface of things. Joyce, for example, projected onto a desolate beach all the theological and ontological conundrums he had learned at school, things very far from his concerns at the time of writing. Yet everything he touched—old shoes, fish eggs, old pots and pans—was utterly transformed to the very depths of its being.

This stratigraphic analysis of reality is carried on today by writers equipped with more modern and precise cultural and epistemological instruments (I will confine myself to mentioning Michel Butor and Uwe Johnson). And it leads to the questioning not merely of the world (that would be a trifling thing) but of the very essence of the work of literature as well. These are risks one has to be prepared to run if one is to follow this path.

The climate dominant today among young writers is more philosophical than ever, but imbued with a philosophy internal to the act of writing. In France the Tel Quel group, headed by Philippe Sollers, concentrates on an ontology of language, of writing, of "the book," a tendency that had its prophet in Mallarmé; in Italy the destructive function of writing appears to be at the heart of the quest; in Germany the main theme is the difficulty of writing the truth. However, there are common characteristics that dominate the general situation in these countries. Literature seems to make itself manifest as an austere and impassive speculative activity, as far from the outcries of tragedy as from the fantasies of happiness. It evokes no colors and no images other than the whiteness of the paper and the arrangement of black lines.

So does my original thesis no longer hold up? A frontal collision between two ways of looking at the world seems to have become impossible, since literature appears to have outflanked the positions of philosophy and to have walled itself up in a philosophical fortress that can hold out with perfect self-sufficiency.

The fact is that if I wish my picture of things to be valid not only for today but also for tomorrow, I must include an element that I have so far neglected. What I have described in terms of a twin-bed marriage must be seen as a *ménage à trois*: philosophy, literature, and science. Science is faced with problems not too dissimilar from those of literature. It makes patterns of the world that are immediately called in question, it swings between the inductive and the deductive methods, and it must always be on its guard lest it mistake its own linguistic conventions for objective laws. We will not have a culture equal to the challenge until we compare against one another the basic problematics of science, philosophy, and literature, in order to call them all into question.

While waiting for this time to come, we have no choice but to dwell on the available examples of a literature that breathes the air of philosophy and science but at the same time keeps its distance, while with a gentle puff it blows away both theoretical abstractions and the apparent concreteness of reality. I am speaking of that extraordinary and indefinable area of the human imagination that produced the works of Lewis Carroll, Queneau, and Borges.

But first I must point out one simple fact, for which I cannot claim to provide any general explanation: whereas the relationship between literature and religion, from Aeschylus to Dostoyevsky, has taken its stand under the banner of tragedy, that between literature and philosophy first became explicit in the comedies of Aristophanes, and was destined to continue to move behind the shield of comedy, irony, and humor. It is no coincidence that what in the eighteenth century were called *contes philosophiques* were in fact lighthearted acts of revenge against philosophy executed by means of the literary imagination.

But in Voltaire and Diderot is the imagination governed by a precise didactic and polemical intention? Does the author know everything he wants to say from the start? Does he know it, or does he think he does? The laughter of Swift or of Sterne is full of shadows. At the same time as the *conte philosophique* or, slightly later, the *conte fantastique* and the Gothic novel unleashed the obsessive visions of the unconscious. Is the real protest against philosophy to be found in lucid irony, in the sufferings of reason (and we Italians think at once of Leopardi's dialogues), in the clarity of the intelligence (and the French immediately think of *Monsieur Teste*); or does it lie in calling up the ghosts that continue to haunt our enlightened houses?

Both these traditions persist here and there to this day. The philosophic writer in the eighteenth-century manner sees his most flourishing reincarnations today in Germany, as poet (Enzensberger), dramatist (Peter Weiss with his *Marat/Sade*), or novelist (Günter Grass). On the other hand, literature in the *fantastique* tradition was relaunched by the Surrealists in their struggle to destroy the barriers between the rational and the irrational in literature. By means of the formula "*hasard objectif*" Breton did away with the irrationality of chance. Associations of words and images responded to a hidden logic no less authoritative than what is commonly called "thought."

As a matter of fact, this new horizon opened up as soon as a certain clergyman, and logic and mathematics don, began to invent the Adventures of Alice. Ever since then we have known that philosophical reason (which "when it sleeps engenders monsters") can have the loveliest of daydreams, absolutely worthy of its loftiest moments of speculation.

Since Lewis Carroll a new relationship has developed between philosophy and literature. We see the advent of those who delight in philosophy as a stimulus to the imagination. Queneau, Borges, Arno Schmidt— all have different relations with different philosophies, and use these to nourish vastly diverse visionary and linguistic worlds. Common to all of them is the habit of holding their cards close to the chest. Their philosophical sorties appear only through allusions to the great texts, metaphysical geometry, and erudition. From one moment to the next we expect the secret filigree of the universe to be made manifest: an expectation that is alway disappointed, as is only right.

Characteristic of this family of writers is the habit of cultivating the most compromising speculative and erudite passions without taking them entirely seriously. On the borders of their kingdom we may find the following writers: Beckett, who is a unique case, to the extent that his atrocious grimace has been suspected of containing tragic and religious elements, whether rightly or wrongly I do not know; Gadda, torn between the desire to write a natural history of the human race every time he sits down, and the fury that chokes him every time, so that he breaks off halfway through his books; and Gombrowicz, torn between a tightrope-walking levity (as in the wonderful duel between a Synthesist and an Analyst) and the all-devouring concentration of Eros.

The eroticization of culture is a game played between signs and meanings, between myths and ideas that can indeed reveal gardens of visionary delights, but it has to be practiced with the utmost detachment. Here I might mention a book that came out a few months ago in France: *Vendredi** by Michel Tournier, a reworking of *Robinson Crusoe* dense with references to the "human sciences," in which Robinson quite literally makes love to the island.

---

*Published in English as *Friday and Robinson's Life on Esperanza Island*, translated by Ralph Manheim (New York: Knopf, 1972).

Robinson Crusoe was a philosophical novel without knowing it, and even earlier *Don Quixote* and *Hamlet*— I do not know with what degree of awareness on the part of their authors—had opened up a new relationship between the phantom lightness of ideas and the heavy weight of the world. When we speak of the relationship between literature and philosophy we must not forget that the whole question begins there.

Literature as
Projection of Desire

On Northrop Frye's
Anatomy of Criticism

Libri Nuovi (Milan), August 1969.

As a recent reader of Northrop Frye's *Anatomy of Criticism* (Princeton: Princeton University Press, 1957 and later editions), I should like to pass on a few impressions and pieces of advice to other recent or future readers. I say at once that my argument will be entirely subjective, since everyone mines every book for the things that are useful to him, especially a book as rich and complex as this one is.

The page on which I realized that this was a book that mattered to me is page 139 in the Italian edition (page 105 in the English):

Civilization is not merely an imitation of nature, but the process of making a total human form out of nature, and it is impelled by the force that we have just called desire. The desire for food and shelter is not content with roots and caves: it produced the human forms of nature that we call farming and architecture. Desire is thus not a simple response to need, for an animal may need food without planting a garden to get it, nor is it a simple response to want, or desire *for* something in particular. It is neither limited to nor satisfied by objects, but is the energy that leads human society to develop its own form. Desire in this sense is the social aspect of what we met on the literal level as emotion, an impulse toward expression that would have remained amorphous if the poem had not liberated it by providing the form of its expression. The form of desire, similarly, is liberated and made apparent by civilization. The efficient cause of civilization is work, and poetry in its social aspect has the function of expressing, as a verbal hypothesis, a vision of the goal of work and the forms of desire.

This passage explains one of Frye's central statements: "The archetypal critic studies the poem as part of poetry, and poetry as part of the total human imitation of nature that we call civilization."

Why does this passage interest me? Because in it, couched in a language that awakens illustrious echoes, I find themes that are still dear to my heart, but that I manage less and less often to put together into a coherent argument. After being in the habit of giving things a "historicist" reading, which guaranteed that I would be able to insert literature into the context of human activity (though doing so garbled both literature and history), I have gone on to look for ways of reading that enable me to get more inside the object, and that therefore I do not feel to be misleading. But these do not fill the void left by that feeling of belonging. I know that I must not on this account rush into excluding the possibility that such a thing exists, though maybe it will only appear at the end of a long road. But I also know that I must restrain myself as far as I can from posing the question at all, unless I am prepared to break the rational spell of methodological stringency.

My reading of this Canadian critic arrives at a good time to link preoccupations of this sort with those that form the theme of the most debated philosophical, sociological, and psychological problems of the moment. The reference to the element of desire, which in literature finds forms that enable it to project itself beyond the obstacles met on its way, seems to me extremely topical, based as it is on the unlivable situation of the present and the drive toward the concept of a desirable society.

I admit that in any other context such a conveniently optimistic interpretation would already seem to me to be suspect, but in this case we are at the center of a vast network of classifications and hypotheses. Perhaps it is because the passage appears on page 105 and not one of the first or last pages (in other words, neither a statement of principles nor a summing up) that the argument deserves to be followed as it radiates outward and spreads in concentric circles over the course of several chapters. Also, the passage may be useful as a clarification and possible correction of the image that we are most likely to get of Frye: that of the critic who interprets literary functions on the basis of anthropology, who has theorized the "seasonal cycle" and the correspondences between literary genres and agricultural rites—someone, therefore, from whom one might at best expect a noble piece of work tending to archaism, using literature perhaps to confirm the immutability of human nature, perhaps to demonstrate the cyclic nature of the movement of history, or perhaps the finalism of it.

Rather than hastening to establish which is the *real* Frye, I would now like to stress one of the contraries on which the *Anatomy of Criticism* is based: the opposition between rite and dream. To the correspondence of literary forms with ritual practices—which is to say, the technical and institutional uses of myth—Frye opposes (or couples, or combines, for with him such things are never clear-cut and unambiguous) their correspondence with dream, the projection of desire and repugnance in opposition to the framework of existing institutions. It is in this key that I enjoy reading the book, rather than in those—legitimate as they may be—of a "cyclic" Frye (though it would be more exact to call him a describer of the cyclic concept of the world that literature has expressed) or of a "teleological" Frye (and we must not forget that this historian and geographer of human desire is a Protestant minister).

For example, the way is still open for a study of the symbol *city* from the Industrial Revolution on, as a projection of the terrors and desires of contemporary man. Frye tells us that the city is the human equivalent of the *mineral* world, in its apocalyptic or paradisiacal aspects (City of God, Jerusalem, soaring architecture, seat of the king and the court) or in its demonic and infernal aspects (City of Dis, City of Cain, labyrinth, modern metropolis). But it has to be said that in the relations between the human world, the animal-vegetable world, and the mineral world, there have been a lot of changes over the last two hundred years: changes in the arrangement and attribution of values that ought to be looked into both on the imaginary-literary and the social levels. *Anatomy of Criticism* allows for and suggests a great number of developments and extensions of this sort. It is a book of continual centrifugal thrusts, which we occasionally have to resist for fear of losing the thread of the author's overall theme.

I would advise readers to concentrate at first on the "modes of invention" both tragic and comic, on the symbol as the archetype, on the apocalyptic and demonic images, and on the *mythoi* of the four seasons. In these chapters the reader will grasp the main thread of the book, which he can then clarify and fill in as he enlarges the area of his reading and goes deeper into its subject matter.

To follow this thread he must go through the history of literature as the representation of exclusion from society and inclusion in society: gods excluded from the society of the immortals and destined to perish; heroes accepted by the society of the gods; nature as the ideal society, which mourns the dead hero (in elegy) or accepts the runaway hero (in pastoral); the fall of the king or chieftain in tragedy; the building of a new society in the comedies of Aristophanes and—from the comedies of Menander and Plautus on—the young married couple as the nucleus of a youthful society that triumphs over the obstacles put in its way by the old; the defeat of Julien Sorel or Emma Bovary in attempting to "climb" a society not his or her own; the ironic, intellectual hero who excludes himself from society; or else the enemy who is hunted down and expelled as a ritual scapegoat.

The study of the history of literary invention from the point of view of the two principal "modes," tragedy and comedy, enables Frye to identify the outcast from society both when the poetic work takes sides with him (the tragic mode, even when this occurs in comedy, romantic poetry, or the realistic novel) and when he is seen as an enemy to be expelled, the ridiculous or repugnant victim, the *pharmakos* (the comic mode, even if in contexts far distant from comedy). The same argument holds good both when the outcast or self-outcast is the hero, and when he is the poet himself, either in the first person or transfigured. Modern literature here opens a case study of this movement of "irony" or self-exclusion.

The identification of the enemy to be expelled is also the mechanism of the detective story, but here Frye (page 47) warns us against the "propagandist" function (the police represent legality in society as it is established) that is part of all literature in which the enemy is identified as someone outside society (the convention of melodrama), whereas the function of genuine comic irony is to define "the enemy of society as a spirit within that society."

The most lively parts of the book, where I found the ideas that for me were the most original and stimulating, were those dealing with comedy, culminating in the chapter on the myth of spring. The most intriguing parts, on account of the largely out-of-the-way material they introduce, are those dealing with romance. The chapters on tragedy hold fewer surprises, because when we come to tragedy it seems that everything has already been said. Irony and satire are perhaps the field in which Frye's inquiry is at its most personal, and here his argument becomes more involved and is left open as a series of suggestions rather than as an organic vision of things.

Frye's dense network of examples is drawn chiefly from the following: the Bible above all, the Homeric poems, the Greek and Latin tragedies and (even more) comedies, the medieval literature of chivalry and learning, Dante, Spenser, a lot of Shakespeare and especially the comedies, a lot of Milton, many eighteenth- and nineteenth-century novels (especially English), with not infrequent incursions into the greater and lesser writers of the twentieth century and even the cinema. Before the eyes of the reader he unravels an argument woven all over with references distant from one another in time and space, but he never ceases to establish correspondences and relationships between them. This in itself is enough to guarantee that a first armchair reading, or foray, without ever turning back or stopping to recapitulate, can be very pleasant and from time to time instructive. Frye calls his chapters "essays," and he has some reason for doing so, for one can follow his digressions like those of an essayist, absorbing the essential unity of the intellectual climate and not asking for more.

If we go on to a systematic reading, at the desk this time, and try to make synopses out of the classifications and subdivisions with which every chapter is studded, we find that the book is far more difficult than it seemed at first, and at times frustrating. This Canadian critic is possessed with the demon of classification and enumeration. He wants to construct systems from which absolutely nothing escapes. Therefore, in every chapter he puts forward new schemes, with terminology that is different though always a little tentative—or, rather, slightly different or with different senses of the same word—while between one scheme and another he traces networks of resemblances (for example, the five *modes* defined in the first essay are matched by the five *phases* of the second, but in reverse order). Moreover, at the back of his mind he always has the Aristotelian and medieval systems of classification, which he compares and superimposes on his own. In a word, he stacks up a series of sieves that are supposed to sift everything at once, the whole of literature in all its parts, and also sift one another reciprocally.

It seems that there is a conflict in him, between his passion for rigid compartments and his sensibility as a critic constantly aware of dimensions that elude every scheme and drive him on to add further schemes. At times he flaunts this demon of systemization and at other times he conceals him in digressions, in approaches from different angles, and in a certain vein of loquacity that every so often runs away with him. For me to take the systematic Frye seriously and settle down to work out synoptic tables has meant finding myself faced with tangles of inextricable lines, and then going back to rely on reading the book as essays.

Here we touch on the crucial point about evaluations of present-day criticism: the possible scientific nature of criticism. Certainly even the most stringent English-speaking criticism finally appears amiably chatty, now that over the last few years French structuralism has accustomed us to a formalization of reading processes that is far leaner and more austere. Let us compare Frye as he catalogues the elements of the medieval romance with a recent structuralist essay on the *Quête du*

Graal. Whereas Frye, at grips with a forest teeming with symbols, seems forever out of breath from chasing the hares that keep popping out on all sides, Tzvetan Todorov the structuralist sees a linear and symmetrical world in which he executes motions of precise elegance and economy: in this thirteenth-century French romance the three levels of meaning refer to one another, and none makes any sense except in relation to the other two; the quest for the Grail is none other than the quest for the tale itself. Whereas Frye sets up a play of mirrors in which the entire encyclopedia of human civilization is refracted, Todorov closes the work in on itself, without leaving any windows to look out of—and, indeed, by his very method rules out the existence of an "out-of-doors" to be looked at.

Maybe the critical analysis I am looking for is one that does not aim directly at the "out-of-doors" but, by exploring the "indoors" of the text and going deeper and deeper in its centripetal movement, succeeds in opening up some unexpected glimpses of that "out-of-doors"—a result that depends less on the method itself than on the way one uses the method. The asceticism I subject myself to in order to enter the "semantic universe" of Greimas, who to the last degree reduces and rationalizes the already skeletal formulas of Propp, has repaid me with the satisfaction of seeing that the "*modèle actantiel*" does enable one to compare the behavior of Ivan the village idiot with that of the financial investor in a program of sociological research; in other words, to establish relationships between types of experience that I would otherwise be quite unable to link together.

If I continue to read books of criticism, it is because

I always hope they will give me surprises of this kind. The greatest of all was to find, hidden in the pages of Bachtin's *Dostoyevsky*, a model of "permanent revolution" (seen as typical of antiquity and the Middle Ages) which could very well be suggested as the society of the future, the only model that would respond to all those requirements that we cannot make fit together: a society based on the regular alternation of destructive periods of consumerism and carnival spirit with periods of productive austerity.

Every true book of criticism may be read like one of the texts it deals with, as a web of poetic metaphors. And this holds good for Frye as well. If efforts have been made to extend these tools of analysis outside the field of creative literature, that is only natural—for example, by going even further than Frye does in his chapter called "The Rhetoric of Non-Literary Prose" and trying to understand the part played by literary modes and symbols and archetypes in every kind of human discourse, in every theoretical model and every vision of the world. I remember an American book I read some years ago (Stanley E. Hyman, *The Tangled Bank: Darwin, Marx, Frazer and Freud as Imaginative Writers* [New York: Atheneum, 1962]). The author examined the writings of four innovators of nineteenth-century thought as if they were imaginative works, mythical cosmogonies, epic poems, tragedies, cycles of novels. He pointed out the characters, situations, images, conflicts, and feeling for nature, but without ever departing from the methods of literary criticism. Was this simply a sophisticated frolic? I must say that Hyman's book has always been a most useful reading lesson for me.

And I think that Frye has also played some part in this lesson, he who for much of his *Anatomy* teaches that even the sacred books must be read by the literary critic exclusively as works of literature. For a clergyman, this is no little thing. On the contrary, if Frye's voice ever takes on tones vibrant with religious controversy it is where he condemns Coleridge's tendency to transform criticism into a kind of natural theology.

Yet there is one point at which Frye's literary and religious worlds do meet: both are in fact biblicocentric worlds. In his chapter on "encyclopedic forms," Frye considers the Bible (Old and New Testaments) as a complete archetypal structure, and also as a compendium of all the modes, symbols, and myths of world literature. From the point of view of literary criticism, the objection might be raised against him that the Bible is not a book, but a library. That is, it is a selection of books placed one after another, which are given particular significance as a whole, and around which we place all other possible books.

The notion of a "library" is not part of Frye's terminology, but it might well be added to it. Literature is not composed simply of books but of libraries, systems in which the various epochs and traditions arrange their "canonical" texts and their "apocryphal" ones. Within these systems each work is different from what it would be in isolation or in another library. A library can have a restricted catalogue, or it can tend to become a universal library, though always expanding around a core of "canonical" books. This is the place where the center of gravity resides, marking off one library from another even more than the catalogue. The ideal library that I would like to see is one that gravitates toward the outside, toward the "apocryphal" books, in the etymological sense of the word: that is, "hidden" books. Literature is a search for the book hidden in the distance that alters the value and meaning of the known books; it is the pull toward the new apocryphal text still to be rediscovered or invented.

Definitions of Territories:
Comedy

Il Caffè (Rome), February 1967; contribution to a symposium on "The Grotesque, Satire, and Literature."

The "comic" element in literature is very important to me, but satire is not the approach that I find most congenial.

One component of satire is moralism, and another is mockery. I would like these two components to remain foreign to me, partly because I do not appreciate them in others. Anyone who plays the moralist thinks he is better than others, whereas anyone who goes in for mockery thinks he is smarter—or, rather, he believes that things are simpler than they appear to be to others. In any case, satire excludes an attitude of questioning and of questing. On the other hand, it does not exclude a large dose of ambivalence, which is the mixture of attraction and repulsion that animates the feelings of every true satirist toward the object of his satire. And if this ambivalence helps to give satire a richer psychological depth, it does not on this account make it a more flexible instrument of poetic knowledge. The satirist is prevented by repulsion from gaining a better knowledge of the world he is attracted to, yet he is forced by attraction to concern himself with the world that repels him.

What I look for in the comic or ironic or grotesque or absurd transformation of things is a way to escape from the limitations and one-sidedness of every representation and every judgment. A thing can be said in more than one way. There is one way in which whoever is saying it wants to say precisely that thing and no other, and another way in which he also wants to say that, certainly, but at the same time wants to point out that the world is far more complicated and vast and contradictory. Ariosto's irony, Shakespeare's comedy, Cervantes's picaresque, Sterne's humor, or the fantasy of Lewis Carroll, Edward Lear, Jarry, or Queneau, are all precious to me insofar as they help one attain that kind of detachment from the particular, that sense of the vastness of the whole.

Nor can one say that this result is obtained only by the greatest. It is, rather, a *method*, a special kind of relationship with the world, capable of imbuing the most varied and everyday manifestations of a civilization. Think how much the sense of humor has counted for in English civilization; and not only that, but how much it has done to enrich literary irony with fundamental dimensions unknown to the classical world. And I am not referring so much to a sort of undercurrent of melancholy good feeling toward the world as to that primary quality of every true humorist: the involvement of himself in his own irony.

It is from these preferences of mine that my reserves about satire arise, for satire is concentrated with exclusive though ambivalent passion on the negative pole of its own world, careful to keep the person of the author out of its protest. But I admire and love the satirical spirit when it emerges without any specific intention, marginal to some broader and more disinterested representation of things. And most certainly I admire satire, and feel homuncular in comparison, whenever the charge of derisive fury is taken to the utmost limits, leaving the threshold of the particular to call the whole human race to account, as in Swift and Gogol, who border on the tragic vision of life.

Definitions of Territories:
Eroticism

Sex and Laughter

Twentieth Century Studies (Canterbury), no. 2 (1969), under the title "Considerations on Sex and Laughter" (translated by Guido Almansi). The issue was devoted to "the treatment of sexual themes in the modern novel." The Italian original later appeared in *Il Caffè*, July–September 1970.

Sexuality in literature is a language in which what is not said is more important than what is. This principle holds good not only for writers who, for good reasons or bad, tackle sexual themes more or less indirectly, but also for those who invest the entire force of their discourse in them. Even writers whose erotic imagination aspires to pass all bounds often use a language that starts off with the utmost clarity and then passes into a mysterious obscurity precisely at the moments of greatest tension, as if its end result could never be anything but inexpressible. This spiral movement to get around or skim over the inexpressible is shared by writers of the most extreme eroticism, such as Sade and Bataille, and also those writers, such as Henry James, from whose pages sex appears to be strictly banned.

The thick symbolic armor beneath which Eros hides is no other than a system of conscious or unconscious shields that separate desire from the representation of it. From this point of view all literature is erotic, just as all dreams are erotic. In the explicitly erotic writer we may therefore recognize one who uses the symbols of sex to give voice to something else, and this something else, after a series of definitions that tend to take shape in philosophical and religious terms, may in the last instance be redefined as another and ultimate Eros, fundamental, mythical, and unattainable.

Most writers are to be found in areas intermediate between these two extremes. Many of them traditionally approach sex by way of the rules of play, of comedy, or at least of irony. Our present intellectual rigor (especially in France, as a reaction against the traditional French wit) tends to condemn the habit of joking and winking at sexual matters as superficial and conformist. A very just argument, above all when it strikes at the (male) habit of diminishing sex, of degrading it; but it runs the risk of making us forget the profound connection between sex and laughter on the anthropological level. For laughter is also a defense of our human trepidation in the face of the revelation of sex; it is mimetic exorcism to enable us to master the absolute turmoil that sexual relations can cause, by means of the lesser turmoil of laughter. The cheerful state of mind that accompanies talk about sex may therefore be understood not only as impatient anticipation of the hoped-for happiness, but also as a recognition of the boundary that is about to be crossed, of entry into a space that is different, paradoxical, and "sacred." Or else, simply, as the modesty of words in the face of what is too far beyond words, as against the crude pretension that sublime or serious language might succeed in providing it with an "equivalent."

What we should establish at this point is whether in this context there is any place for the debunking purpose of a direct, objective, dispassionate representation of sexual relations as facts of life amid all the other facts of life. If this attitude were possible, it would not only occupy a central position, opposed as much to the internal censorship of repression and hypocrisy as to sacred or demonic speculations on Eros, but it would without the least doubt be the victor, clearing the field of all opposition. The literary experience of the last fifty years, however, convinces us that this position remains an intellectual and would-be enlightened pretension. The language of sexuality in fact makes sense only if it is placed at the top of a scale of semantic values. When the musical score needs the highest and the lowest notes, when the canvas requires the most vivid colors: this is when the sign of sex comes into operation. In the world of language, this is the function of the sign of sex: it cannot escape from its privileged position, whether infra-red or ultra-violet; the positive or negative connotation that accompanies the signs of sex in every single literary production determines how values are assigned within the text.

We could say that the axis of values in the literary imagination oscillates between apologia for and vituperation of sexual relations, at the one extreme triumphant exaltation and at the other a descent into the hell of the "anguish of the flesh." The second attitude is largely dominant in literature today. The most typical representation of sexual relations—I am thinking mostly of American novels of the last few years—is in a key of anticlimax, in which the elements of revulsion and desolation, or grotesqueness and caricature, are so strong as to remind us of the sex-hating tradition of preachers and the monstrous erotic temptations of the saints. But it is only in opposition to the complementary attitude that we can place this predominance of theme today, by studying how the apologia for sex has reached such a pitch of rhetorical hoax as to be scarcely practicable except on the level of the mass media.

Here the argument within the text (any possible text) is no longer enough, and this is the right moment to set the text within the social framework from which it emerges. We live in an age of potential desexualization. The struggle for existence in the big cities is such as to encourage asexuality. Sexual mythology on the mass-media level has the function of compensating, of recovering something we feel is already lost or in grave danger.

It is in this context that we may judge the attributions of value within literary texts. And then a writer who represents sex in grotesque or hellish fashion may be seen as one who is warning us of this extreme situation, or putting us on our guard against the illusion that we might easily regain our lost fullness. Meanwhile, the apologist for sex might be a liar, perpetuating an illusion—someone (and we Italians think at once of D'Annunzio) who uses verbal artifice to conceal the unlivableness of the asexual world into which we are sinking. Or else it might be someone who is completely aware of the loss that threatens us and becomes the preacher of a sexual reawakening (which might well take on the regressive aspects of intellectual mythicizing of the primitive, as in D. H. Lawrence); or someone who attempts to establish a more warmly human relationship with reality by giving the sexual encounter a central place and setting up a scale of values based on the vital expression of every human experience and presence (for Henry Miller, who appears to unite the grotesque and apologetic lines, literature is a method of restoring Eros to existence).

Today the situation is more serious and the remedies must be more extreme. The plastic arts have already faced the problem of establishing erotic communication with the materials and objects of our most humdrum everyday lives. Literature can follow on the same path by inventing a communication of sexual signs on the lowest linguistic level (that of the end of the world in Beckett or the regression of the mass-man in Sanguineti), or by imagining sexual relations that are not anthropomorphic (as I have tried to do by narrating the love affairs of mollusks or unicellular organisms).

I have here mentioned literary experiments carried out in the name of laughter. As I wished to demonstrate, only laughter—systematic mockery, giggles of self-derision, the convulsed grimace—can guarantee that our words match up to the terribleness of living and mark a truly revolutionary mutation in us.

Definitions of Territories:
Fantasy

Le Monde, August 15, 1970; contribution (written in French)
to a symposium on the literature of fantasy following the
publication of Tzvetan Todorov's *Introduction à la littérature fantastique*. The numbered questions related to: (1)
the definition of fantasy; (2) the literature of fantasy today;
(3) your own work in relation to fantasy; (4) examples
of short stories and novels of fantasy.

(1) In contemporary French literary language the
term *fantastique* is used chiefly of horror stories, which
involve a somewhat nineteenth-century relationship with
the reader. That is, if the reader wishes to take part in
the game (at least with some part of himself) he has to
believe in what he is reading, and be prepared to be seized
by an almost physiological emotion (usually of terror
or anguish), and seek an explanation of it as he would

in real life. In Italian (as originally in French, I think) the words *fantasia* and *fantastico* by no means involve this leap on the part of the reader into the emotional flood of the text. On the contrary, they imply a detachment, a levitation, the acceptance of a different logic based on objects and connections other than those of everyday life or the dominant literary conventions. And the same, I think, is true of the equivalent words in English (though "fantastic" has been severely corrupted). So we may speak of twentieth-century *fantasy*, or of the *fantasy* of the Renaissance. Ariosto's readers were never faced with the problem of *believing* or *explaining*. For them—as today for the readers of Gogol's "The Nose," of *Alice in Wonderland*, or of Kafka's *Metamorphoses*—the pleasure of fantasy lies in the unraveling of a logic with rules or points of departure or solutions that keep some surprises up their sleeves.

This study by Todorov is very accurate on one meaning of fantasy and full of suggestions with regard to other meanings, aiming at some possible general classification. If we wish to compile an exhaustive atlas of imaginative literature, we will have to start with a grammar of what Todorov calls "wonder" at the level of the earliest combinatorial operations of signs in the primitive myths and fables, and of the symbolic requirements of the unconscious (before any sort of conscious allegory), as indeed at the level of the intellectual games of all times and all cultures.

(2) Nineteenth-century fantasy, a refined product of the Romantic spirit, soon became part of popular literature. (Poe wrote for the newspapers.) During the

twentieth century, intellectual (no longer emotional) fantasy has become uppermost: play, irony, the winking eye, and also a meditation on the hidden desires and nightmares of contemporary man.

(3) I leave the critics the task of placing my novels and stories within (or outside) some classification of fantasy. For me the main thing in a narrative is not the explanation of an extraordinary event, but the *order of things* that this extraordinary event produces in itself and around it; the pattern, the symmetry, the network of images deposited around it, as in the formation of a crystal.

(4) Among the books I have read fairly recently, I will try to find a few little-known names to represent the various literary possibilities of fantasy. First of all, a nineteenth-century novel that might be described as fantageometry: *Flatland* by the English writer Edwin A. Abbott. At the other extreme is a Polish novel of the period between the wars, written by Bruno Schulz. Starting with family memories, he achieves a visionary transfiguration of well-nigh inexhaustible wealth of imagination. And then there are the stories of Felisberto Hernandez, a Uruguayan writer. In these the narrator, who is usually a pianist, is invited to lonely country houses where wealthy maniacs set up complicated charades in which women and dolls change places. He has a few things in common with Hoffmann, but in fact he is like no one else.

Cinema and the Novel:
Problems of Narrative

Cahiers du Cinéma, October 1966; contribution (written in French) to a symposium on "Cinema and the Novel."

To find the elements common to a series of written words (such as a novel) and a series of moving photograms (such as a film) we must examine this flow of words or photograms and isolate the particular chain of narrative images that—even before literature and the novel came into existence—was proper to the oral tradition (myth, fable, folk tale, epic song, legends of saints and martyrs, bawdy tales, etc.). The cinema is derived partly from the storyteller's art (all the James Bond movies are constructed like fairy tales) and partly from the popular literature of the nineteenth century (adventure story, Gothic novel, detective story, love story, romantic novel, social novel), in which the series of successive images has a bearing on the way of writing.

But this inheritance is not enough to enable us to classify as typical of the cinema certain elements such as the comic gag or the suspense created by physical danger. In our analysis we have to bear in mind the debts owed by the cinema to the forms of entertainment that preceded it, not so much the theatre as (above all) the circus with its horses and wild animals and acrobats and clowns, and vaudeville and the Grand Guignol—and, come to that, even sporting events. The mythological and poetic force of the cinema derives from the convergence of many elementary forms of culture. It tends toward repetition rather than innovation.

We therefore have to pinpoint this aspect of a problem that is especially important in the cinema, and is most commonly called sociological, but could even be called ethnological. It is earlier than the novel, and can be termed literary only to the extent to which one might speak of a preliterary or metaliterary aspect of literature.

Yet another aspect of this emerges from the instrument used to tell the story: the camera, in short. For example, the close-up has no equivalent in a narrative fashioned of words. Literature is totally lacking in any working method to enable it to isolate a single vastly enlarged detail in which one face comes forward to underline a state of mind or stress the importance of a single detail in comparison with the rest.

As a narrative device, the ability to vary the distance between the camera and the object may be a small thing indeed, but it makes for a notable difference between cinema and oral or written narrative, in which the distance between language and image is always the same. With language one can create mysterious effects to give the impression of distance, as when Tom Thumb sees a small light far, far away in the forest, or else the impression of proximity that conveys alienation and malaise, like Roquentin looking at himself in the mirror. In cinema the size of the image does not have any affective connotations, but a syntactical function—or, rather, the function of marking "privileged" points in a succession of images. (Printed texts could only use different sizes of type face, and spoken language a heightening of the tone of voice.) But the close-up gives the spectator a special feeling: the larger the image the more he feels directly involved, and this is the reason for the demand for larger and larger screens.

The close-up stems from an ancient institution of painting: the portrait. I do not think that painting has ever managed to exploit the syntactical possibilities of mixing greatly enlarged portraits with "panoramic" scenes. Perhaps this occurs in certain mosaics or frescoes with the head of Christ Pancrator, and on the ceiling of the Sistine Chapel Michelangelo alternated the portraits of prophets and sibyls with Biblical scenes. But these are whole figures and not just heads, nor is the disproportion to the other figures all that great. Above all, the large figures are not part of the narrative. Portraiture has had its applications even in the novel, thanks largely to Balzac. But the minute physiognomic descriptions that Balzac gave us (under the influence of Lavater's theories) are far from being the strong point of his novels. The modern novel, for its part, is more than willing to leave the lineaments of its characters in shadow. But for the cinema, on the contrary, human faces are the stuff of life.

Let us say, then, that what the cinema has that is completely cinematographic ought not to be matched against its literary ancestors. From that standpoint cinema and novel have nothing to teach each other and nothing to learn from each other.

There remains the fact that the cinema is continually being drawn toward literature. In spite of having such power of its own, the cinema has always been afflicted by jealousy of the written text: it wants to "write." The same thing is true of countless upstanding people who occupy important positions in other fields and who one would think were quite satisfied with themselves. Yet one discovers that they spend the night filling reams of paper, urged on by one single ambition: to publish a novel. The cinema's love affair with the traditional novel has bestowed on it several inventions that immediately became commonplaces, such as the off-screen voice to render the first person singular, the flashback to represent the past, the fade-out to convey the passage of time, and so on. Until just the other day literature was a bad master to the cinema. The great novelty of the last few years has been the general awareness that the cinema must look for literary models other than the traditional novel. The challenge of the written word continues to be one of the chief motive forces of invention in the cinema, but—a thing that never happened in the past— literature has begun to function as a model of freedom. The cinema of today employs a wealth of ways to tell a story. It can make a reminiscence film, a diary film, a self-analysis film, a *nouveau-roman* film, a lyric-poem film, and so on. All this is new for the cinema, though less so for literature. From this point of view the cinema is still a tributary of literature, but the situation is fluid and may well change.

At a certain level the opposite might be true.

There is a species of novel that survives simply because its manner of narration, and its themes, do not differ from those of the average film, and aim to satisfy the requirements of the same public, the demands of the same consumer. I am not speaking merely of the *série noire*, in which exchanges between the cinema and the novel are mutually honest, but of that large sector occupied by the average novel with a certain amount of "literary dignity" and, in the best of cases, some interest of subject matter and a construction based on a well-tried recipe.

It is on another level, that of experimental literature, that the cinema has the capacity to render certain narrative techniques obsolete (and, come to that, themes, decor, situations, characters); but I do not think that this capacity stops at the liquidation of the traditional novel. Let us take one of the procedures typical of the *nouveau roman*, such as the imperceptible passage from present to past, from the real to the imaginary, from one "space-time continuum" to another, etc. Two or three films of real quality have sufficed to annex this process to the cinema, and by this time, when we find it in a novel written afterward, the process seems to be "making films" (which in literature still retains its negative character).

But dislocations in time—for example, in Robbe-Grillet—count also (or chiefly) as an operation wrought on language: that absence of emotional and evocative vibrations remains a literary conquest that the cinema cannot poke its nose into. Let us, then, say that the cinema can exercise its power of attrition on those elements of a novel that may be separated from the fact of *writing*. A way of writing can be rendered obsolete only by another way of writing.

More interesting to me today than the novel-film is everything that tends toward the essay-film. The film-questionnaire aspect of *Masculin-Féminin* seems to me indicative of this tendency, in spite of all that this film makes us see directly, all that it represents as a kind of story, and the critical attitude it maintains toward the sociological inquiries to which it turned its attention. The basic point is this: the sociological-inquiry film and the historical-research film make sense only if they are not filmed explanations of a truth that sociology and historiography have already established, but intervene in some way to contest what sociology and historiography are saying. (Incidentally, I think that Rosi is also working along the right lines.) For the true essay-film I envisage an attitude not of pedagogy but of interrogation, with none of that inferiority complex toward the written word that has bedeviled relations between literature and the cinema.

I have always enjoyed the cinema purely as a spectator, without its having anything to do with my literary work. If any part of cinema has in fact influenced some of my work, it is the animated cartoon. The world of drawing has always been closer to me than that of photography, and I find that the art of moving cartoon figures about on a static background is not so different from that of telling a story with words arranged in lines on a blank sheet of paper. The animated cartoon has a lot to teach the writer, above all how to define characters and objects with a few strokes. It is a metaphorical and metonymic art at one and the same time; it is the art of metamorphosis (the great theme of novels ever since Apuleius, and one that the cinema is so bad at) and of anthropomorphism (a pagan vision of the world, far less humanist than is often supposed).

Another visual and graphic way of storytelling to influence me is the comic strip. There, too, one can distinguish aspects of conservation and creation, as in the cinema, but the distinction is much clearer. The adventure-story comic strip tends to retain the viewpoint of the nineteenth-century novel and the cinema. The comic genre, which interests me most, has given our century an entirely new way of storytelling, with the combined use of drawing and writing (or, better, graphic invention linked to spoken and onomatopoeic language). Unfortunately, the study of comic strips has until now been left in the hands of sociologists. A true study of the genre as an art in itself has still to see the light.

Whom Do We Write For?
or
The Hypothetical Bookshelf

Rinascita (Rome), November 24, 1967; contribution to a symposium entitled "For Whom Do We Write a Novel? For Whom Do We Write a Poem?"

Whom do we write a novel for? Whom do we write a poem for? For people who have read a number of other novels, a number of other poems. A book is written so that it can be put beside other books and take its place on a hypothetical bookshelf. Once it is there, in some way or other it alters the shelf, expelling certain other volumes from their places or forcing them back into the second row, while demanding that certain others should be brought up to the front.

If a bookseller knows how to sell his wares, what does he do? He says, "Have you already read that book?

In that case you must take this one." This is not unlike the imaginary or unconscious gesture a writer makes toward his invisible reader, with the sole difference that the writer cannot be content merely to satisfy the reader (and even a good bookseller, come to think of it, has to go a bit further than that); he must also assume a reader who does not yet exist, or else a change in the reader as he is today. This is something that doesn't always happen. In all periods and societies, with the establishment of certain canons of aesthetics, a certain way of interpreting the world, a certain scale of moral and social values, literature can perpetuate itself by a series of confirmations, limited readjustments, and further studies. What interests me, however, is another possibility inherent in literature: that of questioning the established scale of values and code of meanings.

A writer's work is important to the extent that the ideal bookshelf on which he would like to be placed is still an improbable shelf, containing books that we do not usually put side by side, the juxtaposition of which can produce electric shocks, short circuits. And so my initial answer already needs correction. A literary situation begins to get interesting when one writes novels for people who are not readers of novels alone, and when one writes literature while thinking of a shelf of books that are not all literary.

Let me give a few examples on the basis of our experience in Italy. In the years 1945–50 the aim was to write novels for a shelf that was essentially political, or historico-political, to address a reader interested principally in the culture of politics and in contemporary history but whose literary "needs" (or deficiencies) it also seemed urgent to fulfill. Set up in this way, the operation was bound to fail. Political culture was not a "given" thing, with values that literature had to flank with its own, or match up to (and with few exceptions the latter values were also seen as established, "classical" values). On the contrary, it was something that still had to be made. In fact, it is something that needs to be continually constructed and evaluated in light of the entire body of work the rest of culture is producing, which must be evaluated along with it.

In the course of the decade 1950–60 an attempt was made to bring together, on the bookshelf of one and the same hypothetical reader, the problem of European literary decadence between the two wars and the moral and civil sense of Italian historicism. This operation was fairly well suited to the situation of the average Italian reader of those years (the intellectual timidly becoming bourgeois, the bourgeois timidly setting himself problems). But right from the start it was anachronistic on a broader level, and was valid only for the limited range of things that various hegemonies and quarantines had assigned to our culture. In a word, the library of the average Italian intellectual, even with a series of later increments, no longer enabled him to understand anything much of what was going on in the world, or even amongst ourselves. It was inevitable that it should collapse.

Which duly happened in the sixties. The amount of information available to anyone who has studied in the last fifteen years is immeasurably greater than it could possibly have been in prewar, wartime, or post-war Italy. We no longer start by trying to link up with a tradition, but with open questions; the frame of reference is no longer compatibility with a well-proved system, but the state of things on a worldwide scale. (Arguments aiming to show that "we used to be better," even in cases where they are true, are completely useless and serve only to prove the opposite.)

In literature the writer is now aware of a bookshelf on which pride of place is held by the disciplines capable of breaking down the fact of literature into its primary elements and motivations, the disciplines of analysis and dissection (linguistics, information theory, analytical philosophy, sociology, anthropology, a new use of psychoanalysis, a new use of Marxism). To this library of multiple specializations we tend not so much to add a literary shelf as to question its right to be there at all: literature today survives above all by denying itself. Therefore, to the question posed at the beginning, the answer becomes: We will write novels for a reader who has finally understood that he no longer has to read novels.

The weakness of this position does not, as many claim, lie in the nonliterary influences that preside over it, but, on the contrary, in the fact that the nonliterary library posited by the new writers is still too limited. Antiliterature is too exclusively literary a passion to meet our present cultural needs. The reader we have to foresee for our books will have epistemological, semantic, practical, and methodological requirements which he will constantly want to compare, even on the level of literature, as being examples of symbolic procedures and the construction of logical patterns. I speak also, and perhaps chiefly, of the *political* reader.

Having got to this point, I can no longer avoid two problems that are certainly pertinent to this inquiry promoted by *Rinascita*.

First, doesn't the act of supposing an ever more cultured reader detract from the urgency of solving the problem of cultural inequality? This problem exists equally dramatically today in the advanced capitalist societies, in ex-colonial and semicolonial societies, and in the socialist countries. Cultural inequality threatens to perpetuate the social disparities from which it originated. This is the conundrum facing education throughout the world—and, immediately after education, politics. Literature can make only an indirect contribution: for example, by firmly rejecting any paternalistic solution. If we assume a reader less cultured than the writer and take a pedagogical, educational, and reassuring attitude toward him, we are simply underlining the disparity. Any attempt to sweeten the situation with palliatives such as a literature of the people is a step backward, not a step ahead. Literature is not school. Literature must presuppose a public that is more cultured, and *more cultured than the writer himself.* Whether or not such a public exists is unimportant. The writer addresses a reader who knows more about it than he does; he invents a "himself" who knows more than he does, to speak to someone who knows more still. Literature has no choice but to raise the stakes and keep the betting going, following the logic of a situation that can only get worse. It is up to society as a whole to find the solution. (A society, needless to say, of which the writer is also a part, with all the responsibilities that brings with it, even when opposed to the internal logic of his work.) Certainly, in taking this road, literature must be conscious of the risks it is running, even the risk that in order to create an initially egalitarian program the revolution will outlaw literature (along with philosophy, pure science, etc.)— an illusory and disastrously self-injurious solution, but one that has a logic of its own and therefore crops up and will continue to crop up in this and subsequent centuries, at least until people find a better or equally simple solution.

The second question, put in elementary terms, is this: given the division of the world into a capitalist camp and a proletarian camp, an imperialist camp and a revolutionary camp, whom is the writer writing for? Answer: he writes for the one side and the other. Every book—not only of literature, and even if "addressed" to someone—is read by its addressees and by its enemies. It is perfectly possible that the enemies might learn more from it than the addressees. Strictly speaking, this can hold good even for books of revolutionary propaedeutics, from Marx's *Capital* to the manuals on guerrilla warfare. As regards literature, the way in which a "revolutionary" work of art is taken over in a short time by the middle classes and thereby neutralized is a theme that left-wing Italian writers have discussed several times in recent years, coming to pessimistic conclusions that are hard to refute. The argument can be carried forward by putting it on a different footing. For a start, literature has to realize how modest is its impact on politics. The struggle is decided on the basis of general strategic and tactical lines and relative strengths; in this context a book is a grain of sand, especially a literary book. The effect that an important book, literary or scientific, can have on the general struggle in progress is to raise the struggle to a higher level of awareness, to add to its instruments of knowledge, of foresight, of imagination, of concentration, etc. The new level may be more favorable either to revolution or to reaction, depending on how the revolution learns to act, and on how the others act. It does not depend except to a minimal degree on the intentions of whoever wrote the book. The book (or scientific discovery) of a reactionary might be a determining factor in a step forward by the revolution, but the opposite might also be the case. It is not so much the book that is politically revolutionary as the use that can be made of it; even a work intended to be politically revolutionary does not become so except in the course of being used, in its often retarded and indirect effects. Therefore, the decisive element in judging a work with reference to the struggle is the level it is on, the step ahead it enables awareness to take; whereas belonging to one camp or the other, and motivation or intention, are factors that might have a genetic or affective interest, especially as regards the author, but will have scant impact on the course of the struggle. Whether explicit or not, some form of "address" is nearly always discernible in a work, and a writer who thinks of himself as involved in the struggle is naturally led to address his companions-in-arms. But first he must bear in mind the general context in which the work is situated, he must be aware that the front line also passes through the middle of his work, and that it is a front in constant movement, forever shifting the banners we thought had been raised in place for good. There are no safe territories. The work itself is and has to be a battleground.

Right and Wrong
Political Uses of Literature

Paper read in English at a symposium on European politics arranged by the European Studies Program at Amherst College, February 25, 1976.

When I received the invitation to speak here at your symposium, my first thought was one that always comes to me on such occasions: I tried to remember if there was some recent piece of mine on literature and politics, some contribution to one of the numerous debates on the subject. And I realized that I had nothing ready. For some years I had not happened to write or say anything on this subject.

Now that I think of it, this is very odd. In the years of my youth, from 1945 on, throughout the fifties and beyond, the problems then dominant were concerned with the relations between the writer and politics. I might even say that every discussion revolved around this point. My generation could be defined as the one that began to be concerned with literature and politics at the same time.

In recent years, on the other hand, it has often occurred to me to worry about how things are going in politics and how things are going in literature, but when I think about politics I think about politics, and when I think about literature I think about literature. When I confront these two problematical areas today, I feel two quite separate sensations, and both are sensations of emptiness: the lack of a political program that I can believe in and the lack of a literary program I can believe in.

But on a deeper level I am aware that the knot of relationships between politics and literature that we came up against in our youth has not yet been unraveled; its frayed and twisted ends are still getting tangled around our ankles.

What happened in the sixties profoundly changed many of the concepts that we were dealing with, even if we still go on calling them by the same names. We do not yet know what all this will mean in terms of ultimate effects on the future of our society, but we do already know that there has been a revolution of the mind, an intellectual turning point.

If we had to give a brief definition of this process, we could say that the notion of man as the subject of history is finished—the antagonist who has dethroned man must still be called man, but a man very different from what he was before. Which is to say, the human race of the "big numbers" in exponential growth all over the planet; the explosion of the big cities; the ungovernability of society and the economy, whatever system they belong to; the end of economic and ideological Eurocentrism; and the claiming of full rights by the outcasts, the repressed, the forgotten, and the inarticulate. All the parameters, categories, and antitheses that we once used to define, plan, and classify the world have been called into question. And not only those most closely linked to historical values, but even the ones that seemed to be stable anthropological categories—reason and myth, work and existence, male and female—and even the polarity of the most elementary combinations of words—affirmation and negation, above and below, subject and object.

In these last few years, my worries about politics and literature have had to do with their inadequacy with regard to the tasks these changes in our mentality impose.

Perhaps I should begin by giving a better definition of the situation in the tiny domestic microcosm that is Italian literature, in order to explain what fresh tidings the sixties brought us.

During the fifties, Italian literature, and the novel in particular, aspired to represent the ethical and social conscience of contemporary Italy. During the sixties, this claim was attacked on two fronts. On the front of literary form—or, rather, on a front that was not merely formal but also epistemological and eschatological—it was the new avant-garde that attacked and questioned Italian fiction, accusing it of being sentimental, antiquated, and hypocritically consolatory. Only a violent break in the language and the space and time of fiction could represent contemporary life and dispel illusions.

At the same time, in the ranks of politically committed criticism, the most radical critics attacked and destroyed the claim to exemplariness made by committed literature, and accused it of populism.* On this front also, therefore, the ground was prepared for the revenge of the avant-garde, or at least of the literature of negation—that is, for the way of thinking in literature that claims not to provide any positive teaching, but to be merely an indication of the point we are at.

Along with these two attacking forces I must now mention a third, and of no less importance. The cultural hinterland of Italian literature was undergoing a complete change. Linguistics, information theory, the sociology of the mass media, ethnology and anthropology, the structural study of myths, semiology, a new use of psychoanalysis, a new use of Marxism: all these became instruments habitually employed to dismantle any literary object and break it down into its component parts.

I believe that at that moment literature found itself in a more promising situation than it had ever enjoyed before. The ground had been cleared of the vast misunderstandings that had weighed upon the debates of the postwar years. The dismantling of the work of literature might open the way toward a new evaluation and a new structuring. And what came of it? Nothing— or exactly the opposite of what might have been hoped for. This was for reasons both inside and outside the literary movement itself.

---

*I am referring principally to a book by Alberto Asor Rosa, *Scrittori e popolo: Saggi sulla scrittura populista in Italia* (Rome: Samonà e Savelli, 1967).

The new political radicalism of the students of 1968 was marked in Italy by a rejection of literature. It was not the literature of negation that was proposed, but the negation of literature. Literature was accused, in the first place, of being a waste of time in comparison with the one thing that mattered: action. That the cult of action was first and foremost an old literary myth was understood—or is being understood—very slowly.

I would like to say that this attitude was not entirely mistaken. It meant the rejection of a wishy-washy, so-called social literature, the rejection of a wrongheaded notion of the committed writer. And so in some ways it brought us closer to a proper evaluation of the social function of literature, far closer than any fatheaded traditional literary cult could have been.

But it was—and I am speaking in the past tense because I believe that something has already changed—it was also a sign of self-limitation, of narrow horizons, of an inability to perceive the complexity of things.

When politicians and politically minded people pay too much attention to literature, it is a bad sign—a bad sign mostly for literature, because it is then that literature is in most danger. But it is also a bad sign when they don't want to hear the word mentioned, and this happens as much to the most traditionally obtuse bourgeois politicians as to the most ideological revolutionaries. This is a bad sign mostly for *them*, because they are showing themselves afraid of any use of language that calls the certitude of their own language into question.

In any case, the appointment between the two new avant-gardes, literary and political, never took place. The literary avant-garde suffered from the loss of the potential reserves of readers that it was looking forward to, and soon enough the defeated writers of the fifties slid back into their seats. Places cannot stay empty for long in literature without being occupied, in the worst hypothesis by bad writers, and at best by writers of the traditional stamp.

In recent years all the more oversimplified political viewpoints have failed, and our awareness of the complexity of the society we live in has grown, even if no one can claim to have a solution in his pocket. The situation in Italy today is on the one hand a state of deterioration and corruption in our institutional framework, and on the other of a growing collective maturity and search for ways of governing ourselves.

What is the place of literature in such a situation? I have to admit that the situation is no less confused in this field than in that of politics. There is an extensive nationwide public for the Italian novel, particularly when it deals with recent politics or history—not in the didactic manner of thirty years ago, but as a set of problems. On the other hand, there is the pressure of the mass media urging the writer to write for the newspapers, to take part in round-table discussions on television, to give his opinion on anything that he might or might not know about. The writer is given a chance to fill the space left vacant by any intelligible political discussion. But this task turns out to be too easy (it is too easy to make generalizations without having any responsibility in practice), whereas it ought to be the most difficult task a writer could undertake. The more flaccid and abstract the language of politics becomes, the more we are conscious of a tacit demand for a different language, more direct and personal. More provocative, too. Provocation is the public function most in demand in present-day Italy. The life and death and posthumous life of Pasolini have consecrated the provocative role of the writer.

There is a fundamental error in all this. What we ask of writers is that they guarantee the survival of what we call *human* in a world where everything appears inhuman; guarantee the survival of *human* discourse to console us for the loss of humanity in every other discourse and relationship. And what do we mean by *human*? Usually, whatever is temperamental, emotional, ingenuous, and not at all austere. It is very hard to find someone who believes in the austerity of literature, superior to and opposed to the false austerity of language that runs the world today.

The Nobel Prize this year was awarded to Eugenio Montale, but few now remember that the strength of his poetry has always lain in his keeping his voice low, without emphasis of any kind, using modest and doubtful tones. It is precisely for this reason that he has made himself heard to many, and his presence has had a great impact on three generations of readers. This is how literature tunnels its way forward; its "efficacy," its "power," if they exist at all, are of this type.

But society today demands that the writer raise his voice if he wants to be heard, propose ideas that will have impact on the public, push all his instinctive reactions to extremes. But even the most sensational and explosive statements pass over the heads of readers. All is as nothing, like the sound of the wind. Any comment appears no more than a shake of the head, as at a naughty boy. Everyone knows that words are only words, and produce no friction with the world around us: they involve no danger either for the reader or the writer. In the ocean of words, printed or broadcast, the words of the poet or writer are swallowed up.

This is the paradox of the power of literature: it seems that only when it is persecuted does it show its true powers, challenging authority, whereas in our permissive society it feels that it is being used merely to create the occasional pleasing contrast to the general ballooning of verbiage. (And yet, should we be so mad as to complain about it? Would to God that even dictators realized that the best method of freeing themselves from the dangers of the written word is to treat it as counting for nothing!)

In the first place, we have to remember that wherever writers are persecuted it means not only that literature is persecuted, but also that there is a ban on many other kinds of discussion and thought (and political thought in the forefront). Fiction, poetry, and literary criticism in such countries acquire unusual political specific gravity, insofar as they give a voice to all those who are deprived of one. We who live in a state of literary freedom are aware that this freedom implies a society on the move, in which a lot of things are changing (whether for better or worse is another problem); in this case, too, what is in question is the relationship between the message of literature and society, or, more precisely, between the message and the possible creation of a society to receive it. This is the rapport that counts, not the one with political authority, now that those in government cannot claim to hold the reins of society, either in the democracies or in the authoritarian regimes of right or left. Literature is one of a society's instruments of self-awareness—certainly not the only one, but nonetheless an essential instrument, because its origins are connected with the origins of various types of knowledge, various codes, various forms of critical thought.

In a word, what I think is that there are two wrong ways of thinking of a possible political use for literature. The first is to claim that literature should voice a truth already possessed by politics; that is, to believe that the sum of political values is the primary thing, to which literature must simply adapt itself. This opinion implies a notion of literature as ornamental and superfluous, but it also implies a notion of politics as fixed and self-confident: an idea that would be catastrophic. I think that such a pedagogical function for politics could only be imagined at the level of bad literature and bad politics.

The other mistaken way is to see literature as an assortment of eternal human sentiments, as the truth of a human language that politics tends to overlook, and that therefore has to be called to mind from time to time. This concept apparently leaves more room for literature, but in practice it assigns it the task of confirming what is already known, or maybe of provoking in a naïve and rudimentary way, by means of the youthful pleasures of freshness and spontaneity. Behind this way of thinking is the notion of a set of established values that literature is responsible for preserving, the classical and immobile idea of literature as the depository of a given truth. If it agrees to take on this role, literature confines itself to a function of consolation, preservation, and regression—a function that I believe does more harm than good.

Does this mean that all political uses of literature are wrong? No, I believe that just as there are two wrong uses, there are also two right ones.

Literature is necessary to politics above all when it gives a voice to whatever is without a voice, when it gives a name to what as yet has no name, especially to what the language of politics excludes or attempts to exclude. I mean aspects, situations, and languages both of the outer and of the inner world, the tendencies repressed both in individuals and in society. Literature is like an ear that can hear things beyond the understanding of the language of politics; it is like an eye that can see beyond the color spectrum perceived by politics. Simply because of the solitary individualism of his work, the writer may happen to explore areas that no one has explored before, within himself or outside, and to make discoveries that sooner or later turn out to be vital areas of collective awareness.

This is still a very indirect, undeliberate, and fortuitous use for literature. The writer follows his own road, and chance or social and psychological factors lead him to discover something that may become important for political and social action as well. It is the responsibility of the sociopolitical observer not to leave anything to chance, and to apply his own method to the business of literature in such a way as not to allow anything to escape him.

But there is also, I think, another sort of influence that literature can exert, perhaps not more direct but certainly more intentional on the part of the writer. This is the ability to impose patterns of language, of vision, of imagination, of mental effort, of the correlation of facts, and in short the creation (and by creation I mean selection and organization) of a model of values that is at the same time aesthetic and ethical, essential to any plan of action, especially in political life.

So it comes about that, having excluded political education from the functions of literature, I find myself stating that I do believe in a type of education by means of literature; a type of education that can yield results only if it is difficult and indirect, if it implies the arduous attainment of literary stringency.

Any result attained by literature, as long as it is stringent and rigorous, may be considered firm ground for all practical activities for anyone who aspires to the construction of a mental order solid and complex enough to contain the disorder of the world within itself; for anyone aiming to establish a method subtle and flexible enough to be the same thing as an absence of any method whatever.

I have spoken of two right uses, but now I can discern a third, which is connected to the critical manner in which literature regards itself. If at one time literature was regarded as a mirror held up to the world, or as the direct expression of feelings, now we can no longer neglect the fact that books are made of words, of signs, of methods of construction. We can never forget that what books communicate often remains unknown even to the author himself, that books often say something different from what they set out to say, that in any book there is a part that is the author's and a part that is a collective and anonymous work.

This kind of awareness does not influence literature alone: it can also be useful to politics, enabling that science to discover how much of it is no more than verbal construction, myth, literary *topos*. Politics, like literature, must above all know itself and distrust itself.

As a final observation, I should like to add that if it is impossible today for anyone to feel innocent, if in whatever we do or say we can discover a hidden motive—that of a white man, or a male, or the possessor of a certain income, or a member of a given economic system, or a sufferer from a certain neurosis—this should not induce in us either a universal sense of guilt or an attitude of universal accusation.

When we become aware of our disease or of our hidden motives, we have already begun to get the better of them. What matters is the way in which we accept our motives and live through the ensuing crisis. This is the only chance we have of becoming different from the way we are—that is, the only way of starting to invent a new way of being.

Levels of Reality
in Literature

Paper read at an international conference on "Levels of
Reality," Florence, September 1978.

Different levels of reality also exist in literature; in
fact literature rests precisely on the distinction among
various levels, and would be unthinkable without an
awareness of this distinction. A work of literature might
be defined as an operation carried out in the written
language and involving several levels of reality at the
same time. From this point of view, some consideration
of works of literature might not be completely useless
even to the scientist or philosopher of science.

In a work of literature, various levels of reality may
meet while remaining distinct and separate, or else they
may melt and mingle and knit together, achieving a
harmony among their contradictions or else forming an
explosive mixture. Shakespeare's plays provide us with

a number of clear examples. For distinction between the different levels we might think of *A Midsummer Night's Dream*, in which the complications in the plot occur where three levels of reality intersect, though these remain quite distinct: (1) the aristocratic characters at the court of Theseus and Hippolyta; (2) the supernatural characters Titania, Oberon, and Puck; (3) the rustic comic characters, Bottom and his friends. This third level borders on the animal kingdom, which may be seen as a fourth level, entered by Bottom when he is changed into an ass. In addition there is one further level to consider, that of the performance of the story of Pyramus and Thisbe, the play within the play.

Hamlet, on the other hand, constitutes a sort of short circuit, or a whirlpool that sucks in all the various levels of reality; it is from their very irreconcilability that the drama comes into being. There is the ghost of Hamlet's father with his demand for justice, which is the level of archaic values, of knightly virtues, with its moral code and supernatural beliefs; there is the level we might call realistic, that of "Something is rotten in the state of Denmark" (i.e., the court at Elsinore); there is the level of Hamlet's inner life, of the modern psychological and intellectual awareness that is the great novelty of the play. To hold these three levels together, Hamlet disguises himself in a fourth, the linguistic barrier of his feigned madness. But, as if by induction, this feigned madness leads to real madness, and the level of madness seizes and eliminates one of the few positive elements remaining in the play: the delicate figure of Ophelia. This drama also has a play within the play, the performance of the troupe of strolling players; and this constitutes a level of reality on its own, separate from the rest, though interacting with them.

Up till now I have confined myself to distinguishing the various levels of reality within the work of art considered as a world of its own, but we cannot stop there. We have to consider the work as a product, in its relation to the outside world in the age when it was created and the age when we received it. In all periods and in all literatures we find works that at a certain time turn around on themselves, look at themselves in the act of coming into being, and become aware of the materials they are made of. Just to stick to Shakespeare, in the last act of *Antony and Cleopatra*, before killing herself, Cleopatra imagines her fate as a prisoner taken to Rome for Caesar's triumph, mocked by the crowds; even now she thinks that her love for Antony will become the subject of theatrical performances:

> . . . the quick comedians
> Extemporally will stage us, and present
> Our Alexandrian revels. Antony
> Shall be brought drunken forth, and I shall see
> Some squeaking Cleopatra boy my greatness
> I' the posture of a whore.

There is a fine passage by Middleton Murry about this dazzling piece of mental acrobatics. On the stage of the Globe theatre a piping boy dressed up as Cleopatra represents the real, majestic Queen Cleopatra in the act of imagining herself being represented by a boy dressed up as Cleopatra.

These are the tangles we have to start with in saying anything about the levels of reality in a work of literature. We cannot lose sight of the fact that these levels are part of the *written* world.

"I write." This statement is the one and only real "datum" a writer can start from. "At this moment I am writing." Which is also the same as saying: "You who are reading are obliged to believe only one thing: that what you are reading is something that at some previous time someone has written; what you are reading takes place in one particular world, that of the written word. It may be that likenesses can be established between the world of the written word and other worlds of experience, and that you will be called on to judge upon these likenesses, but your judgment would in any case be wrong if while reading you hoped to enter into a direct relationship with the experience of worlds other than that of the written word." I have spoken here of "worlds of experience," not of "levels of reality," because within the world of the written word one can discern many levels of reality, as in any other world of experience.

Let us then agree that the statement "I write" serves the purpose of pinning down a first level of reality, which I have, explicitly or otherwise, to take account of in any operation that creates a rapport between diverse levels of reality in writing, and even between things written and things not written. This first level may be useful to me as a platform on which to erect a second level, which may even belong to a reality utterly different from the first, and indeed refer to a different stratum of experience.

For example, I might write, "I write that Ulysses listens to the song of the Sirens," an incontrovertible statement that bridges the gap between two worlds that are not contiguous: the immediate and empirical world in which I am and am writing, and the mythical one in which it always happens that Ulysses, tied to the ship's mast, is listening to the Sirens' song.

The same thing might also be written, "Ulysses listens to the song of the Sirens," leaving the "I write" understood. But if we do leave this understood we must be prepared to risk the reader's getting confused between two levels of reality, and believing that the act of listening on the part of Ulysses takes place on the same level of reality as my act of writing this sentence.

I have said "the reader believes," but it is clear enough that the credibility of what is written can be understood in very different ways, each one corresponding to more than one level of reality. There is nothing to prevent anyone from believing in the encounter of Ulysses with the Sirens as a historical fact, in the same way as one believes in the landing of Christopher Columbus on October 12, 1492. Or else we may believe it by feeling ourselves struck by the revelation of a truth beyond perception that is contained in the myth. But here we enter a field of religious phenomenology in which the written word would merely act as a spur to meditation. However, the credibility that interests us here is neither of these, but the kind of credibility peculiar to the literary text, in parentheses, as it were, matched on the reader's part by an attitude Coleridge defined as "suspension of disbelief." This suspension of disbelief is the condition on which the success of every literary invention depends, even if it is admittedly within the realm of the fabulous and incredible.

We have considered the possibility that the level of "Ulysses listens" might be put on a par with that of "I write." But this balance between the two levels could occur only if you, the reader, believed that the statement "I write" also belonged on a literary or mythological level. The "I" that is the subject of "I write" would then become the "I" of a fictional or mythological character—such as Homer, in fact. For clarity's sake, let us put our sentence in the following manner: "I write that Homer tells that Ulysses listens to the Sirens." The statement "Homer tells" may be placed on a level of mythical reality, in which case we will have two levels of mythical reality, that of the fable narrated and that of the legendary blind bard inspired by the Muses. But the same statement might be placed on a level of historical or (better) philological reality. In that case, by "Homer" we mean the individual or collective author with whom scholars busy themselves over the "Homeric question," and the level of reality would then be identical or contiguous to that of "I write." (Notice that I have not written "Homer writes" or "Homer sings," but "Homer tells," so as to leave both possibilities open.)

The way in which I have formulated the sentence makes it natural to think that Homer and I are two distinct persons, but this could be a wrong impression. The phrase would be exactly the same if it had been written by Homer in person, or in any case by the real author of the *Odyssey*, who at the moment of writing splits into two first persons: the empirical "I" who pens the words on the page (or dictates them to a scribe) and the mythical character of the blind bard, visited by divine inspiration, with whom he identifies himself.

In the same way, nothing would change if the "I" were the "I" who is speaking to you, while Homer, of whom I speak, were also "I": that is, if what I attribute to Homer were my own invention. This procedure would be clear at once if the phrase ran: "I write that Homer tells that Ulysses discovers that the Sirens are mute." In this case, in order to obtain a particular literary effect, I apocryphally attribute to Homer my own inversion, or distortion, or interpretation of the Homeric narrative. (In fact, the idea of the silent Sirens is Kafka's, and we must realize that the "I" who is the subject of the sentence is Kafka.) But even without turning things upside down, the countless authors who in recasting an earlier author have rewritten or interpreted a mythical (or at least a traditional) tale have done this to communicate something new, while still remaining faithful to the image of the original; and with all of them, in the "I" of the writing first person one can distinguish one or more levels of mythical or epic reality that draw material from the collective imagination.

Let us go back to the sentence we started with. Every reader of the *Odyssey* knows that more exactly it ought to be written, "I write that Homer tells that Ulysses says: I have listened to the song of the Sirens."

In the *Odyssey*, in fact, the adventures of Ulysses in the third person surround and contain other adventures of Ulysses in the first person, narrated by him to Alcinoüs, king of the Phaeacians. If we compare one with the other, we find that the difference between them is not simply grammatical. The adventures told in the third person have a psychological and emotional dimension that the others lack, and in them the supernatural presence consists in appearances of the Olympian gods in the guise of ordinary mortals. On the other hand, the adventures of Ulysses in the first person belong to a more primitive repertoire of myth, in which ordinary mortals and supernatural beings meet face to face; a world peopled by monsters, Cyclopses, Sirens, enchantresses who change men into pigs, and in fact the whole pre-Olympian pagan world of the supernatural. We may therefore define these as two different levels of mythical reality, to which there are two corresponding geographical realities. One corresponds to the historical knowledge of the time (the voyages of Telemachus and the homecoming to Ithaca), while the other belongs to fable and results from a juxtaposition of the most heterogeneous traditions (the travels of Ulysses as told by Ulysses himself). We may add that between the two levels is the island of the Phaeacians, which was the ideal place that gave birth to the narrative—a utopia of human perfection, outside the bounds of history and geography.

I have dwelt on this point because it serves to show how the different levels of reality may be matched by different levels of credibility—or, to put it better, a different suspension of disbelief. Assuming that a reader "believes" in the adventures of Ulysses as told by Homer, this same reader might judge Ulysses to be a mere braggart in all that Homer makes him say in the first person. But let us be careful not to confuse levels of reality (within the work) with levels of truth (referring to things outside it). For this reason we ought always to bear in mind the entire sentence: "I write that Homer tells that Ulysses says: I have listened to the song of the Sirens."

This is the formula that I put forward as the most complete, and at the same time the most compact, model of the connecting links between levels of reality in works of literature. Every part of this sentence may be linked to various sets of problems. I shall now give a number of suggestions, starting again from the beginning.

I write

This statement, "I write" (or "I am writing"), is connected with the whole field of problems—particularly fertile in this century—concerning what has been called metaliterature, and the analogous problems of metatheatre, metapainting, and so on. We already mentioned the play within the play while speaking of Shakespeare; there is no dearth of examples in the work of other playwrights, from Corneille's *Illusion comique* to Pirandello's *Six Characters in Search of an Author*. But in the last few decades these metatheatrical and metaliterary processes have acquired fresh importance, with foundations of a moral or epistemological nature, in opposition to the illusoriness of art, to the claim made by realism to lead the reader or spectator to forget that what he has before his eyes is an operation performed by means of language, a fiction worked out with an eye toward a strategy of effects.

The moral and indeed pedagogical motive is dominant in Brecht, with his theory of the epic theatre of alienation: the spectator must not abandon himself passively and emotionally to the illusion on the stage, but must be urged to think and to participate.

A process of theorization based on structural linguistics, on the other hand, forms the background to research carried out in French literature during the past fifteen years, and in both critical thought and creative practice this puts the material side of writing—the text itself—firmly in the foreground. We need only mention the name of Roland Barthes.

I write that Homer tells

Here we enter a very extensive field, the splitting or multiplication of the subject of the verb "to write"; and it is a field in which any really exhaustive theoretical work has yet to be done.

We might begin with a habit characteristic of the writers of chivalric romances, that of claiming a hypothetical manuscript as a source. Even Ariosto pretends to refer back to the authority of Turpin. And Cervantes introduces the figure of an Arab writer, Cid Hamet Benengeli, between himself and Don Quixote. Not only that, but Cervantes supposes a kind of contemporaneousness between the action narrated and the writing of the Arabic manuscript, so that Don Quixote and Sancho Panza are aware that the adventures they are having are those written by Benengeli, and not the ones written about by Avellaneda in his apocryphal second part of *Don Quixote*.

A still simpler method is that of suggesting that the book is written in the first person by the protagonist. The first novel that may be considered entirely *modern* was not published under the name of the author, Daniel Defoe, but as the memoirs of an obscure sailor from York, a certain Robinson Crusoe.

All this brings me little by little to the heart of the problem: the successive layers of subjectivity and feigning that we can discern underneath the author's name, and the various "I"s that go to make up the "I" who is writing. The preliminary condition of any work of literature is that the person who is writing has to invent that first character, who is the author of the work. That a person puts his whole self into the work he is writing is something we often hear said, but it is never true. It is always only a projection of himself that an author calls into play while he is writing; it may be a projection of a real part of himself or the projection of a fictitious "I"—a mask, in short. Writing always presupposes the selection of a psychological attitude, a rapport with the world, a tone of voice, a homogeneous set of linguistic tools, the data of experience and the phantoms of the imagination—in a word, a *style*. The author is an author insofar as he enters into a role the way an actor does and identifies himself with that projection of himself at the moment of writing.

The author-*cum*-character is both something less and something more than the "I" of the individual as an empirical subject. He is something less because (for example) Gustave Flaubert the author of *Madame Bovary* excludes the language and visions of Gustave Flaubert the author of *La Tentation de Saint Antoine* or *Salammbô*. He rigorously cuts down his inner world to the set of data that make up the world of *Madame Bovary*. And he is something more because the Gustave Flaubert who exists only in relation to the manuscript of *Madame Bovary* partakes of a far more compact and well-defined state of being than does the Gustave Flaubert who, while writing *Madame Bovary*, knows that he was the author of *La Tentation* and is about to be the author of *Salammbô*. He knows that he is continually oscillating between one world and another, and that in the end all these worlds flow together and unify in his mind.

The example of Flaubert may be used to verify the formula I have suggested if we translate this into a series of projections or lantern slides. Gustave Flaubert the author of the complete works of Gustave Flaubert projects outside himself the Gustave Flaubert who is the author of *Madame Bovary*, who in turn projects from himself the character of a middle-class married woman in Rouen, Emma Bovary, who projects from herself that Emma Bovary whom she dreams of being.

$$\{GF\} \rightarrow \boxed{GF} \rightarrow \boxed{EB} \rightarrow \{EB\}$$

Each element projected reacts in its turn on the element that projects it; it transforms and conditions it. So the arrows go not in one direction only, but in both:

$$\{GF\} \rightleftarrows \boxed{GF} \rightleftarrows \boxed{EB} \rightleftarrows \{EB\}$$

All we then have to do is connect the last term with the first—that is, establish the circular movement of these projections. It was Flaubert himself who gave us a precise clue to this with his famous phrase "*Madame Bovary, c'est moi.*"

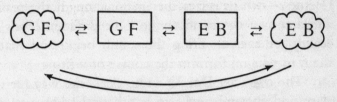

How much of the "I" who shapes the characters is in fact an "I" who has been shaped by the characters? The further we go toward distinguishing the various levels that go to make up the "I" of the author, the more we realize that many of these levels do not belong to the author as an individual but to collective culture, to the historical period or the deep sedimentary layers of the species. The starting point of the chain, the real primary subject of the verb "to write," seems ever more distant from us, more rarefied and indistinct. Perhaps it is a phantom "I," an empty space, an absence.

In order to acquire more solid substance, the "I" can become a character, and indeed the protagonist of the written work. But we need only think of the extremely subtle pages that Gianfranco Contini devotes to the "I" of the *Divine Comedy* to realize that it, too, can be split into a number of persons, rather like the "I" who is speaking in Proust's *A la recherche du temps perdu.*

With the "I" who becomes a character we are shifting our focus from "I write that Homer tells" to "Homer tells that Ulysses . . ."

Homer tells that Ulysses

The author-protagonist brings an internal subjectivity to the written world, a figure endowed with a distinctness of his own—often a visual and iconic distinctness—which seizes the imagination of the reader and acts as a device to connect the different levels of reality, or even to bring them into being and enable them to take on form in the course of writing.

The character Don Quixote clears the way for the clash and encounter of two antithetical languages, or, rather, of two literary worlds without any ground in common: the chivalric-supernatural and the picaresque-comic. It opens up a new dimension, or, rather, two: an extremely complex level of mental reality and a representation of the environment which we might call realistic, but in a completely new sense compared with picaresque "realism," which consisted of a repertoire of stereotyped images of poverty and squalor. The sun-drenched country roads on which Don Quixote and Sancho Panza meet with friars carrying parasols, muleteers, ladies in sedan chairs, and flocks of sheep constitute a world that had never before been written about. It had never before been written about because there had never been a reason for writing about it, whereas here it fulfills a need: it is the reverse of the inner reality of Don Quixote, or, better still, the background against which Don Quixote projects his own codified interpretation of the world.

Don Quixote is a character endowed with an unmistakable iconic quality and inexhaustible inner riches. But this does not mean that to perform the function of protagonist a character necessarily has to have such depth. The function of the character may be likened to that of an "operator," in the mathematical sense of the word. As long as his function is well defined, he can be merely a name, a profile, a hieroglyphic, a sign.

When we read *Gulliver's Travels* we know very little about Dr. Lemuel Gulliver, ship's doctor in the Royal Navy. His substance as a character is infinitely scantier than that of Don Quixote, yet his is the personality that we follow throughout the book, and the one that brings it into being. This is because, even though it is hard to define Lemuel Gulliver psychologically or facially, his function as an "operator" is very clear, in the first place as a giant in a world of dwarfs and then as a dwarf in a world of giants. And this operation in terms of size is the easier interpretation, whereby Gulliver "works" as a character even for children who read Swift's book in simplified texts. But the real operation which he manifests (and here I am thinking of a very persuasive essay on this subject by an Italian scholar, Giuseppe Sertoli, published this year) is that of the contrast between the world of logico-mathematical reason and the world of bodies, of their physiological materiality and various cognitive experiences and various ethical and theological concepts.

Ulysses says:

Punctuated with a colon. This colon is a very important articulated "joint," and I would call it the headstone of narrative at all times in all lands. Not only because one of the most widespread structures of written narrative has always been that of stories inserted into another story that acts as a frame, but also because where the frame does not exist we may infer an invisible colon that starts off the discourse and introduces the whole work.

I will confine myself to touching on the salient problem. In the West, the novel was born in Hellenistic Greece, taking the form of a main narrative into which secondary narratives, told by the various characters, were inserted. This method is characteristic of ancient Indian narrative, where, however, the structure of the story in relation to the point of view of the narrator obeys rules far more complicated than in the West. (I am here relying on a monograph published in 1914, *Sur l'origine indienne du roman grec*, by F. Lacôte, an expert on Indian literature.) Also based on Indian models are those collections of stories inserted into a narrative that acts as a frame, both in the Islamic world and in medieval and Renaissance Europe.

All of us have in mind *The Arabian Nights*, in which all the stories are contained within the general framework of the tale of the Persian king, Shahryar, who kills his brides after their wedding night, and of his bride Scheherazade, who succeeds in postponing this fate by telling wonderful stories and stopping just at the climax. Besides the tales told by Scheherazade, there are others narrated by characters in her tales. In other words, the stories are like boxes within boxes—as many as five of them at a time. Here I am relying on an essay called *Les Hommes-récits* by Tzvetan Todorov, who has studied the *enchâssement* of the tales in *The Arabian Nights* and in

Potocki's *Manuscrit trouvé à Saragosse* (*Poétique de la prose* [Paris: Seuil, 1971]).

Borges speaks of one of the *Arabian Nights*, number 602, the most magical of all, in which Scheherazade tells Shahryar a tale in which Scheherazade tells Shahryar a tale, etc., etc. In the translations of *The Arabian Nights* that I have at hand, I have never been able to find this 602nd Night. But even if Borges invented it he did well, because it represents the natural culmination of the *enchâssement* of the tales.

From the point of view of levels of reality, I should say that the *enchâssement* of *The Arabian Nights* does indeed create a structure in perspective, but to my reading, at least in the only way we can read them, these tales appear to be all on the same plane. In them we can distinguish two very different types of narrative: the magical type of Indian and Persian origin, with its genies, flying horses, and metamorphoses, and the Arab-Islamic storytelling type of the Baghdad cycle, with the caliph Harun-al-Rashid and Jafar the vizier. But the tales of both types are put on the same plane, both structurally and stylistically, and as we read we slide from one type to the other, as the eye slides over the surface of a tapestry.

In the prototype of literary storytelling in the West, Giovanni Boccaccio's *Decameron*, between the tales and the framework there is a clean stylistic split that highlights the distance between the two planes. The framework of the ten days of the *Decameron* describes the pleasant life lived in their country abode by the seven women and three men of this happy band of storytellers. We are on a plane of stylized reality, uniformly pleasant, refined in a mannered fashion, without contrasts, without characterization; nothing but descriptions of the weather and the landscape, of the pastimes and conversations of this playful little court that every day elects a queen and ends the day with a poem. The tales narrated, however, constitute a catalogue of the narrative possibilities becoming available to language and culture at a time when the variety of living forms was a new thing, coming into its own at that very moment. Each novella reveals an intensity of writing and of representation that radiates outward in all sorts of different directions in such a way as to stress these directions in comparison with the frame. Does this mean that the frame is a merely decorative element? If we said this, we would be forgetting that the framework of the tales, that earthly paradise of the elegant court, is itself contained within another frame, tragic, deathly, hellish: the plague in Florence in 1348, described in the introduction to the *Decameron*. It is the stark reality of a world at the end of the world, the plague as a biological and social catastrophe, that makes sense of the utopia of an idyllic society governed by beauty, gentleness, and intelligence. The chief product of this utopian society is the short story, and the story reproduces the variety and nervous intensity of a world that is lost, the laughter and tears by now erased by Death the Leveler.

Let us now see what is inside the frame.

I have listened to the Sirens' song

I could also have said: I have blinded Polyphemus the Cyclops, or: I have eluded the enchantments of Circe.

But if I have chosen the episode of the Sirens it is because this enables me to introduce a further transition in perspective with the narrative of Ulysses, a further level of reality, contained in the Sirens' song.

What do the Sirens sing? One possible hypothesis is that their song is nothing more or less than the *Odyssey*. The tendency of the poem to incorporate itself, to reflect itself as in a mirror, appears a number of times in the *Odyssey*, especially at banquets when the bards sing. And who better than the Sirens could endow their own song with this function of magic looking glass?

In this case we would have a case of the literary process that André Gide defined by the heraldic term *mise en abyme*. This occurs when a work of literature includes another work resembling the first—that is, when a part of it reproduces the whole. We have already mentioned the play within the play in *Hamlet* and the 602nd Night according to Borges. Examples also extend to painting, as in the mirror effects in the pictures of van Eyck. I will not dwell on the *mise en abyme*, because I need only refer you to an exhaustive study published a few months ago: Lucien Dällenbach, *Le Récit spéculaire* (Paris: Seuil, 1977).

But what the text of the *Odyssey* tells us about the Sirens' song is that the Sirens say they are singing and wish to be heard, and that their song is the best that can be sung. The final experience taken into account in the narrative of Ulysses is a lyrical and musical experience on the borders of the ineffable. One of the finest passages in Maurice Blanchot interprets the Sirens' song as a "beyond" of expressive possibilities from which Ulysses, having experienced its ineffability, withdraws, falling back from the song itself to his account of the song.

In order to verify my formula I have so far made use of narrative examples, choosing from the classics in verse or prose or in the theatre, but always with a story to tell. Now that I have got to the Sirens' song, I ought to go back over my entire argument to see if it can be applied, as I think it can, point by point to lyric poetry, and shed light on the various levels of reality that the "operation" of poetry traverses. I am convinced that this formula, with very small modifications, can be transcribed with Mallarmé in Homer's place. Such a formulation might perhaps enable us to pursue the Sirens' song, the ultimate point writing can attain, the final core of the written word, and perhaps in the wake of Mallarmé we would arrive at the blank page, at silence, at absence.

The path that we have followed—the levels of reality evoked by literature, the whole gamut of veils and shields—may perhaps stray off into infinity, may perhaps encounter nothingness. As we have witnessed the disappearance of the "I," the primary subject of the verb "to write," so the ultimate object eludes us. Perhaps it is in the field of tension between one vacuum and another that literature multiplies the depths of a reality that is inexhaustible in forms and meanings.

Now, right at the end of my talk, it occurs to me that I have been speaking throughout of "levels of reality," whereas the topic of this conference reads "The Levels of Reality." Perhaps the fundamental point of my talk is exactly this: literature does not recognize Reality as such, but only *levels*. Whether there is such a thing as Reality, of which the various levels are only partial aspects, or whether there are only the levels, is something that literature cannot decide. Literature recognizes the *reality of the levels*, and this is a reality (or "Reality") that it knows all the better, perhaps, for not having come to understand it by other cognitive processes. And that is already a great deal.

2

Why Read the Classics?

L'Espresso (Rome), June 28, 1981.

Let us begin with a few suggested definitions.

(1) The classics are the books of which we usually hear people say, "I am rereading . . . " and never "I am reading. . . ."

This happens at least among those who consider themselves "very well read." It does not hold good for young people at the age when they first encounter the world, and the classics as a part of that world.

The reiterative prefix before the verb "read" may be a small hypocrisy on the part of people ashamed to admit they have not read a famous book. To reassure them, we need only observe that, however vast any person's basic reading may be, there still remain an enormous number of fundamental works that he has not read.

Hands up, anyone who has read the whole of Herodotus and the whole of Thucydides! And Saint-Simon? And Cardinal de Retz? But even the great nineteenth-century cycles of novels are more often talked about than read. In France they begin to read Balzac in school, and, judging by the number of copies in circulation, one may suppose that they go on reading him even after that, but if a Gallup poll were taken in Italy, I'm afraid that Balzac would come in practically last. Dickens fans in Italy form a tiny elite; as soon as its members meet, they begin to chatter about characters and episodes as if they were discussing people and things of their own acquaintance. Years ago, while teaching in America, Michel Butor got fed up with being asked about Emile Zola, whom he had never read, so he made up his mind to read the entire Rougon-Macquart cycle. He found it was completely different from what he had thought: a fabulous mythological and cosmogonical family tree, which he went on to describe in a wonderful essay.

In other words, to read a great book for the first time in one's maturity is an extraordinary pleasure, different from (though one cannot say greater or lesser than) the pleasure of having read it in one's youth. Youth brings to reading, as to any other experience, a particular flavor and a particular sense of importance, whereas in maturity one appreciates (or ought to appreciate) many more details and levels and meanings. We may therefore attempt the next definition:

(2) We use the word "classics" for books that are treasured by those who have read and loved them; but they are treasured no less by those who have the luck

to read them for the first time in the best conditions to enjoy them.

In fact, reading in youth can be rather unfruitful, due to impatience, distraction, inexperience with the product's "instructions for use," and inexperience in life itself. Books read then can be (possibly at one and the same time) formative, in the sense that they give a form to future experiences, providing models, terms of comparison, schemes for classification, scales of value, exemplars of beauty—all things that continue to operate even if a book read in one's youth is almost or totally forgotten. If we reread the book at a mature age, we are likely to rediscover these constants, which by this time are part of our inner mechanisms, but whose origins we have long forgotten. A literary work can succeed in making us forget it as such, but it leaves its seed in us. The definition we can give is therefore this:

(3) The classics are books that exert a peculiar influence, both when they refuse to be eradicated from the mind and when they conceal themselves in the folds of memory, camouflaging themselves as the collective or individual unconscious.

There should therefore be a time in adult life devoted to revisiting the most important books of our youth. Even if the books have remained the same (though they do change, in the light of an altered historical perspective), we have most certainly changed, and our encounter will be an entirely new thing.

Hence, whether we use the verb "read" or the verb "reread" is of little importance. Indeed, we may say:

(4) Every rereading of a classic is as much a voyage of discovery as the first reading.

(5) Every reading of a classic is in fact a rereading.

Definition 4 may be considered a corollary of this next one:

(6) A classic is a book that has never finished saying what it has to say.

Whereas definition 5 depends on a more specific formula, such as this:

(7) The classics are the books that come down to us bearing the traces of readings previous to ours, and bringing in their wake the traces they themselves have left on the culture or cultures they have passed through (or, more simply, on language and customs).

All this is true both of the ancient and of the modern classics. If I read the *Odyssey* I read Homer's text, but I cannot forget all that the adventures of Ulysses have come to mean in the course of the centuries, and I cannot help wondering if these meanings were implicit in the text, or whether they are incrustations or distortions or expansions. When reading Kafka, I cannot avoid approving or rejecting the legitimacy of the adjective "Kafkaesque," which one is likely to hear every quarter of an hour, applied indiscriminately. If I read Turgenev's *Fathers and Sons* or Dostoyevsky's *The Possessed*, I cannot help thinking how the characters have continued to be reincarnated right down to our own day.

The reading of a classic ought to give us a surprise or two vis-à-vis the notion that we had of it. For this reason, I can never sufficiently highly recommend the direct reading of the text itself, leaving aside the critical biography, commentaries, and interpretations as much as possible. Schools and universities ought to help us understand that no book that talks *about* a book says more than the book in question, but instead they do their level best to make us think the opposite. There is a very widespread topsy-turviness of values whereby the introduction, critical apparatus, and bibliography are used as a smokescreen to hide what the text has to say and, indeed, can say only if left to speak for itself without intermediaries who claim to know more than the text does. We may conclude that:

(8) A classic does not necessarily teach us anything we did not know before. In a classic we sometimes discover something we have always known (or thought we knew), but without knowing that this author said it first, or at least is associated with it in a special way. And this, too, is a surprise that gives a lot of pleasure, such as we always gain from the discovery of an origin, a relationship, an affinity. From all this we may derive a definition of this type:

(9) The classics are books which, upon reading, we find even fresher, more unexpected, and more marvelous than we had thought from hearing about them.

Naturally, this only happens when a classic really works as such—that is, when it establishes a personal rapport with the reader. If the spark doesn't come, that's a pity; but we do not read the classics out of duty or respect, only out of love. Except at school. And school should enable you to know, either well or badly, a certain number of classics among which—or in reference to which—you can then choose *your* classics. School is obliged to give you the instruments needed to make a choice, but the choices that count are those that occur outside and after school.

It is only by reading without bias that you might

possibly come across the book that becomes *your* book. I know an excellent art historian, an extraordinarily well-read man, who out of all the books there are has focused his special love on *Pickwick Papers*; at every opportunity he comes up with some quip from Dickens's book, and connects each and every event in life with some Pickwickian episode. Little by little he himself, and true philosophy, and the universe, have taken on the shape and form of the *Pickwick Papers* by a process of complete identification. In this way we arrive at a very lofty and demanding notion of what a classic is:

(10) We use the word "classic" of a book that takes the form of an equivalent to the universe, on a level with the ancient talismans. With this definition we are approaching the idea of the "total book," as Mallarmé conceived of it.

But a classic can establish an equally strong rapport in terms of opposition and antithesis. Everything that Jean-Jacques Rousseau thinks and does is very dear to my heart, yet everything fills me with an irrepressible desire to contradict him, to criticize him, to quarrel with him. It is a question of personal antipathy on a temperamental level, on account of which I ought to have no choice but not to read him; and yet I cannot help numbering him among *my* authors. I will therefore say:

(11) *Your* classic author is the one you cannot feel indifferent to, who helps you to define yourself in relation to him, even in dispute with him.

I think I have no need to justify myself for using the word "classic" without making distinctions as to age, style, or authority. What distinguishes the classic, in the argument I am making, may be only an echo effect that holds good both for an ancient work and for a modern one that has already achieved its place in a cultural continuum. We might say:

(12) A classic is a book that comes before other classics; but anyone who has read the others first, and then reads this one, instantly recognizes its place in the family tree.

At this point I can no longer put off the vital problem of how to relate the reading of the classics to the reading of all the other books that are anything but classics. It is a problem connected with such questions as "Why read the classics rather than concentrate on books that enable us to understand our own times more deeply?" or "Where shall we find the time and peace of mind to read the classics, overwhelmed as we are by the avalanche of current events?"

We can, of course, imagine some blessed soul who devotes his reading time exclusively to Lucretius, Lucian, Montaigne, Erasmus, Quevedo, Marlowe, the *Discourse on Method*, *Wilhelm Meister*, Coleridge, Ruskin, Proust, and Valéry, with a few forays in the direction of Murasaki or the Icelandic Sagas. And all this without having to write reviews of the latest publications, or papers to compete for a university chair, or articles for magazines on tight deadlines. To keep up such a diet without any contamination, this blessed soul would have to abstain from reading the newspapers, and never be tempted by the latest novel or sociological investigation. But we have to see how far such rigor would be either justified or profitable. The latest news may well be banal or mortifying, but it nonetheless remains a point at which to stand and look both backward and forward. To be able to read the classics, you have to know "from where" you are reading them; otherwise both the book and the reader will be lost in a timeless cloud. This, then, is the reason why the greatest "yield" from reading the classics will be obtained by someone who knows how to alternate them with the proper dose of current affairs. And this does not necessarily imply a state of imperturbable inner calm. It can also be the fruit of nervous impatience, of a huffing-and-puffing discontent of mind.

Maybe the ideal thing would be to hearken to current events as we do to the din outside the window that informs us about traffic jams and sudden changes in the weather, while we listen to the voice of the classics sounding clear and articulate inside the room. But it is already a lot for most people if the presence of the classics is perceived as a distant rumble far outside a room that is swamped by the trivia of the moment, as by a television at full blast. Let us therefore add:

(13) A classic is something that tends to relegate the concerns of the moment to the status of background noise, but at the same time this background noise is something we cannot do without.

(14) A classic is something that persists as a background noise even when the most incompatible momentary concerns are in control of the situation.

There remains the fact that reading the classics appears to clash with our rhythm of life, which no longer affords long periods of time or the spaciousness of humanistic leisure. It also conflicts with the eclecticism of our culture, which would never be capable of compiling a catalogue of things classical such as would suit our needs.

These latter conditions were fully realized in the case of Leopardi, given his solitary life in his father's house (his "*paterno ostello*"), his cult of Greek and Latin antiquity, and the formidable library put at his disposal by his father, Monaldo. To which we may add the entire body of Italian literature and French literature, with the exception of novels and the "latest hits" in general, which were left to beguile the leisure of his sister Paolina ("*your* Stendhal," he wrote her once). Even with his intense interest in science and history, he was often willing to rely on texts that were not entirely up-to-date, taking the habits of birds from Buffon, the mummies of Fredrik Ruysch from Fontanelle, the voyage of Columbus from Robertson.

In these days a classical education like the young Leopardi's is unthinkable; above all, Count Monaldo's library has multiplied explosively. The ranks of the old titles have been decimated, while new ones have proliferated in all modern literatures and cultures. There is nothing for it but for all of us to invent our own ideal libraries of classics. I would say that such a library ought to be composed half of books we have read and that have really counted for us, and half of books we propose to read and presume will come to count—leaving a section of empty shelves for surprises and occasional discoveries.

I realize that Leopardi is the only name I have cited from Italian literature—a result of the explosion of the library. Now I ought to rewrite the whole article to make it perfectly clear that the classics help us to understand who we are and where we stand, a purpose for which it is indispensable to compare Italians with foreigners and foreigners with Italians. Then I ought to rewrite it yet again, lest anyone believe that the classics ought to be read because they "serve any purpose" whatever. The only reason one can possibly adduce is that to read the classics is better than not to read the classics.

And if anyone objects that it is not worth taking so much trouble, then I will quote Cioran (who is not yet a classic but will become one): "While they were preparing the hemlock, Socrates was learning a tune on the flute. 'What good will it do you,' they asked, 'to know this tune before you die?' "

The Odysseys
Within the Odyssey

La Repubblica (Rome), October 21, 1981.

How many odysseys are there in the *Odyssey*? At the beginning of the poem, the story of Telemachus is the search for a story that is not there, the story that will be the *Odyssey*. Phemius, the bard at the royal palace of Ithaca, already knows the *nostoi* of the other heroes. Only one is lacking, that of his own king. For this reason Penelope doesn't want to hear him sing any more. Then Telemachus goes off in search of this story among the veterans of the Trojan War. If he finds the story, whether it ends happily or not, Ithaca will emerge from the timeless, lawless, and chaotic situation in which it has been for many years.

Like all the veterans, Nestor and Menelaus have a lot to tell, but not the story Telemachus is seeking, until, finally, Menelaus comes out with a truly fantastic adventure: disguising himself as a seal, he captured the Old Man of the Sea (that is, Proteus of the countless metamorphoses) and forced him to tell him the past and the future. Proteus of course knew the whole *Odyssey* word for word, and he began to recount the adventures of Ulysses at the same point that Homer does, with the hero on Calypso's island. Then he broke off, for at that point Homer could take over and continue the story.

Arriving at the court of the Phaeacians, Ulysses hears a bard (who is blind like Homer) singing about the adventures of Ulysses. The hero bursts into tears and then decides to take up the narrative himself. In this story he gets as far as Hades to question Tiresias, and Tiresias tells him how his story ends. Then Ulysses meets the Sirens, who are singing. What are they singing? Still the *Odyssey*, perhaps the same one we are reading, perhaps a very different one. The story of this return is already there before the return is accomplished: it exists before being acted out.

Even in the Telemachus episode we find expressions such as "think of the return," "tell of the return." Zeus did not "think of the return" of the sons of Atreus; Menelaus asks the daughter of Proteus to "tell of the return" and she explains how to force her father to do so, so that Menelaus is able to capture Proteus and say, "Tell me of the return, and how I will go on the fish-laden sea."

The return must be discerned and thought about and remembered. The danger is that it might be forgotten about before it has happened. Indeed, one of the first stages of the journey recounted by Ulysses, the episode of the Lotus Eaters, involves the risk of losing his memory by eating the sweet fruit of the lotus. It may seem strange that the test of forgetfulness occurs at the beginning of the journeyings of Ulysses, not at the end. If, after overcoming so many trials, bearing so many setbacks, learning so many lessons, Ulysses had forgotten everything, his loss would have been far graver: not to have gained any experience from what he had suffered, or any meaning from what he had lived through.

But, if we look more closely, this threat of the loss of memory comes up a number of times in books IX–XII: first in the encounter with the Lotus Eaters, then with Circe's drugs, then again in the song of the Sirens. Each time Ulysses has to be wary, lest he forget on the instant. Forget what? The Trojan War? The siege of Troy? The wooden horse? No. His home, the course to steer, the purpose of the voyage. The expression Homer uses on these occasions is "forget the return."

Ulysses must not forget the route he has to travel, the form of his destiny. In short, he must not forget the *Odyssey*. But the bard who composes by improvising, the rhapsodist who memorizes and sings passages from poems that have already been sung—they, too, must not forget if they are to "tell the return." For anyone who sings verses without the aid of a written text, "forget" is the most negative verb in existence. And for them to "forget the return" means to forget the poems known as *nostoi*, which were the warhorse of their whole repertoire.

I wrote a few comments some years ago on the subject of "forgetting the future" (in *Corriere della Sera*, August 10, 1975), and concluded as follows: "What Ulysses preserves from the lotus, from Circe's drugs and the Sirens' song, is not merely the past or the future. Memory really matters—for individuals, for the collectivity, for civilization—only if it binds together the imprint of the past and the project of the future, if it enables us to act without forgetting what we wanted to do, to become without ceasing to be, and to be without ceasing to become."

My piece was followed by an article by Edoardo Sanguineti in *Paese Sera* (reprinted in *Giornalino 1973– 1975* [Turin: Einaudi, 1976]) and by a whole string of answers, his and mine. Sanguineti objected as follows:

For we must not forget that the wanderings of Ulysses were not an outward journey at all, but a return journey. Therefore we should ask ourselves for a moment what sort of future he really has before him; because the future that Ulysses was seeking was really his past, in point of fact. Ulysses overcomes the flatteries of regression because he is totally bent toward a Restoration.

We gather that one fine day, out of spite, the real Ulysses, the great Ulysses, became the Ulysses of the Ultimate Journey, for whom the future is by no means a past, but the Realization of a Prophecy—that is, a true Utopia. Whereas the Homeric Ulysses comes to the recovery of his past as a present; his wisdom is Repetition, and we can easily realize this from the scar he bears, which marks him forever.

In reply to Sanguineti I pointed out (in *Corriere della Sera*, October 14, 1975) that "in the language of myth, as in that of folk tales and of the popular novel, every undertaking that brings justice, repairs wrongs, or relieves a miserable situation is usually represented as the restoration of an earlier, ideal order. The desirability of a future to be conquered is guaranteed by the memory of a lost past."

If we take a close look at fairy stories, we find that they present two types of social transformation, always with a happy ending: either from high to low and then again to high, or simply from low to high. In the first type a prince is by mischance reduced to being a swineherd or some such lowly station, and then regains his royal status. In the second type there is a young man impoverished from birth, a shepherd or a peasant, and maybe simple-minded into the bargain, who by his own courage or with the help of magic powers succeeds in marrying the princess and becoming king.

The same patterns hold good for tales with a female protagonist. In the first type a girl of royal, or at any rate wealthy, status falls to the condition of a derelict because of the rivalry of a stepmother (like Snow White) or her half-sisters (like Cinderella), until a prince falls in love with her and raises her to the very top of the social ladder. In the second type we have a real shepherdess or peasant girl who overcomes all the disadvantages of her humble birth and marries a prince.

One might think that it is tales of the second type that give the most direct expression to the people's desire for a reversal of social roles, whereas those of the first type reveal this desire in a more attenuated form, as the restoration of a previous, hypothetical order. But, on closer consideration, the extraordinary good fortune of the shepherd or shepherdess represents nothing but a miraculous and consolatory illusion, which in large part has been carried on by the popular romantic novel. On the other hand, the misfortunes of the unlucky prince or princess link the notion of poverty to the idea of a *right* that has been *trodden under foot*, of justice to be vindicated. That is (on the plane of fantasy, where ideas can put down roots in the form of elementary figures), this second type of story puts its finger on a spot that was destined to be fundamental to the entire development of the social conscience in the modern age, from the French Revolution on.

In the collective unconscious, the prince in beggar's rags is proof that every beggar is in fact a prince who is the victim of a usurpation and must regain his realm. Ulysses or Robin Hood, kings or kings' sons or knightly aristocrats fallen on evil days, when they triumph over their enemies will restore a society of the Just in which their true identity will be revealed.

But is it the same identity as before? It may be that the Ulysses who arrives in Ithaca as a poor beggar unrecognized by everyone is no longer the same person as the Ulysses who departed for Troy. It is no coincidence that he had once saved his life by pretending his name was Nobody. The only immediate and spontaneous recognition comes from his dog, Argos, as if the continuity of the individual could make itself manifest through signs perceptible only to an animal.

For the nurse the proof of his identity was the scar left him by a boar's tusk, for his wife the secret of the manufacture of their marriage bed out of the roots of an olive tree, and for his father a list of fruit trees. These signs have nothing regal about them; they put the hero on the level of a poacher, a carpenter, a gardener. To them are added the qualities of physical strength and pitiless aggressiveness toward his enemies, and, above all, the favor shown by the gods, which is what convinces Telemachus, if only by an act of faith.

In his turn, the unrecognizable Ulysses wakes up in Ithaca and does not recognize his own country: Athena has to intervene to assure him that Ithaca is really and truly Ithaca. In the second half of the *Odyssey* the identity crisis is general. Only the story assures us that the characters and places are the same characters and places; but even the story changes. The tale that the unrecognizable Ulysses tells the shepherd Eumaeus, then his rival Antinoüs, and even Penelope, is another and completely different *Odyssey*: the wanderings that have brought the fictitious person whom he claims to be all the way there from Crete, a story far more likely than the one he himself had told to the king of the Phaeacians. Who is to say that this is not the "real" *Odyssey*? But this new *Odyssey* refers to yet another *Odyssey*, for in his travels the Cretan had come across Ulysses. So here we have Ulysses speaking of a Ulysses traveling in countries where the "real" Ulysses never set foot.

That Ulysses is a hoaxer is already known before the *Odyssey*. Wasn't it he who thought up the great swindle of the wooden horse? And at the beginning of the *Odyssey* the first recollections of his character are two flashbacks to the Trojan War, told to each other consecutively by Helen and Menelaus. Two tales of trickery. In the first he disguises himself in order to enter the besieged city and wreak havoc; in the second he is shut up inside the wooden horse with his colleagues, and is able to prevent Helen from unmasking them by inducing them to talk.

In both these episodes Ulysses is associated with Helen—in the first she is an ally and an accomplice in his trick, in the second an adversary, who imitates the voices of the Achaeans' wives to tempt them to betray themselves. The role of Helen seems contradictory, but it is always marked by trickery. In the same way, Penelope's web is a stratagem symmetrical with that of the Trojan Horse, and like the latter is a product of manual dexterity and counterfeiting, so that the two main characteristics of Ulysses are also those of Penelope.

If Ulysses is a hoaxer, the entire account he gives to the king of the Phaeacians might be a pack of lies. In fact, these seagoing adventures of his, concentrated in four central books of the *Odyssey*, a rapid series of encounters with fantastic beings (the ogre Polyphemus, the winds bottled up in a wineskin, the enchantments of Circe, sirens and sea monsters), clash with the rest of the poem, which is dominated by grave tones, psychological tension, and a dramatic crescendo gravitating toward an end: the reconquest of his kingdom and of his wife besieged by suitors. Here, too, we find motifs in common with folk tales, such as Penelope's web and the test of drawing the bow, but we are on ground far closer to modern criteria of realism and likelihood. Supernatural interventions are concerned solely with the appearance of the Olympian gods, usually concealed in human forms.

We should remember, however, that the same adventures (especially the one with Polyphemus) are mentioned elsewhere in the poem, so that Homer confirms them. Not only that: the gods themselves discuss them on Olympus. And Menelaus also recounts an adventure of the same folk-tale stamp, his encounter with the Old Man of the Sea. We can only attribute these excursions into the realm of fantasy to a montage of traditions of diverse origins, handed down by bards and meeting up later in the Homeric *Odyssey*, which in the account given by Ulysses in the first person probably reveals its most archaic stratum.

Most archaic? According to Alfred Huebeck, things might have happened the other way around. Before the *Odyssey*—even in the *Iliad*—Ulysses had always been an epic hero, and epic heroes, such as Achilles and Hector in the *Iliad*, do not have fabulous adventures based on monsters and enchantments. But the author of the *Odyssey* has to keep Ulysses away from home for ten years, lost, unaccounted for by his family and his ex-companions-in-arms. Therefore, he must make Ulysses leave the known world, pass into a different geography, an extra-human world, a "beyond" (it is no coincidence that his wanderings culminate in a journey to the Underworld). For this excursion outside the bounds of the epic, the author of the *Odyssey* resorts to traditions (which really are more archaic) such as the feats of Jason and the Argonauts. It is thus the *novelty* of the *Odyssey* to have put an epic hero such as Ulysses at grips with "witches and giants, monsters and maneaters"—that is, in situations typical of a more *archaic* saga, the roots of which must be sought "in the world of antique fable, and even of primitive magical and shamanistic concepts."

According to Huebeck, it is here that the author of the *Odyssey* shows his true modernity, the quality that makes him so close to us, so up-to-date. Traditionally the epic hero was a paradigm of aristocratic and military virtues, and Ulysses is all this, but over and above it he is the man who bears the hardest trials, labors, sorrows, and solitude. "Certainly he draws his public into the mythical world of dreams, but this dream world becomes the mirror image of the world in which we live, dominated by need and anguish, terror and sorrow, into which man is thrust with no escape."

Elsewhere in the same volume Stephanie West, starting from premises different from Huebeck's, suggests a hypothesis that supports his argument: the idea that there had been an "alternative" *Odyssey*, another route for the return, earlier than Homer. Homer (or whoever wrote the *Odyssey*), finding this travelogue too poor and scant of meaning, replaced it with the fabulous adventures while retaining a trace of it in the voyages of the pseudo-Cretan. And, in fact, in the Proem there is a line that might be seen as the synthesis of the entire *Odyssey*: "He saw the cities and learned the thoughts of many men." What cities? What thoughts? This hypothesis would fit better with the wanderings of the pseudo-Cretan. . . .

However, as soon as Penelope recognizes him in his reconquered marriage bed, Ulysses goes back to talking about the Cyclops, the Sirens. . . . Isn't the *Odyssey* perhaps the myth of every journey there is? For Homer-Ulysses, the distinction between truth and falsehood may not have existed, and he told of the same experience at one time in the language of actual experience, at another in the language of myth, just as even for us today every journey, long or short, is always an odyssey.

Ovid and
Universal Contiguity

Preface to an edition of the *Metamorphoses* of Ovid, 1979.

On high in the sky there is a Way, which one sees when the night is clear. It is called Milky, and it catches the eye because it is so white. Here the gods pass by on their way to the dwelling of the great Thunderer, at the palace. To right and left, with open doors, are the atria of the nobles, forever crowded. The populace lives dispersed in other places. The most powerful and illustrious gods have here established their dwelling, at the front [*a fronte potentes/caelicolae clarique suos posuere penates*]. If the expression did not seem irreverent, I would dare to say that this place is the Palatine of the great heaven.

Thus, at the beginning of the *Metamorphoses*, to introduce us to the world of the celestial gods, Ovid starts by making it so similar as to be identical to everyday Rome, with regard to layout, division into social classes, and matters of custom (the throng of *clientes*, for instance). And religion also: the gods keep their penates in the houses where they dwell, which implies that the sovereigns of heaven and earth also devote a cult to their little household gods.

Comparison does not imply irony or belittling. We are in a universe in which the forms densely pack the allotted space, constantly exchanging qualities and dimensions, and the flux of time is filled with a proliferation of stories and cycles of stories. Terrestrial forms and stories echo celestial forms and stories, but each entwines the other by turns in a double spiral. The contiguity between gods and human beings—related to the gods and the object of their compulsive loves—is one of the dominant themes of the *Metamorphoses*, but this is no more than a particular instance of the contiguity between all the figures and forms of existing things, anthropomorphic or otherwise. Fauna, flora, mineral kingdom, and firmament embrace within their common substance what we are accustomed to think of as human, in the sense of an aggregate of bodily, psychological, and moral qualities.

The poetry of the *Metamorphoses* is rooted above all in these indistinct borderlands between diverse worlds, and as early as book II it seizes an extraordinary opportunity in the myth of Phaëthon, who dares to take the reins of the sun chariot. The sky appears in this as absolute space, abstract geometry, and at the same time as the scene of a human adventure rendered with such precision of detail that we do not lose the thread for an instant, as it carries emotional involvement to an agonizing pitch.

This is not merely precision in the most concrete and material facts, such as the motion of the chariot swerving and bumping because of the unusual lightness of the load, or the emotions of the clumsy young charioteer, but in the visualization of idealized patterns, such as the map of the heavens. I should say at once that this is only apparent precision, one of contradictory facts that convey their effect when taken one by one, and even in terms of general narrative impact, but cannot weld together into a coherent vision. For example, the sky is a sphere traversed by roads going up and going down, recognizable by the wheel ruts, but at the same time the sky is whirling in the opposite direction to the sun chariot. It is suspended at a dizzying height above the lands and the oceans that are seen in the background. At one time it appears as an overarching vault in the loftiest part of which the stars are fixed, at another as a bridge that carries the chariot over the void, causing Phaëthon to be equally terrified of going on or turning back: "*Quid faciat? Multum caeli post terga relictum / ante oculos plus est. Animo metitur utrumque.*" It is an empty wilderness (and therefore not the sky city of book I: "Do you think, perhaps, that there are sacred woods and cities of gods and temples rich with gifts?" asks Phoebus), a wilderness populated by the figures of ferocious beasts that are only *simulacra*, shapes of constellations, but no less menacing for all that. There one discerns an oblique track, halfway up, that skirts the

South Pole and the Bear; but if one swerves off the road and is lost among the precipices, one ends up falling beneath the moon, to scorch the clouds and set fire to the earth.

After the ride through the heavens, suspended in space, which is the most engrossing part of the story, there begins the grandiose description of the earth on fire, of the boiling sea with the bodies of seals floating on it belly up. One of the classic passages of Ovid as a depictor of catastrophe, this is a twin to the flood in book I. All around Alma Tellus, Mother Earth, the waters recede. The shriveled springs attempt to turn back and seek refuge in the maternal womb (*"fontes / qui se condiderant in opacae viscera matris"*). And the earth, with singed hair and eyes bloodshot from the ashes, implores Jove with what little voice is left in her parched throat, warning him that if the poles catch fire even the palaces of the gods will crumble. (The terrestrial or the celestial poles? It has also been suggested that this means the axis of the earth, which Atlas can no longer hold because it is incandescent. But the poles at that time were an astronomical notion, and besides, the next line clearly states *"regia caeli."* Was the sky palace really up there, then? How is it that Phoebus left it out and Phaëthon didn't come across it? Anyway, such contradictions are found not only in Ovid: in Virgil and the other supreme poets of antiquity, it is also hard to get a clear idea of how the ancients really "saw" the skies.)

The episode culminates in the wrecking of the sun chariot by a thunderbolt from Jove, in an explosion of shattered bits and pieces: *"Illic frena iacent, illic temone*

revulsus / axis, in hac radii fractarum parte rotarum. . . ."
(This is not the only traffic accident in the *Metamorphoses*:
another high-speed skid off the road is that of Hippol-
ytus, in the last book of the poem; the wealth of detail
in relating *this* disaster passes from mechanics to anatomy, with descriptions of the rending of the bowels
and severed limbs.)

This interpenetration of gods, men, and nature does
not imply an unequivocal hierarchical order, but an intricate system of interrelations in which each level can
influence the others, though to differing extents. Myth,
in Ovid, is the field of tension in which these forces
clash and balance. Everything depends on the spirit in
which the myth is related. Sometimes the gods themselves recount the myths in which they are involved, as
moral examples intended as warnings to mortals; at other
times mortals use the same myths to challenge or argue
with the gods, as do the daughters of Pierus or Arachne.
Or it may be that there are some myths that the gods
love to hear told, and others they prefer to have si-
lenced.

The daughters of Pierus know a version of the Titans' ascent to Olympus seen from the point of view of
the Titans, including the terror of the gods as they are
put to flight (book V). They recount it after challenging
the Muses in the art of storytelling, and the Muses come
back with another series of myths that re-establish the
viewpoint of Olympus. Then they punish the mortals
by turning them into magpies. A challenge to the gods
implies irreverent or blasphemous intentions in the
story.

Arachne the weaver challenges Minerva in the art of the loom and makes a tapestry depicting the sins of the libertine gods (book VI). The technical precision with which Ovid describes the working of the looms in this challenge might suggest a possible identification of the poet's work with the weaving of a tapestry in various shades of purple. But which? That of Athena-Minerva, in which we see the grandiose figures of Olympus with their traditional attributes, while in tiny scenes at the four corners of the web, framed by olive leaves, are depicted four divine punishments inflicted on mortals who have challenged the gods? Or that of Arachne, in which the insidious seductions of Jove, Neptune, and Apollo, which Ovid has already recounted at some length, reappear as sarcastic comments among garlands of flowers and festoons of ivy (not without the addition of some delightful details, such as Europa, carried across the sea on the bull's back, lifting her feet so as not to get them wet: ". . . *tactumque vereri / adsilientis aquae timidasque reducere plantas*")?

Neither one nor the other. In the vast catalogue of myths that the entire poem in fact is, the myth of Athena and Arachne may in its turn contain two smaller catalogues aimed in opposing ideological directions: one to induce holy terror, the other to incite people to irreverence and moral relativity. Anyone who inferred from this that the poem as a whole should be read in the first manner (since Arachne's challenge is cruelly punished) or in the second (since the poetic rendering favors the guilty victim) would be making a mistake. The *Metamorphoses* aim to represent all that is worth telling of what has been passed down by literature, and with all the force of images and meanings that this implies, without deciding between the various keys in which it can be read—in accord with the ambiguity that is proper to myth. Only by giving a place in the poem to all the stories or implied stories that flow in every direction, that push and shove to channel themselves into the well-ordered expanse of his hexameters, can the author of the *Metamorphoses* be sure of presenting no partial design, but rather a living multiplicity that excludes no god known or unknown.

The case of a new, foreign god, not easy to recognize as such, a scandalous god clashing with each and every model of beauty and virtue, is amply exemplified in the *Metamorphoses* in the case of Bacchus-Dionysus. It is his orgiastic cult that the devotees of Minerva, the daughters of Minyas, refuse to join, continuing to spin and card wool on the days of the Bacchic festivals and alleviating their long labors by telling stories. Here, then, is another use for storytelling, which in lay terms is justified as pure entertainment ("*quod tempora longa videri / non sinat*") or as an aid to productivity "*utile opus manuum vario sermone levemus*"), but which is also pleasing to Minerva, *melior dea* for those industrious girls disgusted by the orgies and dissipation of the cults of Dionysus that were fast spreading through Greece after triumphing in the East.

It is certain that the art of storytelling, so dear to the hearts of weaving women, is linked to the cult of Athena-Minerva. We have seen this in the instance of Arachne, who for scorning the goddess was turned into a spider; but we see it also in the opposite case, that of an excessive cult of Athena which led to the other gods being neglected. In fact, in book IV the daughters of Minyas, also guilty of being too certain of their talents, too exclusive in their worship ("*intempestiva Minerva*"), are punished horrendously by being changed into bats by the god who knows not labor but drunkenness, who listens not to stories but to impetuous, dark song. To avoid being changed into a bat himself, Ovid was extremely careful to leave all the doors of his poem open to gods past, present, and future, indigenous and foreign; to the East, which exerted pressure on the world of fable from beyond the bounds of Greece, and to the Augustan restoration of the Roman spirit, which weighed upon the contemporary political and intellectual situation. But he was not able to convince the nearest and most "executive" god, Augustus Caesar, who transformed him forever into an exile, an inhabitant of distant places—Ovid, who longed to bring everything together into one close-knit whole.

From the East ("from some ancestor of the *Thousand and One Nights*," says L. P. Wilkinson) he got the romantic tale of Pyramus and Thisbe (which one of the daughters of Minyas chooses from a list of tales of the same mysterious origin), with its wall that opens a way for whispered words to pass but not for kisses, with the night flooded with moonlight beneath the bright mulberry tree—a tale destined to cast its reflections as far as the midsummer of the Elizabethan age.

Also from the East, by way of the Alexandrian romance, Ovid obtained the technique of multiplying the space within the poem by means of stories inserted into other stories and thereby increasing the impression of density, of intricacy, of being packed in. An example is the forest in which a wild-boar hunt intrudes into the destinies of illustrious heroes (book VIII), not far from the whirlpools of the Achelous, which halt the survivors of the hunt on their way home. They are welcomed to the dwelling of the river-god, who represents an obstacle as well as a refuge, a pause in the action and an opportunity for reflection and storytelling. Since one of the hunters is Theseus, eager to know the origin of everything he sees, and another is Peirithoüs, insolent and unbelieving ("*deorum / spector erat mentisque ferox*"), the river feels encouraged to tell some wonderful stories of metamorphosis, and is then emulated by his guests. Thus, in the *Metamorphoses*, new incrustations of stories are constantly being added, as on shells that might bring forth a pearl. In this case the pearl is the humble idyll of Philemon and Baucis, which embraces a whole minutely delineated world and moves at a totally different pace.

It should be said that Ovid only occasionally makes use of these structural complexities. The passion that dominates his compositional talents is not arrangement but accumulation, along with the varying of perspective and changing of pace. Thus, when Mercury wishes to bring sleep to Argus, whose hundred eyelids never close all at once, and begins to recount the metamorphosis of the nymph Syrinx into a clump of reeds, one part of her story is told in detail, another summed up in a single phrase; the rest is left moot when the god falls silent as soon as he sees that all of Argus's eyes have yielded to sleep.

The *Metamorphoses* are above all the poem of rapidity. Everything has to happen at high speed, strike the imagination; every image has to overlap another image, come into focus, and then vanish. This is the principle of the cinema: each line, like each frame, must be full of visual stimuli in motion. The abhorrence of the vacuum dominates both space and time. For page after page all verbs are in the present, so that everything is happening before our eyes; events pursue each other, and anything distant is rejected. When Ovid wishes to change pace, the first thing he does is to change not the tense of the verbs but the person, switching from the third person to the second, which means introducing the character whom he is just going to speak about and addressing him directly as "you"; "*Te quoque mutatum torvo, Neptune, invenco. . . .*" The "present" resides not simply in the tense of the verb, but in the very presence of the character who is being called up to the eyes. Even when the verbs are in the past, the vocative suddenly closes the gap. This method is often used when several subjects are performing parallel actions, to avoid the monotony of making lists. If he has spoken of Tityus in the third person, then Tantalus and Sisyphus are summoned with the vocative "You." Even plants have a right to the second person ("*Vos quoque, flexipedes hederae, venistis*"), and no wonder, seeing that they are plants that move like human beings, and run toward the sound of the lyre of the widowed Orpheus, crowding together into a dense bed of Mediterranean flora (book IX).

There are also times—and the one I mentioned just now is one of them—when the story has to slow down, change to a calmer gait, render the passage of time as if it were suspended, and depict a vague distance. What does Ovid do in such cases? To make it clear that the story is not in any hurry, he stops to gaze at the most minute details. For example, Philemon and Baucis are welcoming some unknown visitors (the gods) to their humble dwelling. *"Mensae sed erat pes tertius impar: / testa parem fecit; quae postquam subdita clivum / sustulit, aequatem mentae tersere virentes. . . ."*: "But of the three legs of the table one is too short. A bit of pottery corrects that; slipped underneath, it gets rid of the incline, and the tabletop is then cleaned with leaves of green mint. And on it they put olives of two colors, sacred to chaste Minerva, and autumnal dogberries steeped in liquid juice, and endives and radishes and some curdled milk, and eggs carefully turned on ashes that are not too hot: and all in earthenware dishes" (book VIII).

It is by making his picture ever richer in detail that Ovid achieves an effect of rarefaction, and a pause. For Ovid's way is always to add, never to remove; to go in for more and more detail, never to become blurred and vague. This method achieves different results according to the intonation. In this case it is quiet and sympathetic to humble things, but elsewhere it is agitated and eager to saturate the wonder of the fable with objective observation of real natural phenomena. For instance, Perseus fights with the sea monster whose back is encrusted with shells, laying Medusa's head, bristling with snakes, face down on a rock, but only after covering the rock with a layer of seaweed and underwater plants, so that her face does not have to suffer contact with the gritty sand. Seeing the foliage turn to stone on touching Medusa, the nymphs amuse themselves by making other twigs undergo the same transformation. This is the origin of coral, which is soft underwater but petrifies on contact with the air. Thus Ovid concludes this fantastic adventure in an etiological key, in keeping with his taste for the bizarre forms in nature.

A law of the greatest internal economy dominates this poem, which on the surface is devoted to unbridled extravagance. It is the economy proper to metamorphosis, which demands that the new forms should recover the materials of the old ones as far as possible. After the flood, during the transformation of stones into men (book I), "if there was in them a part damp with some moisture, or earthy, this came to serve as the body; what was solid, unable to bend, changed into bone; those that were veins remained, with the same name." Here the economy extends to the very name: "*quae modo vena fuit, sub eodem nomine mansit.*" What most catches the attention about Daphne (book I) is her disheveled hair (so much so that Phoebus's first thought on seeing her is "Think, if she were to comb it!" ("*Spectat inornatus collo pendere capillos / et 'Quid, si comantur?' ait*"), so that in the flowing lines of her flight she is already predisposed toward metamorphosis into a plant: "*in frondem crines, in ramos bracchia crescunt / pes modo tam velox pigris radicibus haeret. . . .*" Cyané, in book V, merely takes her dissolution into tears to the last degree ("*lacrimisque absumitur omnis*"), until she turns into the little lake of which she was the nymph. And the Lycian peasants (book VI) who hurled insults at the vagabond Latona (who wanted to quench the thirst of her newborn twins) and fouled the lake waters by stirring up the mud, were already not much different from the frogs into which they were then changed by just retribution. Enough that the neck should disappear, the shoulders join to the head, the back turn green and the belly a dirty white.

This technique of metamorphosis has been studied by Shcheglov in a very clearly stated and convincing essay.

All these transformations are concerned with physio-spatial traits that Ovid was in the habit of isolating even apart from metamorphosis ("hard stone," "long body," "curved back"). . . . Thanks to his knowledge of the properties of things, the poet makes transformation take the shortest route, for he knows in advance what man has in common with the dolphin, what he lacks, and what he has more of in comparison. The essential thing is that, thanks to the representation of the entire world as a system of elementary properties, the process of transformation—this improbable and fantastic phenomenon—is reduced to a series of comparatively simple processes. The event is no longer represented as a fable, but as a set of habitual and likely facts: growth, diminution, hardening, softening, curving, straightening, compression, rarefaction, etc.

Ovid's writing, as defined by Shcheglov, would contain the coldest and most rigorous model, or at least program, of Robbe-Grillet. It goes without saying that such a definition does not exhaust all that we can look for in Ovid. But the important thing is that this way of describing objects *objectively* (whether animate or inanimate), "as different combinations of a relatively small number of basic, utterly simple elements," corresponds to the one certain philosophy of the *Metamorphoses*: "that of the unity and kinship of all that exists in the world, things and living beings alike."

With the cosmogonical account in book I and Pythagoras's profession of faith in the last book, Ovid attempted to endow this philosophy of nature with a theoretical system, perhaps in competition with his remote predecessor Lucretius. A lot has been argued about what weight to give these pronouncements, but maybe the only thing that counts for us is the poetic coherence of Ovid's way of expressing his world: this swarm and tangle of events that are often similar yet always different, in which he celebrates the continuity and mobility of all that is.

Ovid has not yet finished the chapter on the origins of the world and the primordial catastrophes when he starts in on the series of love affairs of the gods with nymphs or mortal girls. The love stories (which make up the most vivid part of the poem, the first eleven books) reveal a number of constants. Love here is love at first sight, an impelling demand, without psychological complications, and one that cries out for immediate satisfaction. Since the creature desired usually refuses and flees, the motif of a chase through the woods is recurrent. Metamorphosis can occur at different moments, either as a disguise on the part of the seducer, or as an escape for the trapped girl, or else as a punishment meted out to the victim of seduction by some jealous goddess.

Compared with the continual pressure of male desires, cases of female initiative in love are relatively rare, but in compensation they are more complex, not matters of momentary whim but of the passions, bearing a greater psychological depth (Venus in love with Adonis, for instance). They often involve a morbid erotic element (the nymph Salmacis, who in embracing Hermaphroditus melts into a bisexual creature). In a few cases we have illicit passions, incestuous (like the tragic characters of Myrrha and Byblis; the way in which the latter's passion for her brother is revealed to her, her dream, her suffering—these make up one of the finest passages of Ovid as a psychologist), or homosexual (Iphis), or criminally jealous (Medea). In the heart of the book the stories of Jason and Medea open up enough space for a genuine novel, with the interweaving of adventure, dark passions, and the "black" grotesque of witches' potions that will later reappear in *Macbeth*.

The passage without intervals from one story to the next is underlined, as Wilkinson observes, by the fact that the end of a story rarely coincides with the end of one of the books into which the poem is divided. Ovid may even begin a new story when he has only a few lines left until the end of a book. This is partly the old expedient used by writers of serials, who whet the reader's appetite for the next installment; but it is also a sign of the contiguity of the work, which would not have been divided into books if its length had not necessitated a certain number of scrolls. We are thus given the impression of a real and coherent world in which there is an interaction between events that are usually considered in isolation.

The stories may resemble one another, but they never repeat one another. Not for nothing is the most heartbreaking story the one (in book III) concerned with the unrequited love of the nymph Echo—condemned to the repetition of sounds—for the youth Narcissus, condemned to gaze upon his own image "repeated" in the watery mirror. Ovid races through this forest of love stories, all similar and all different, pursued by the voice of Echo reverberating among the rocks: "*Coeamus! Coeamus! Coeamus!*"

The Structure of
Orlando Furioso

Radio broadcast, 1974; written on the occasion of the five
hundredth anniversary of the birth of Lodovico Ariosto.

Orlando Furioso is a poem that refuses to begin and
refuses to end. It refuses to begin because it is presented
as the continuation of another poem, Matteo Maria
Boiardo's *Orlando Innamorato*, left unfinished at the author's death. And it refuses to end because Ariosto never
stopped working on it. Having published it in the first
edition of forty cantos in 1516, he went on trying to
make it grow, at first attempting to give it a sequel which
remained incomplete (the so-called *Cinque canti*, published after his death), and then inserting new episodes
in the middle cantos, so that in the third and definitive
version, dating from 1532, the number of cantos jumped
to forty-six. In between there was a second edition (1521),

which bears witness to another aspect of the poem that cannot be considered finished: the polishing, the tuning up of language and versification that Ariosto constantly busied himself over. All his life long, one might say, because to achieve the 1516 edition he worked for twelve years, and then he toiled for another sixteen on the 1532 edition; the next year he died. This process of expanding from the inside, making episodes proliferate from other episodes, creating new symmetries and new contrasts, seems to me to explain Ariosto's method of construction rather well. And for him it remained the best method of enlarging this poem, with its polycentric and contemporaneous structure, the events of which branch out in every direction, continually intersecting and diverging.

So that one can follow the vicissitudes of such a mass of main and secondary characters, the poem requires a type of "assembly" that enables it to leave one character or theatre of operations and pass on to another. Sometimes these shifts occur without breaking the continuity of the narrative, as when two people meet and the story, which has been following the first, parts from him and follows the second; and at other times by means of clear breaks that interrupt the action right in the middle of a canto. It is usually the last two lines of an *ottava* (the eight-line stanza used by Ariosto and also, for example, by Spenser in *The Faerie Queene*) that warn us of the suspension and interruption of the narrative. They are rhymed couplets such as these:

> Segue Rinaldo, e d'ira si distrugge:
> ma seguiamo Angelica che fugge.

[Rinaldo follows, consumed with rage. But let us follow Angelica, who is fleeing.]

Or else:

> Lasciànlo andar, che farà buon cammino,
> e torniamo a Rinaldo paladino.

[Let him go, for he will have a safe journey, and let us return to Rinaldo the Paladin.]

Or again:

> Ma tempo è omai di ritrovar Ruggiero
> che scorre il ciel su l'animal leggiero.

[But now it is time to find Ruggiero again, as he rides through the skies on that fleet animal.]

While these breaks in the action are placed in the middle of the cantos, the end of each individual canto promises us that the story will continue in the next one. Here, too, this informative function is assigned to the rhymed couplet at the end of the *ottava*:

> Come a Parigi appropinquosse, e quanto
> Carlo aiutò, vi dirà l'altro canto.

[How they approached Paris, and how much Charles helped them, the next canto will tell you.]

To end the canto Ariosto often pretends to be a bard reciting his lines at a court soirée:

Non più, Signor, non più di questo canto;
ch'io son già rauco, e vo' posarmi alquanto.

[No more, my lord, no more of this canto; for I am already hoarse, and am inclined to rest.]

Or else he shows himself in the very act of writing:

Poi che da tutti i lati ho pieno il foglio,
finire il canto, e riposar mi voglio.

[Since my paper is full on all sides, I would like to finish the canto and rest.]

The start of the following canto, on the other hand, nearly always involves a widening of the horizon, a detachment from the impetus of the narrative, in the form either of an aphoristic introduction, or of an amorous peroration, or again of an elaborate metaphor, before taking up the story where it left off. It is in fact at the beginning of the cantos that we find those digressions about contemporary Italy, especially plentiful in the last part of the poem. It is as if, by means of these linking passages, the times in which the author lived and wrote made irruptions into the fabled times of the narrative.

To give a brief description of the form of *Orlando Furioso* is therefore impossible, because we are not confronted with any rigid geometry. We might have recourse to the image of a force field, continually generating new force fields within itself. The movement is always centrifugal: at the outset we are already right in the middle of the action, and this holds good for the poem as a whole as well as for each canto and episode.

The trouble with any preamble to *Orlando Furioso* is that if one begins by saying, "It is a poem that is a continuation of another poem, which in turn continues a cycle of innumerable other poems," the reader is at once discouraged. If before he starts reading he has to find out all about its precedents, and the precedents of the precedents, when on earth will he be able to start on Ariosto's poem? But any preamble is immediately seen to be superfluous. The *Furioso* is a book unique in its kind, and can be—or should I say, must be?—read without reference to any other book either before or after it. It is a world of its own that one can travel the length and breadth of, going in, coming out again, and losing oneself in it.

That the author would pass off the construction of this world as a continuation, an appendix, or what he called a "*gionta*" (adjunct) to another man's work, may be interpreted as a sign of Ariosto's extraordinary modesty, an extreme example of understatement, of that special spirit of irony vis-à-vis himself that makes a man minimize great and important things. But it may also be viewed as a concept of time and space that rejects the closed configuration of the Ptolemaic cosmos, and opens out limitlessly toward past and future, as indeed toward an incalculable plurality of worlds.

From the very start the *Furioso* introduces itself as the poem of movement; or, better, it introduces the particular kind of movement that is going to run through it from top to bottom: movement in broken, zigzag lines. We could trace the general pattern of the poem by following the continual intersection and divergence of these lines on a map of Europe and Africa, but to define it we have only to look at the first canto, in which three horsemen are pursuing Angelica, who is fleeing through a wood, in a frenzied dance comprising strayings and chance encounters, blunders and changes of plans.

It is with this zigzag traced by galloping horses and the fitfulness of the human heart that we are introduced to the spirit of the poem. The pleasure of speedy action is mingled at once with a sense of breadth and the availability of time and space. Absent-minded behavior is characteristic not only of Angelica's pursuers, but also of Ariosto himself. One is tempted to say that the poet, as he starts his narrative, does not yet know the outline of the plot that later on will guide him with such precise premeditation. But one thing he already has perfectly clear in his head: this dash, and at the same time this leisureliness of narration, which—in a word pregnant with meaning—we might describe as the *errant* movement of Ariosto's poetry.

Such characteristics of Ariosto's "space" can be discerned on the scale of the poem as a whole or in single cantos, and even on a minute scale such as that of the stanza or the single line. The *ottava* is the measure in which we are best able to recognize what is unique about Ariosto. In the *ottava* he can twist us around his little finger; he is at home. His miracle is above all that of casual ease. This is mainly for two reasons. One is intrinsic to the nature of the *ottava*, a stanza that lends itself even to long discourses, and to the alternation of sublime and lyrical tones of voice with tones more prosaic and jocular. The other is intrinsic to Ariosto's way of writing poetry, which is not confined to limitations of any kind;

he did not decide (as Dante did) on a rigid division of the material, or a rule of symmetry that would make him adhere to a pre-established number of cantos and a certain number of stanzas in each canto. In the *Furioso* the shortest canto has seventy-two stanzas, while the longest has 199. The poet could take his time if he wished and use several stanzas to say something that others would say in a line, or he could concentrate in a single line what could well be material for a lengthy peroration.

The secret of the *ottava* in Ariosto's hands lies in the way he follows the varied rhythms of the spoken language, in the abundance of what the great nineteenth-century critic De Sanctis called the "inessential accessories of language," and also in the swiftness of his ironic sallies. But colloquialism is only one of his registers, which extend from the lyrical to the tragic to the aphoristic, and can occur together in the same stanza. Ariosto can write with memorable concision, and many of his lines have become proverbial: "*Ecco il giudicio umano come spesso erra!*" ("Behold how often human judgment errs!"), or "*O gran bontà de' cavallieri antiqui!*" ("Ah, the great courtesy of the knights of old!"). But it is not only with these parentheses that he achieves his changes of pace: the very structure of the *ottava* is based on the interruption of the rhythm. The six lines linked by two alternating rhymes are followed by the couplet, producing an effect that we would now call an anticlimax, a brusque change not only of rhythm but of psychological and intellectual climate as well, from the cultured to the popular, from the evocative to the comic.

Naturally, Ariosto plays with these "turnarounds" to his stanzas as he sees fit, but the game could become monotonous without the poet's agility in giving life to the stanza by introducing pauses, making stops in different positions, adapting different syntactical speeds to the metrical scheme, alternating long sentences with short ones, breaking the stanza and in some cases running on into the next, jumping from the past tense to the imperfect to the present to the future—in short, creating a series of planes and perspectives in his story.

The freedom and ease of movement that we have encountered in the versification are still more evident on the level of narrative structures and the composition of the plot. The main themes, let us remember, are two. The first recounts how Orlando, as a rejected lover of Angelica, became a furious madman, and how the Catholic armies, lacking their champion, very nearly lost the whole of France; and how the lost reason of the madman was found by Astolfo on the moon and driven back into the person of its rightful owner, enabling him to regain his place in the ranks. Parallel with this unwinds the second plot, that of the predestined but constantly frustrated love of Ruggiero, champion of the Saracen camp, for the Christian warrior-woman Bradamante, and of all the impediments that stand in the way of their nuptial destiny until the Saracen manages to change sides, receive baptism, and wed his robust beloved. The Ruggiero-Bradamante plot is no less important than that of Orlando and Angelica, because it is from that couple that Ariosto (like Boiardo before him) intends to trace the descent of the Este family, which means not only to justify his poem in the eyes of his patrons, but above all to link the mythical times of chivalry with contemporary events, with his own times in Ferrara and in Italy.

The two main themes and their numerous ramifications therefore proceed entwined together, but they in turn are wound around the trunk of the truly epic part of the poem, the events in the war between the Emperor Charlemagne and Agramante, king of Africa. This epic is largely concentrated in a block of cantos dealing with the siege of Paris by the Moors, the Christian counter-offensive, and the quarrels in Agramante's camp. The siege of Paris is more or less the center of gravity of the poem, just as the city of Paris appears as its geographical heart:

> Siede Parigi in una gran pianura
> ne l'ombilico a Francia, anzi nel core;
> gli passa la riviera entro le mura
> e corre et esce in altra parte fuore:
> ma fa un'isola prima, e v'assicura
> de la città una parte, e la migliore;
> l'altre due (ch'in tre parti è la gran terra)
> di fuor di fossa, e dentro il fiume serra.
>
> Alla città che molte miglia gira
> da molte parti si può dar battaglia;
> ma perché sol da un canto assalir mira,
> né volontier l'esercito sbarraglia,
> oltre il fiume Agramante si ritira
> verso ponente, acciò che quindi assaglia;
> però che né cittade né campagna
> ha dietro (se non sua) fino alla Spagna.
>
> (XIV. 104–105)

[Paris stands in a great plain in the navel of France, or rather, the heart. The river passes within its walls, and flows, and issues forth at the other side. But first it creates an island, and I assure you this is the best part of the city. The other two (for the great town is in three parts) are enclosed on the outside by the moat, and inside by the river. Against the city, which encircles many miles, one can bring battle on many sides. But because he only plans to assault on one side, and is not willing to risk his army, Agramante retires beyond the river toward the west, so that he can attack from there; for there is no town or countryside at his back (except his own) from there to Spain.]

From what I have said it might be thought that the wanderings of all the main characters end by converging at the siege of Paris. But this does not occur. Most of the most famous champions are absent from this collective epic, and only the gigantic bulk of Rodomante towers above the fray. Where are all the others hiding out?

We have to confess at this point that the poem has another center of gravity, a negative center, a trapdoor, or a sort of maelstrom that one by one swallows all the main characters. This is the enchanted palace of Atlante the wizard. Atlante's magic takes special delight in illusory architecture. As early as canto IV, among the crests of the Pyrenees, he causes a solid steel castle to rise up, and then makes it vanish into thin air. In cantos XII to XXII we see, not far from the English Channel, the rise of a castle that is a kind of abyss, a void in which all the images of the poem are reflected.

Orlando himself, while seeking Angelica, has the misfortune to fall victim to this enchantment, by a process that is repeated almost identically for each of these valiant knights: he sees his beloved being carried off, he pursues the kidnapper, enters a mysterious palace, and wanders around and around in empty halls and corridors. Or, rather, the palace is empty of what is sought, and peopled only by seekers.

These men wandering through the loggias and down the back stairs, groping behind tapestries and canopies, are the most celebrated Christian and Moorish knights. All of them have been drawn to the palace, by the vision of a beloved woman, of an enemy they cannot catch up with, of a stolen horse, of a lost object. And now they can no longer escape from those walls. If one of them makes as if to leave, he hears his name called and turns— and the apparition sought in vain is there, the woman he has to rescue is looking out of a window begging for help. Atlante has given shape and form to the kingdom of illusion. If life is always varied, unexpected, and changing, illusion is monotonous, forever harping on the same string. Desire is a race toward nothingness, and Atlante's enchantment concentrates all unsatisfied longings in the prison of a labyrinth. But he does not change the rules that govern the movements of men in the open spaces of the poem and of the world.

Astolfo also ends up in the palace, chasing (or thinking he is chasing) a peasant boy who has stolen his horse, Rabicano. But with Astolfo no enchantment holds. Having a magic book that explains all about such palaces, Astolfo goes straight to the marble flagstone at the doorstep and has only to lift it for the whole palace to go up in smoke. At that moment he is joined by a troop of knights. Nearly all of them are friends of his, but instead of greeting him they hurl themselves upon him as if they mean to make mincemeat of him with their swords. What has happened? Atlante the wizard, perceiving himself in trouble, has had recourse to one last enchantment, making Astolfo appear to the many and various prisoners in the palace as the adversary who lured them in. But Astolfo has only to set his lips to his horn to dispel the magic, the wizard, and the victims of wizardry alike. The palace, a spider's web of dreams and desires and envy, simply melts away. Or, rather, it ceases to be a place outside ourselves, with doors and stairs and walls, and returns to hiding in our minds, in the labyrinth of thought. To those he had captured, Atlante grants freedom to roam the roads of the poem once more. Is this Atlante or Ariosto? The enchanted palace stands revealed as an astute structural stratagem on the part of the narrator, who, given the downright impossibility of developing a great number of parallel events at the same time, felt he had to withdraw certain characters from the action for the space of a few cantos, to lay certain cards aside and get on with his game, and then pull the cards out of his sleeve at the opportune moment. The enchanter who wants to delay the accomplishment of destiny and the poet-strategist who now swells, now thins the ranks of the figures on the stage, first regrouping and then dispersing them, merge until the two are virtually identical.

The word "game" has come up several times in this talk, but we must not forget that games, whether of children or grown-ups, always have a serious basis. First and foremost they are techniques for training the faculties and attitudes that will be required in life. Ariosto's is the game of a society that feels itself to be the creator and repository of a particular vision of the world, but also feels that it is digging an abyss beneath its feet, to the accompanying rumble of distant earthquakes.

The forty-sixth and last canto opens by listing a whole crowd of people who in fact make up the public for which Ariosto thought he was writing his poem. This is the real dedication of *Orlando Furioso*, not the compulsory bow made at the beginning of canto I to Cardinal Ippolito d'Este, the "munificent offspring of Hercules" to whom the poem is addressed.

The vessel of the poem is sailing into harbor, and waiting to greet it on the quayside it finds the most gracious and beautiful ladies in all the cities of Italy, as well as the knights and the poets and the learned men. What Ariosto does here is make a swift review of names and rapid profiles of his contemporaries and friends. It is a description of his perfect public, and at the same time a picture of his ideal society. By a kind of structural *volte-face*, the poem steps out of itself and looks at itself through the eyes of its readers, defining itself by means of a census of those to whom it is addressed. And in its turn it is the poem that does duty as a definition or an emblem of a society of readers present or future, of all those people who will take part in his game, and who will recognize themselves in it.

Candide:
An Essay in Velocity

Preface to an Italian edition of Voltaire's *Candide* with illustrations by Paul Klee, 1974.

Wiry figures, animated by an eel-like mobility, flex and writhe in a dance of whiplash nimbleness: it was in such a way that in 1911 Paul Klee illustrated Voltaire's *Candide*, giving visual (I would almost say "musical") form to the joyous energy that—over and above the dense web of references to an age and culture—this book still communicates to the reader of our times.

In *Candide* today it is not the "philosophical tale" that most enchants us, or the satire, or the emergence of a moral or a vision of the world: it is the sheer pace of the thing. With lightness and rapidity a whole series of disasters, tortures, and massacres scampers across the page, bounds from chapter to chapter, is ramified and multiplied, without afflicting the reader's emotions with any effect but that of an exhilarating and primordial vitality. If the three pages of chapter VIII suffice for Cunégonde to relate how, having had her father, mother, and brother hacked to pieces by the invaders, she was raped, disemboweled, cured, reduced to being a washerwoman, prostituted in Holland and Portugal, and shared on alternate days by two "protectors" of different faiths, and in this way chanced to witness the *auto-da-fé* of which Pangloss and Candide were the victims, and finally to meet up with the latter again, less than two pages in chapter IX are needed for Candide to find himself with two corpses on his hands and for Cunégonde to exclaim: "However did you do it, you who were born so gentle, to slaughter a Jew and a prelate in the space of two minutes?" And when the old servant has to explain why she only has one buttock, and starts to tell her life story from when, as the daughter of a pope, at the age of thirteen, in the space of three months, she experienced destitution and slavery, was raped nearly every day, saw her mother cut into four pieces, suffered war and hunger, and was dying in the plague in Algiers, all to get to the point of telling us about the siege of Azov and the unusual source of nourishment that the starving janissaries found in female buttocks—well, at that point things go on a bit longer: two whole chapters or (say) six pages and a half.

Voltaire's great discovery as a humorist was destined to become one of the sure-fire effects of comic films—the high-speed accumulation of disasters. And there is no lack of sudden accelerations of pace that carry the sense of the absurd to the point of paroxysm, as when the series of disasters already told so swiftly "in full" is repeated in résumé at breakneck speed. What Voltaire projects with his lightning "shots" is a great world-embracing movie, *Around the World in Eighty Pages*, that carries Candide from his native Westphalia to Holland to Portugal to South America to France to England to Venice and finally to Turkey, while branching out into the supplementary world tours of the "co-stars," both men and women, the latter easy prey to pirates and slave traders from Gibraltar to the Bosporus. Above all, it is a great movie on current events in the world, with the massacre of whole villages in the Seven Years' War between France and Germany (the "Bulgars" and the "Avars"), the Lisbon earthquake of 1755, the *auto-da-fé* of the Inquisition, the Jesuits in Paraguay who refused Spanish and Portuguese domination, the mythical riches of the Incas, with a few briefer flashes on Protestantism in Holland, the spread of syphilis, piracy in the Mediterranean and the Atlantic, the civil wars in Morocco, and the exploitation of Negro slaves in Guyana, all the while leaving a certain margin open for the literary and social gossip of Paris and for interviews with the many dethroned monarchs of the time, who had all gathered for the Carnival in Venice.

A topsy-turvy world, in short, in which nobody comes off well anywhere, if we except the only wise and happy land, El Dorado. Any connection here between happiness and wealth should be put out of mind, given that the Incas do not know that the gold dust on their roads and the cobblestones of diamonds have such value for the men of the Old World. And yet, just think: Candide finds a wise and happy society right there among the gold fields. It is there that Pangloss might finally be right, and the best of all possible worlds might be a reality. The trouble is that El Dorado is hidden among the most inaccessible peaks of the Andes, perhaps located in a crack in the map. It is a no-place, a utopia.

But if Voltaire's Bengodi has some of the vagueness and unconvincing quality that is proper to utopias, the remainder of the world, with all its painful vexations, even if these are mentioned very briefly, is by no means represented artificially. "This is what it costs for you to eat sugar in Europe!" says the Negro in Dutch Guyana, after telling us his sufferings in a few lines. And the courtesan in Venice: "Ah, monsieur, if you could imagine what it is like to have to caress, indiscriminately, an aged merchant, a lawyer, a monk, a gondolier, an abbot; to be exposed to every insult and affront; to be often reduced to borrowing a skirt just to go and have it taken off again by some repulsive fellow; to be robbed by one man of what one has earned from another; to be taxed by the officers of justice, and to have no prospects other than a horrendous old age, a hospital, a dungheap. . . ."

Certainly the characters in *Candide* seem to be made of rubber. Pangloss is rotting with syphilis, they hang him, they tie him to the oar of a galley, and we find him still alive and well; but it would be wrong to say that Voltaire skips over the price of suffering. What other novelist has the courage to show us his heroine, who at the beginning is "rosy-cheeked, fresh, plump, and appetizing," transformed into a Cunégonde who is "faded, with gummy eyes and flattened breasts, and chapped, reddened arms"?

We are aware at this point that our reading of *Candide*, intended to be completely detached, completely

"superficial," has led us to the heart of the "philosophy,"
of Voltaire's vision of the world. This is perceived not
only in Voltaire's quarrel with Pangloss's providential
optimism. When we come down to it, the mentor who
is the longest at Candide's side is not the unfortunate
Leibnizian pedant at all, but the "Manichean" Martin,
who is inclined to see nothing in the world but the
triumphs of the devil. And if Martin plays the role of
the anti-Pangloss, one can by no means say that he has
things all his own way. It is vain, says Voltaire, to seek
a metaphysical explanation of evil, as do both Pangloss
the optimist and Martin the pessimist, because this evil
is totally subjective, indefinable, and incapable of measurement. Voltaire's creed is antifinalist; or, rather, if
his god does have an end and purpose, then it is an
inscrutable purpose. A design for the universe does not
exist; or if it exists, it is up to God to know it, not up
to man. Voltaire's "rationalism" is an ethical and vol-
untaristic attitude depicted against a theological background as incompatible with man as that of Pascal.

If this merry-go-round of catastrophes can be con-
templated with something approaching a smile, it is
because human life is a brief, limited thing. There is
always someone who can claim to be more unlucky than
we are, and if by any chance there were some person
who had nothing to complain about and possessed every
good thing that life had to offer, he would end up like
Signor Pococurante, senator of Venice, who forever has
a stench under his nose and finds fault where in all conscience he ought to find only reasons for satisfaction and
admiration. The really and truly negative character in
the book is this one, Pococurante the bored-to-tears.

For in the last analysis Pangloss and Martin, although they give absurd answers to meaningless questions, are in fact struggling amid the sufferings and the risks that are the very stuff of life.

The subdued vein of "wisdom" that emerges in this book, through marginal spokesmen such as Jacques the Anabaptist, the Inca elder, and the Parisian savant who closely resembles the author, is stated at the end (and put into the mouth of the Dervish) in the famous moral *"il faut cultiver notre jardin"*: "we must tend our own garden." A very restricted moral, certainly, and one that should be understood primarily in its anti-metaphysical, intellectual sense—you must not saddle yourself with problems other than the ones you can solve by your own direct, practical efforts—and then in its social sense, as the first affirmation of work as the substance of every value. To our ears today the exhortation to "tend our own garden" comes laden with selfish, bourgeois overtones, totally out of tune with our own anguish and concerns. It is no coincidence that this injunction appears on the last page, almost outside this book in which work appears only as damnation and gardens are regularly devastated. It is also utopian, no less than the kingdom of the Incas is: the voice of "reason" in *Candide* is utterly utopian. But neither is it pure chance that this phrase from *Candide* is the one that has become most famous, and indeed proverbial. We must not forget the radical ethical and epistemological change that this statement marked (we are in 1759, exactly thirty years before the storming of the Bastille). Man is no longer judged in his relations with transcendental good and evil, but by that little or much that he can in fact do. From this stem both an ethic of strictly "productive" work, in the capitalistic sense of the word, and an ethic of practical, responsible, and concrete commitment without which no common problems can be solved. The real choices of man today, in a word, start from this point.

The City as Protagonist
in Balzac

Introduction to an Italian translation of Balzac's *Ferragus*,
1973.

To make a novel out of a city, to represent the
streets and the various districts as *dramatis personae*, each
one with a character in conflict with every other; to give
life to human figures and situations as if they were spontaneous growths from the cobbles of the streets, or else
protagonists in such dramatic contrast with them as to
cause a whole string of disasters; to work in such a way
that at every changing moment the true protagonist was
the living city, its biological continuity, the monster that
was Paris—this is what Balzac felt impelled to do when
he began to write *Ferragus*.

I should say that he started out with a completely
different idea in his head: the power wielded by mysterious personages by means of the invisible network of

secret societies. But in fact he had two particular cores
of inspiration, which he aimed to blend into a single
cycle of novels. On the one hand were the secret societies, and on the other the mysterious omnipotence of
a single individual on the fringes of society. The myths
destined to mold both popular and cultured fiction for
over a century all pass through Balzac. The Superman
who takes his revenge on the society that has outlawed
him by transforming himself into a totally elusive demi-
urge features throughout all the volumes of *La Comédie
humaine* in the manifold guises of Vautrin, and was later
reincarnated in all the Counts of Monte Cristo, the
Phantoms of the Opera, and even the Godfathers whom
best-selling novelists are now putting into circulation.
The sinister conspiracy that stretches its tentacles on
every side was destined—part in jest and part in ear-
nest—to obsess the most urbane English novelists from
the beginning to the end of the nineteenth century, and
rise again in our own age with the mass production of
tough spy thrillers.

With *Ferragus* we are still in the full flood of Byronic
Romanticism. In a March 1833 issue of the *Revue de
Paris* (a weekly to which Balzac was bound by contract
to contribute forty pages a month, amid continual re-
bukes from the publisher for the lateness of the copy
and for making too many corrections on the proofs),
we find the preface to the *Histoire des treize*, in which
the author promises to reveal the secrets of thirteen resolute outlaws bound by a secret pact of mutual aid that
rendered them invincible. He announced the appearance
of a first part: *Ferragus, chef des dévorants*. (The word
dévorants, or *devoirants*, traditionally meant the members

of a trade association, "companions-in-duty," but Balzac was certainly playing on a false etymology of *dévorer*, which is far more suggestive and would mean "devourers."

Though the preface is dated 1831, Balzac did not begin work on the project until February 1833, and he did not succeed in delivering the first chapter for the week following the publication of the preface; so, two weeks later, the *Revue de Paris* brought out the first two chapters together. The third chapter held up publication of the next issue, and the fourth and last came out later in a supplement during the month of April.

But the novel as published was very different from the one that had been announced. The old project no longer interested the author. He was concerned with quite a different thing, which made him sweat over his manuscripts instead of tossing off pages at the rate demanded, and led him to scatter the proofs with corrections and additions that made a hash of the typographer's work. The plot he used is still breathtaking, with its mysteries and totally unexpected *coups de théâtre*, and the shady character going by the Ariostian *nom de guerre* of Ferragus has a central position in it, but the adventures to which he owes his secret authority as well as his public infamy are left unsaid, and Balzac only showed him in his decline. And as for the "thirteen"—or, rather, the twelve other members—it almost seems as if the author forgot about them, for he showed them only in the distance, as decorative "extras" at a splendidly pompous funeral Mass.

What was now arousing Balzac's enthusiasm was the topographical epic poem of Paris, following his first intuition of the city as language, as ideology, as the conditioning factor of every thought and word and gesture, the streets that *"impriment par leur physiognomie certaines idées contre lesquelles nous sommes sans défense,"* the city as monstrous as a giant crustacean, whose inhabitants are no more than motor articulations. For years Balzac had been publishing sketches of Paris life, cameos of typical characters, and now he aimed to organize this material into a kind of Parisian encyclopedia with space for a mini-treatise on how to follow women down the street, for the genre painting (worthy of Daumier) of passers-by caught in the rain, for the classification of tramps, for the satire on the building mania then afflicting the city, for the portrayal of a slut, for a record of the speech of the various social classes. When Balzac's dialogues shed their habitual declamatory emphasis, they succeed in conveying fashionable fads and neologisms and even tones of voice, as when we hear a saleswoman say that marabou feathers give a lady's hair style *"quelque chose de vague, d'ossianique et de très comme il faut."* The treatment of the exteriors is matched by that of the interiors, luxurious or squalid as they may be, with studied pictorial effects such as that of the vase of *géroflées* in Widow Gruget's hovel. The description of the Père-Lachaise cemetery and the intricacies of the bureaucracy of "funeral directors" crowns the whole design, as if the novel that opened with a vision of Paris as a living organism were to close on the level of the Paris of the dead.

The *Histoire des treize* has been transformed into an atlas of the continent called Paris. And when Balzac had finished *Ferragus* (for his obstinacy did not permit him to stop a project in the middle) and, having quarreled with the *Revue de Paris*, wrote two further parts to complete the trilogy for other publishers, the result was two novels vastly different from the first and from each other. But what they do have in common, far more than the fact that their protagonists turn out to be members of the mysterious association (a detail quite secondary to the plot), is the presence of ample digressions that add further items to his Parisian encyclopedia. The second chapter of *La Duchesse de Langeais* (a love story lent impetus by an event in his own life) provides a sociological study of the aristocracy of the Faubourg Saint-Germain; *La Fille aux yeux d'or* (which is far more substantial, and is one of the central texts in a line of French culture extending without interruption from Sade to the present day, to, for example, Bataille and Klossowski) opens with a kind of anthropological museum of Parisians divided into social classes.

If this wealth of digressions is greater in *Ferragus* than in the two other novels of the trilogy, this does not mean that Balzac puts the whole elaborate force of his writing into them alone. The inner psychological drama of the relations between the Desmarets couple also engages the author to the height of his powers. We may be less interested in the story of this all-too-perfect pair, given our own reading habits, which at a certain pitch of sublimity enable us to see only dazzling clouds and prevent us from distinguishing movements and contrasts. And yet the way in which the shadow of a doubt, which cannot be dispelled, does not succeed in making any external dent in their loving faith in each other, but corrodes it from inside, is achieved in a way that is very far from banal. Nor must we forget that pages that might appear to us as mere exercises in conventional eloquence, such as Clémence's last letter to her husband, were *tours de force* that Balzac was especially proud of, as he himself confessed in a letter to Madame Hańska.

As for the other psychological drama, the one concerned with excessive fatherly love, it is less convincing to us, even as a first sketch of *Père Goriot* (though in this case the egoism is all on the father's side, and all the sacrifices on the daughter's). How differently Dickens managed to deal with the reappearance of a convict father in that masterpiece *Great Expectations*.

But even granting that the stress laid on psychology tends to push the adventure plot into the background, we still have to admit how much the plot has to do with our pleasure as readers. The suspense works, even though the emotive core is constantly shifting from one character to another. The speed of events is hectic, even if many parts of the plot do limp slightly because of inaccuracy or illogic. The mystery of Madame Jules's visits to the street of ill repute is one of the earliest criminal enigmas to confront a self-made detective, even if the solution does come too soon and is disappointingly simple.

The strength of the whole novel is maintained and condensed by its being based on a mythology of the metropolis—a metropolis in which, as in the portraits of Ingres, all the characters appear to be the owners of their faces. The era of the anonymous crowd has not yet begun; there is only a little while to go, the twenty years or so that separate Balzac and the apotheosis of the city in the novel from Baudelaire and the apotheosis of the city in poetry. To make this shift clear, we might use two quotations from readers of a century later, both of whom, in their different ways, were interested in such problems.

Balzac discovered the big city as a den of mysteries, and the sense he keeps ever-alert is that of curiosity. It is his Muse. He is never either tragic or comic; he is curious. He is always delving into a tangle of things with the air of a man who scents a mystery and promises one, and dismantles the machine piece by piece with biting, lively, triumphant gusto. Look at how he approaches new characters. He scrutinizes them from every angle as rarities, he describes them, he sculpts them, he defines and comments on them, he brings out all their singularities and promises marvels. His judgments, observations, harangues, and maxims are not psychological truths, but the tricks of a suspicious examining magistrate with his hands on a mystery that must at all costs be solved. Therefore, when the search, the hunt for the mystery, abates, and—at the beginning of a book or in the course of it (never at the end, for by that time all is revealed, along with the mystery)— Balzac discourses on his craze for mystery with sociological, psychological, and lyrical enthusiasm, then he is truly admirable. Look at the beginning of *Ferragus* or the opening of the second part of *Splendeurs et misères des courtisanes*. He is sublime. It is Baudelaire who is being heralded here.

The writer of these sentences was Cesare Pavese, in his diary of October 13, 1936, when he was still a young man.

At more or less the same time, in his essay on Baudelaire, Walter Benjamin wrote a passage in which we have only to replace the name of Victor Hugo with the even more fitting name of Balzac to continue and complete the argument quoted above:

One may look in vain, in the *Fleurs du mal* or *Spleen de Paris*, for anything analogous to those frescoed townscapes at which Victor Hugo was peerless. Baudelaire describes neither the population nor the city. And it is just this renunciation that enabled him to evoke the one in the image of the other. His crowd is always that of the metropolis; his Paris is always overpopulated. . . . In the *Tableaux parisiens* one can nearly always feel the secret presence of a crowd. When Baudelaire is concerned with the light of dawn, in the deserted streets there is something of the "swarming silence" that Hugo feels in Paris at night. . . . The crowd was the wafting veil through which Baudelaire saw Paris.

The Novel as Spectacle

Il Giorno (Milan), October 14, 1970; contribution to a
debate between Carlo Cassola and Pietro Citati.

When one visits the exhibition the Victoria and Albert Museum in London put on this year for the cen-
tenary of Dickens, the things that best give the sense of
what it meant to be a novelist in the middle of the last
century are the popular magazines that Dickens published throughout his life and in which his novels came
out in installments. Bearing various titles, all good-
naturedly homely (*Bentley's Miscellany, Master Hum-
phrey's Clock, Family Words, All the Year Round*), these
weekly or monthly booklets, of which Dickens was
often the publisher, editor, and sole contributor, served
chiefly (or exclusively) as an outlet for the novel the
writer was writing, with illustrations at climactic moments. Concerning the importance of the illustrators

(Seymour, who began *Pickwick* but never finished it; Cruikshank, with whom Dickens quarreled after *Oliver Twist*; Browne, known as "Phiz," who remained his faithful interpreter for almost all the rest of his production) the exhibition provides a lot of documents. We see that Dickens marked the manuscript at points where a drawing was called for, and by looking at the sketches we see how a character, under the author's guiding hand, acquired the face that would make him popular and recognizable to thousands of readers.

Dickens had a strong sense of theatre. He tried to be an actor, but without success. On the other hand, at the height of his fame, he had enormous success at reading episodes from his novels in theatres in London, the provinces, and the United States. Storytelling returned to its roots as word-of-mouth communication, and the public paid for the novelist's recitals as for a spectacle. But this element of spectacle extended also to the written page. To be the author of a novel meant for Dickens not just writing it, but also guiding its visual interpretation by directing the illustrator, and imposing his own rhythm on the emotions of the public by leaving the installments in suspense; thus the making of a novel, like the making of a spectacle, took place as it were before the reader's eyes, in a kind of dialogue with his reactions of curiosity, fear, laughter, or tears.

In one of these little magazines of Dickens's the novels were presented by a sort of buffoon who claimed to have found the manuscripts in the case of an old clock in a mysterious house. As with the old writers of novellas, one fiction served as a framework for other fictions. The stories that people were to follow like events in the lives of people they knew made no attempt to conceal their conventional and spectacular nature—and, in a word, their purely fictional nature. Letters to Dickens from his readers begging him not to kill off a certain character were not written out of any confusion of fiction and reality, but from enthusiasm for the game, the ancient game played between storyteller and listener, demanding the physical presence of a public to act as chorus, as if aroused by the very voice of the narrator.

Narrative continued to have this quality of collective spectacle even after centuries of being no longer a recitation by a storyteller or troubadour, but the object of silent, solitary reading. We might say that the quality has been lost in comparatively recent times; perhaps it is still too early to say whether this is a final nightfall, or merely a temporary eclipse.

Carlo Cassola very rightly attributes the end of the "romanesque" to Flaubert, and for this reason Flaubert should be recognized as the writer who started the dissolution of literary forms that led to the programs of the various avant-gardes; very justly, Cassola clings to Flaubert as the constant model for his own poetics. But when he claims to draw a universal dogma from this, he goes against the innermost spirit of his own inspiration. To look at life without any mythical or cultural middlemen, and to wait for "the revelation of truth from the speechless language of things," implies not only a particular notion of the world of objects and one's own ego, but also a quite exceptional relationship between the two terms, a spiritual journey, a state of grace. Anyone who gets that far may well forget that he set foot on that road just to write a novel. The poetics of the ineffability of existence are and always will be bound to rare individual experiences and particular historical circumstances. Cassola says that those poetics have triumphed, but doesn't he realize that this triumph is a defeat? What could such a triumph mean nowadays? Novels as dull as dishwater, with the grease of random sentiments floating on top. For someone like Cassola, who is right to express his love for what he has learned from Flaubert, it would be better to recognize that we have never been further from that time than we are now, that the state of mind cannot be reproduced at will, and proudly to reassert one's own lonely position as an epigone.

If at this time I am driven to take sides with Citati in his rehabilitation of the "romanesque" and to take a bet on its future reincarnation, it is not only because the aspects of "craftsmanship" in the art of fiction have always interested me, but also because it seems to me that reasons within the literary effort itself will end by urging us in that direction.

Dwelling on what is happening today in the most specialized literary laboratories, we find two contradictory things. On the one hand the novel (or what in experimental literature has taken the place of the novel) has, as its very first rule, not to rely on a story (or a world) outside its own pages, and the reader is called upon only to follow the process of writing, the text in the act of being written. On the other hand there is a move toward studies and analyses of what is (or was) the traditional narrative in all its forms. Never before has this human act of telling a story, always operative at all stages of a civilization, been so often analyzed, dismantled, and reassembled in all its most basic mechanisms, both as oral narrative (primitive myth, fairy story, epic) and as written narrative (novella, popular novel, newspaper reporting), or as a story told in visual images (films or comic strips). One might even say that storytelling is at one and the same time reaching the nadir of its eclipse in creative texts and the zenith of critical and analytical interest in it.

Certainly if Roland Barthes devotes his most recent book to a minute analysis of a Balzac story,* in which every detail turns out to be functional in producing a certain effect and nothing remains insignificant, he says he can do this because a text so *full of meaning*, readable by means of "deciphering codes" that include all the conscious and unconscious commonplaces of a society, cannot be written today. In other words, if we can finally achieve an in-depth reading of a classic novel (which in this case means Romantic and romanesque), it is because we are dealing with a dead form.

But we can also turn this argument upside down. If we now know the rules of the "romanesque game," we can construct "artificial" novels, born in the laboratory, and we can play at novels like playing at chess, with complete fairness, re-establishing communications between the writer, who is fully aware of the mechanisms he is using, and the reader, who goes along with

---

*Roland Barthes, *S/Z* (Paris: Seuil, 1970). The Balzac story analyzed is "Sarrazine."

the game because he, too, knows the rules, and knows he can no longer have the wool pulled over his eyes. But since the design of a novel is that of an initiation rite, of an apprenticeship in mastering our emotions, fears, and processes of cognition, the novel (even when practiced ironically) ends by overwhelming us in spite of ourselves, author and readers alike; in the end it calls into question everything that we have in us and everything outside of us. By "outside," of course, I mean the historical and social context, all of it "impure," that nourished the novel in its Golden Age.

Manzoni's *The Betrothed*:
The Novel of
Ratios of Power

Paper read at a conference on Manzoni at the University of Nijmegen, October 1973.

The Libraries of Renzo and Lucia

Renzo and Lucia can neither read nor write. In *I promessi sposi* (*The Betrothed*) this fact is of a decisive importance that I think has never received the attention it deserves. Not being able to read or write is (or may be presumed to be) a common characteristic of the heroes and heroines of many works of literature before and after them, but I cannot think of another great book in which the fact of being illiterate is so constantly present in the author's awareness. Renzo and Lucia cannot read or write in a world in which the written word is always parading before their eyes, and this cuts them off from making their modest dream come true.

The written word crops up in the world of Renzo and Lucia in two ways: as an instrument of power and as an instrument of information.

As an instrument of power it is systematically antagonistic to the two poor fiancés. It is the written word as wielded by Dr. Azzecca-Garbugli, the "paper, pen, and inkpot" with which the host of the Luna Piena attempts to register the names and address of his two customers. Or, worse still, the invisible paper, pen, and ink with which Ambrogio Fusella succeeds in catching Renzo in a trap.

The lack of the written word as instrument of information becomes a recurrent theme in what is to such an extent a novel of separation. More attention ought to be paid to certain pages in chapter XXVII, one of the most significant parts of the book, dealing with the difficulties of Renzo and Lucia's correspondence by means of letters written and read aloud by third parties. To the question of how illiterates communicate by letter Manzoni devotes a paragraph that I would certainly call one of the finest in the whole book:

The peasant who knows not how to write, and who needs to write, applies to one who knows that art, choosing as far as he can one of his own station, for with others he is hesitant, or a little untrusting. He informs him, with more or less clarity and orderliness, of who his ancestors were, and in the same manner tells him what to set down on paper. The literate person understands part and guesses at the rest, gives a few pieces of advice, suggests a few changes, and says, "Leave it to me." He picks up his pen, puts the other's thoughts as well as he can into literary form, corrects them, improves them, embellishes them, tones them down, or even omits them, according to how he thinks best, because—and there's nothing to be done about it—someone who knows better than others has no wish to be a mere tool in their hands, and when he is concerned with the business of others he wants it to go a little in his own way. All the same, the above-mentioned literate does not always succeed in saying everything he wants to: sometimes he ends up saying something else entirely. This happens even to us, who write for publishers. When the letter thus composed gets into the hands of the recipient, who also has no skill in the ABCs, he takes it to another learned person of the same stamp who reads it and explains it to him. Questions of interpretation arise, because the person concerned, judging by previous events, claims that certain words mean certain things, while the reader, judging by the experience he has of composition, insists that they mean something else. In the end the one who does not know has to put himself in the hands of the one who does, and give him the task of answering; an answer that, since it follows upon the question, is then open to a similar interpretation. So, to take a case, if the subject of the correspondence is the least bit jealous; if there is a question of secret business, such as one would not like a third party to know; if, for example, the letter were to get lost; and if, in a case such as this, there were no intention to come out with things in particularly clear terms—well, then, however long the correspondence lasts, the two correspondents end up understanding each other about as well as two scholastics of an earlier day who have been disputing about entelechy—not to take a simile from contemporary life, which might well have earned us a box on the ear.

The struggle between the urgency of feeling, the resistance of the written language, and the deformations inherent in the transmission of it are described in terms of a shared view of social life, but also of an implicit confession by the author, who makes himself explicit in the comment that it "happens even to us, who write for publishers." And we can only regret that, in telling us about this disappointing exchange of letters along such a stormy channel, Manzoni did not take a little more time, and extend the postal network between Renzo and Agnese to include Lucia as well.

However, in the same chapter, the role of the written word returns to the limelight a moment later, and it is a very different role, though still a negative one. We have a description of Don Ferrante's library, a catalogue of Renaissance letters that could well fit into one of the early chapters of Michel Foucault's *Les Mots et les choses*, and regarded by Manzoni with an eye utterly devoid of any historical filial piety, regarded, in fact, as a museum of false knowledge. It is not just the rejection by the Enlightenment of the dark sides of the past that agitates Manzoni; on the contrary, he is motivated here by one of the recurrent motifs in his moral polemic, an indictment of everything that represents the corruption of culture. Culture for Manzoni was an area in which human weakness manifested itself in the most blameworthy ways. For him the error of culture was an emblem of condemnation, a manifestation of the Fall. Hence his severity in judging Italian literature of the sixteenth and seventeenth centuries. His *Storia della colonna infame* does not just draw its strength from the stringency of its "enlightened" battle against a prejudice and a judicial error. Indeed, in the last part of the argument, directed against the responsibility of intellectuals, Manzoni spares absolutely no one.

In contrast to Don Ferrante's library, we might

mention the library of the village tailor, in whose house Lucia is given hospitality after the conversion of the "Innominato." He is "a man who knew how to read, and had in fact more than once read the *Legends of the Saints* and *Puerin Meschino* and the *History of the Kings of France*, and passed in those parts for a man of knowledge and talent." It is the library of small-town country culture, which Manzoni regards with sympathy, as a use of the written word that has not yet been corrupted and still has something to be said in its favor: "From this comes the best dough in the world." Manzoni's attitude is not yet the Romantic vindication of folklore, but neither is it the disdain of the Enlightenment for traditional old-wives' tales. It is curiosity with a touch of diffidence, such as the modern sociologist feels about the rights and wrongs of mass culture.

In short, the novel about the two illiterates is a book that contains a number of libraries. Looked at in one way, the entire novel takes place inside a library that contains the "faded, scratched-up manuscript" of the anonymous seventeenth-century author of this story of Milan. Similarly, the whole book culminates in the foundation of the Ambrosian Library, to crown the ideal center of the novel, the life of Cardinal Federigo Borromeo. This is a library to which Manzoni eventually entrusts the realization of his ideal of culture, not without some barbed remarks about the bad upkeep of Italian libraries. But even here the emphasis is on the spirit that animates Federigo in conceiving the library and organizing it in practice, rather than on the results, on the effects that the library will have on man's history: "Do not ask what have been the effects of this foundation of Borromeo's on public culture; it would be easy to demonstrate in two phrases, in the way in which one demonstrates these things: that they were miraculous, or that they were nil." And when he goes on to consider the shelf bearing the hundred works written by the cardinal in person, Manzoni pulls back, not without having given us to understand that the stature of Federigo as a writer was not, alas, comparable to that of Federigo as a man.

Several times in the novel, Manzoni dwells upon the mistaken use of books. The use made by Don Abbondio, for example: the casual reader of grandiloquent panegyrics in which Saint Charles is compared to a little-known Carneades. "You should know that Don Abbondio liked to read a little every day, and a neighboring curate who had a bit of a library used to lend him one book after another, the first that came to hand." Or, worse still, the use that is made of books in Don Rodrigo's house, where the *Gerusalemme liberata* is bandied about in convivial disputes as a code of the rules of chivalry for the convenience of arrogant swordsmen.

But never is writing so ill-used as it is in legal documents. The contrast between the formality of the written law and the reality of the ratios of power dominates the entire book. It is no coincidence that this conflict starts in the very first chapter, with the proclamations against brigands, to show the impotence of lawmaking, and reappears in the third chapter, to show how the law is exploited by the Azzecca-Garbuglis according to two sets of weights and measures. Nor does church law fare any better. It counts for little, for example, that this law safeguards novices' freedom to choose their vocation, when in order to conserve their patrimonies the families condemn their younger sons to the priesthood and their daughters to the nunneries. Parental authority and the pressures of the environment will certainly succeed in curbing the unruliness of Gertrude.

From all these features there emerges one common factor: Manzoni's distrust of the written word; that is, distrust of the ideological masquerades of power. Defeated both on the plane of practical strength and on that of the written word, the two poor illiterate wretches have on their side a truth that writing nearly always conceals rather than reveals, a truth that is not at all consoling or edifying: the brute experience of the ratios of power.

The Triangle of Power

Around Renzo and Lucia and their bitterly opposed marriage, the forces in play are arranged in a triangle, with three authorities at the angles: social power, false spiritual power, and true spiritual power. Two of these forces are adverse and one is favorable. Social power is always adverse; the church is divided into a good and a bad church, one of which works to get around the obstacles set up by the other. This triangular figure is presented twice, more or less identically: in the first part of the book with Don Rodrigo, Don Abbondio, and Fra Cristoforo, and in the second with the Innominato, the nun of Monza, and Cardinal Federigo Borromeo.

To extract a geometrical scheme from such a complex and modulated book is not a misrepresentation. Never was a book calculated with greater precision than *The Betrothed*. Every poetic and ideological effect is regulated by predetermined but essential clockwork, by diagrams of perfectly balanced stresses. Certainly, the Manzonian quality of the book is rendered not so much by the skeleton as by the flesh, and the skeleton itself could have served for quite a different book—for example, a Gothic novel. The ingredients and characters to create even a Sade, with torture-house castles and convents rife with perversion, could have been there if Manzoni had not been allergic to the portrayal of evil. But to give Manzoni a chance to include in the novel all that he really wanted to say, and draw a veil over what he preferred not to say, the bone structure had to be absolutely functional. And there is no story more functional than the fable in which there is an objective to be reached in spite of impediments created by opponents, but with the aid of helpers; in which the hero and heroine have nothing to think of except doing the right thing and abstaining from doing the wrong things. This is the case with poor Renzo and Lucia.

In the two triangles, a slightly repetitive and general resemblance links Don Rodrigo and the Innominato, and the same can almost be said for Fra Cristoforo and Federigo. In the third angle, that of false spiritual power, there is a clean break. Don Abbondio and Gertrude are such different and individual characters that they determine the general tone of the narrative surrounding them, a comedy of humors when Don Abbondio is at center stage, a drama of conscience when Gertrude is dominant. (We may also see *The Betrothed* as a "poly-novel" in which a number of novels succeed one another and cross one another's paths, with the novels of Don Abbondio and Gertrude merely the chief and most fully achieved ones.)

It is clear that of the three forces in operation in this triangle, the one Manzoni knows best—or, shall we say, the one that best expresses the eighteenth-century basis of his taste and culture—is the bad church. The good church, in spite of the ample space occupied in the novel by Cristoforo and Federigo, remains an external (though functional) presence. Around Cristoforo there still move those complex ratios of power that form one of the great dimensions of Manzoni: in this case the position of the Order of Capuchins, suspended between being independent of the system and being a necessary part of it, thanks to the immunity of the monasteries, which is valuable to both sides (as it was once valuable to the then arrogant Cristoforo), and capable of making even criminals respect the friars. For Federigo, on the other hand, in spite of the historical character presented fully within his context, it is only fictional predetermination that moves both him and his fearsome penitent. In the famous conversion episode, the die is cast from the moment the characters enter the scene, and there is no margin left for diversions or setbacks. From the very first moment, the Innominato displays "if not remorse, a certain boredom with his wickednesses," while the cardinal is so sure of his power over souls that, when the visit of the wicked knight is announced to him, he thinks at once of the lost sheep and not of a formal move of political convenience.

Even the role of the tyrant is a character part. Between Don Rodrigo and the Innominato there is only a quantitative difference. The second enjoys more authority than the first (though we do not quite know why) and a more sinister reputation (though we know little of his evil deeds). His "*castellaccio*" ("grim castle") repeats in darker colors the scenic function of Don Rodrigo's "*palazzotto*" ("little palace"). Who exactly Don Rodrigo and the Innominato are is never clear, not just as psychological characters but with regard to their social positions. Manzoni is always punctilious in delineating hierarchies, the distribution of powers in the church or in political organs both central and peripheral—a Spanish châtelain, a mayor, a consul—but when he touches on feudal law as such, he is overcome with an unusual reticence. That Don Rodrigo is a feudal overlord is to be presumed, but it is never actually stated. We know only that he exploits the political power of his "uncle the count," and that after his death the palace is inherited by a marquis. As for the Innominato, in an earlier version he is given the title of "count," but Manzoni tries to make him appear more as an outlaw and a brigand than as the title holder of a feudal estate, with the right to exact taxes and demand forced labor. It is as if in Manzoni's conscience, very attentive to institutional structures, it was precisely the normal institutions of feudalism, the mainspring of all the mechanisms of power in the book, that were concealed by a mechanism of self-censorship.

In fact, it is hard to establish the internal rules of *The Betrothed*, for Manzoni is constantly changing the focus of his telescope. Once certain that his narrative and conceptual machinery works in the main, he sets about adjusting the focus on different characters and different aspects, adopting for each of them a different light plot, with a greater or lesser degree of filter or of contrast. His technique of portrayal proceeds by a series of approximations in the various versions of the book, and the last is not necessarily better than the first.

What really and truly interests Manzoni is not so much the characters as the forces in operation in life and society, and their conditionings and clashes. The ratios of power are the real driving force of his narrative, and the crucial core of his moral and historical preoccupations. In representing these stresses—Fra Cristoforo at Don Rodrigo's banquet, or the "free choice" of Gertrude's vows as a nun, or the "vicar for provisions" in Ferrer's carriage surrounded by the angry mob—Manzoni's touch is always light and sure, and he puts his finger within a millimeter of the spot. It is no coincidence that *The Betrothed* is the most read Italian political book, one that all parties agree has helped to shape Italian political life, a text more than any other in which a person who practices politics, and finds himself day by day measuring an overall idea against objective conditions, can see himself reflected. But it is also the *antipolitical* book *par excellence*, starting as it does from the conviction that politics can change nothing, either through laws that claim to put restraints on *de facto* power or through the assertion of collective strength on the part of the outsiders. And Manzoni is not simply inventing. In actual fact, the proclamations against the brigands must be enforced by the Azzecca-Garbuglis, and the crowd assaulting the bakeries of Milan will always come up against the provocation of some Ambrogio Fusella, impelled by the "captain of justice" to lay his hands on the usual scapegoat. The book is an Italian classic in this sense as well, and it has never ceased to model reality after its own image.

There is also a "revolutionary" novel in *The Betrothed* that peeps out from time to time from among the folds of the "moderate" novel. For example, in the famous "reflection" on the roles of oppressor and victim in the midst of the mob on the "night of deceits," or the way Renzo vents his own personal thirst for justice in the Milanese uprising over the price of bread. And if as a "revolutionary" novel it is only a novel of missed opportunities, even the opportunities of the "moderate" novel, however much more obvious, are relinquished time and again. The virtue of Fra Cristoforo fails to touch the heart of Don Rodrigo, and the decisive turning, postponed until it can reach a higher level with Federigo and the Innominato, does not bring the expected solution but simply marks a new stage. The "revolutionary" novel of an impossible revolution and the "moderate" novel of a mendacious conciliation would be equally false. Manzoni, who belongs to a world scarred by the trauma of the French Revolution, and who writes with the leaden cloak of the Restoration on his shoulders, has to work out the solution to his novel on a different level.

History, Famine, and Pestilence

It was only by passing from the viewpoint of individuals to a universal one that he could resolve the vicissitudes of the betrothed couple from Lecco. And when we realize that the part of Providence is played by the plague, then we understand that the theme of petty political ideology went up in smoke some time ago. The real forces at work in the novel stand revealed as natural and historical disasters of slow incubation and sudden conflagration, upsetting the little game of the ratios of power. The picture expands, the link between macrocosm and microcosm remains close and at the same time uncertain, rather like our questions concerning the biological and anthropological future of the world today. On closer examination, *The Betrothed* is from the very outset a novel of famine, of devastated lands, from the beginning of chapter four, when Fra Cristoforo arrives from Pescarenico with his baggage of skeletal images: "the skinny girl, holding a gaunt cow on a rope in the pasture," and so on. (There is in Manzoni a painter of genre pictures, Northern and grotesque almost in the manner of Brueghel, which crops up from time to time. Another example of this "school" is Don Rodrigo's village in chapter five, and yet another is the scene in the hospital of the plague victims.)

What Manzoni portrays is a nature forsaken by God— something other than the rule of Providence! And when God manifests himself to put things right, he does it with the plague. Some people today tend to see Manzoni, beneath the paintwork of edifying ideology, as a kind of nihilist, and with a brand of nihilism that we are to find more radical only in Flaubert.

As far as mankind is concerned, there are nothing but failures: bad government, rotten economy, wars, the invasion of the *Landsknechte*. It is a history book wrapped up in the pages of a novel, and, moreover, history as we now understand it, with the "eventful" parts (such as Wallenstein's battles or the succession to the dukedom of Mantua) confined to the table talk of Don Rodrigo, while what commands the field are the crises in agriculture, the price of grain, the demand for labor, the intensity of epidemics. *The Betrothed* gives us a vision of history as a constant confrontation with catastrophe.

To go back to our triangles—corrupt potentates, bad church, good church—we can now superimpose on them a new triangle with angles representing human history (bad government, wars, uprisings), nature forsaken by God (famine), and divine justice, terrible and inscrutable (the plague). Manzoni's plague, as well as being a grandly orchestrated set piece, is a new dimension in which all the characters and stories turn out differently. Even Renzo's picaresque journey is transformed into a journey of mystical initiation, culminating in the leap onto the gravediggers' cart and punctuated by the carnival riotousness of death. This point deserves to be better remembered, not only for the phrase "*povero untorello*" ("poor plague-spreader") but also because this unexpected *danse macabre* is one of the few moments at which Manzoni writes without restraint. We even have the apparition of the madman carried away riding backward on a black horse (in an earlier version it was Don Rodrigo in person), dragged off to hell as if in a religious drama.

To complete the scheme of the opposing and supporting forces in the "religious drama" of *The Betrothed*, we have only to find a place for mankind's hankering to force God's designs, as a counterbalance to the world forsaken by God. It is a "resolving" force that turns into an obstacle. On the individual level this force is represented by Renzo's attempts at resistance, from the first vague efforts, which fail because his friends withdraw, to the complex orchestration of the "night of deceits." On the collective level the same force acts, and is defeated, on the day the Milanese storm the bakeries.

Under this heading I would not list only these two episodes, which are among Manzoni's supreme poetic achievements, but also one of the murkiest parts of the book: Lucia's vows. Manzoni places little stock in justification by works, and considers Lucia's vows on a level with all the gestures of human voluntarism, as a vain attempt to force God's designs, a legalistic error, smacking of the legalism that he abhorred, and almost as a wish to press God into making a contract. As an invalid contract the vow is easily annulled by Fra Cristoforo—a Fra Cristoforo who has risen again from the hospital of the plague victims, almost a shadow of his former self, returning now to die as soon as he has accomplished his task, like the magical helper in folk tales who often takes the form of a beneficent animal destined for sacrifice.

The target is always one and the same: the vanity of human voluntarism in the face of the inexorable, complex forces at work. And these forces can be recognized as much in the lineaments of severe transcendency as in the natural forces investigated by science. More than once in Manzoni the language of an abrasive theology gets mingled with that of a science that looks only at the facts. The *Colonna infame* is not the work of an "enlightened" Manzoni precedent to or parallel with the "providentialistic" Manzoni: the two are one and the same man. The persecution of supposed plague-spreaders is an execrable error, both in the light of scientific knowledge about the spread of bacterial epidemics and in the light of Manzoni's theology, according to which a scourge like the plague cannot depend on an act of the human will, or on the actions of a handful of men, but only on the hand of God, or the chain of human failings that move God to punishment and the most extreme remedies of His Providence.

In *The Betrothed* the same line is taken in the discussions about the famine. As early as Don Rodrigo's banquet in chapter five, such discussions are based on the mistake of thinking that bread is scarce because of deliberate acts by hoarders or bakers; as far along as chapter twelve, Manzoni the historian and economist explains the complexity of the climatic, social, military, and administrative causes that lead to famine. The arguments of science, even here, are also the arguments for a belief in the measureless might of God, for a religious feeling that in its heart of hearts is no more optimistic than the atheism of Leopardi.

These two poets, still so imbued with the crisis of eighteenth-century culture, reacted on two opposing ideal planes, and in ways between which we can now recognize the parallel aspects, not simply the contrasts in which the moral and stylistic choices of our youth became polarized. Leopardi was more drastic in rejecting all that faith in both human progress and the bounty of nature had to offer in terms of facile illusions. Manzoni was more cautious and contradictory in rejecting any consoling religiosity that concealed the pitilessness of the world. For both of them, simply because they started with an exact knowledge of the forces they had to confront, human action had some meaning.

On Fourier, I:
Brief Introduction to the
Society of Love

L'Espresso, April 18, 1971; written on the occasion of the publication of a selection from the writings of Charles Fourier, edited by Italo Calvino (see headnote to the next essay).

Fourier was distinguished by the particular quality of his visionary imagination even in his own times. Someone described him then as "the Ariosto of utopians," though this was not meant to prevent his being taken seriously. Yet he had followers eager to put his detailed instructions for the foundation of "phalanxes" and "phalansteries" into practice point by point, and not only in France. Dostoyevsky was, as it were, a Fourierist who found himself one day in front of a firing squad, and in the United States the phalanx at Brook Farm had illustrious supporters, including Hawthorne. Stendhal called Fourier a "sublime dreamer"; Engels called him "one of the greatest satirists of all time." But the modern reputation of this utopian from Besançon begins with André Breton, who in the *Ode à Charles Fourier* celebrated him as the forefather of the Surrealist revolution.

A businessman who went from financial disaster to disaster during the French Revolution and the Napoleonic Wars, Fourier worked out a radical critique of commercial civilization—indeed, of Civilization *tout court*, because for him Civilization was a determinate period, preceded by Barbarism, and as it had begun so it was destined to end, giving place to Harmony.

Another target of his furious polemic was the family. His analysis of the hypocrisies of marriage was considered scandalous even by his own disciples, while his vindication of the freedom of women makes him today a precursor of women's liberation.

Fourier had an obsession with classifying everything in long lists divided into genera and species. He even drew up a classification of the various types of cuckolded husbands, which along with other lists (for example, the various types of financial bankruptcy) was to have been part of a general analysis of the defects of Civilization.

This aspect—the critique of Civilization—occupies a large part of Fourier's work, but there have always been and continue to be numerous critiques of Civilization. What makes Fourier a writer unique in his kind is his ability to see a completely different world, to describe it in the most minute detail, and to analyze the mechanisms of its motivations.

Unlike almost all social thinkers before and after

him, Fourier does not want to change human "passions": the "passions" are the sole essence of man, positive by definition, and the negative thing is what checks and represses them, which is to say Civilization. Starting from an analysis of these "passions," Fourier piece by piece constructs a model of society in which everyone's passions can be satisfied; indeed, a society in which the satisfaction of the passions of others guarantees the fulfillment of one's own. The result is a vastly complex organization. Contrary to what one might think, an antirepressive theory taken to its ultimate consequences, as is this one of Fourier's, leaves precious little margin for spontaneity, or chance, or the vagueness of psychological impulses. Everything is calculated, ordered, and precise.

The organization of a working day in the phalanx—in which everyone moves on from one job to another without spending more than two hours on any one, assuming different tasks and roles in the various "series" with which he or she is associated—is based chiefly on the fulfillment of the feeling known as "butterflying," the wish to change occupations and company. Shows and masquerades, uniforms and parades have great importance in social life—and, indeed, in productive life as well, because "splendor in the workshop" and mythological or exotic get-ups and decorations for every social category are big incentives to social productivity.

The aspect of life in Harmony that the author described most exhaustively is the educational system, and these are the most surprising pages. Fourier considered motherly virtues to be useless, and life with fathers actually damaging. While still at the breast, children begin a collective life in the care of professional nannies. At three years of age, while amusing himself by shelling peas, the child begins to do useful work, a perfectly natural thing in a world in which it is difficult to draw the line between work and play.

The most famous and extraordinary *trouvaille* of Fourier as an educator is that of the Little Hordes. Those children who like to play with muck—which is to say the vast majority—are organized into Little Hordes and are responsible for collecting the garbage. Thus what in Civilization is a vice becomes in Harmony a passion much appreciated by society, and what in Civilization is a repellent chore becomes in Harmony a game that answers to an inner vocation. Instead of being looked down upon, the Little Hordes are surrounded by the veneration of the public, their members are thought of as little saints, and this prestige stimulates their dedication to the common welfare. The children of the Little Hordes wear hussar uniforms, blow trumpets, and ring bells, as wll as ride ponies (whereas the Little Bands, composed of gentler children who tend flowers, are mounted on zebras, animals of which Fourier was very fond). Making noise and using rough language are the prerogatives of the Little Hordes, indivisible from their social duties, which include catching reptiles and preparing tripe in the butcher shops. (Psychoanalysts find an exact coincidence between the description of the Little Hordes and what Freud says of the anal-aggressive phase of infancy.)

The path of social sanctity, on which one starts in infancy with the Little Hordes, can be pursued in adulthood in two main fields: gastronomy and the love life.

When he writes of "gastronomic science" (or "gastrosophy") Fourier, who not for nothing was a relative, fellow townsman, and friend of Brillat-Savarin, is always in top form. The classification of gastronomic tastes and the association of lovers of this food or that, or of this or that way of cooking a certain foodstuff, is fundamental to the smooth working of the phalanx. An old hen, which when put on the table by an imprudent bride can cause a conjugal squabble, can gladden the hearts of fanciers of elderly poultry, who in Civilization do not know one another and rarely find those who understand them, whereas in Harmony they can get together periodically to enjoy their favorite dish.

The classification of tastes also regulates the perfect working of the system in matters of love. Before Krafft-Ebing and the Kinsey Report, Fourier felt the need to explore the world of sexual manias. A contemporary of Sade, and like him a visionary and compulsive writer, Fourier is not tempted by sadism. Where there is sadism there is the suffocation of a passion. The Princess Stroganoff, who tortured her serfs, was lesbian without knowing it. If her passion had been truly fulfilled, it would not have caused the suffering of others, only pleasure.

Lesbianism receives particularly close attention from Fourier, and he is very much aware of the predilection. He also shows himself to be solicitous about the amorous satisfaction of old men and women. But of all amorous passions, it is Platonic love that appears to him to arouse the most consuming desires. This aspect, better than any other, defines Fourier's character, his extreme freedom of thought, and his fundamental candor.

The recently discovered manuscripts of *Le Nouveau Monde amoureux* contain a real and proper novel, *Fakma, or The Whirlwind of Cnidos*. It is an erotic fantasy set in a stylized Orient such as we find in Barbarella cartoons. A host of beautiful women and young men take part in erotic warfare. Having fallen into an ambush, the lovely prisoners have to earn their ransoms by giving sexual services that are also trials of virtue. Fakma, a gigantic queen who aspires to sanctity, has been seized by the desire for a chaste Platonic affair. She may fulfill her dream only on the condition that she yields carnally to fifty-six people.

On Fourier, II:
The Controller of Desires

Introduction to Charles Fourier, *Theory of the Four Movements and The New World of Love, with Other Writings on the Work, Education and Architecture of the Society of Harmony*, selected and introduced by Italo Calvino (Turin: Einaudi, 1971). The writing of this introduction, dated April 1971, and the publication of the volume concluded a period of reading works on and by Fourier that began in 1968.

An inexhaustible inventor of words, Fourier did not have linguistic good luck on his side. Of all the bizarre neologisms that cram his pages, only one was accepted and consecrated by common use in all the languages of Europe: "phalanstery." Having little by little lost its futuristic connotations, the term has ended up by standing for the enormous monotonous low-rent complexes on the outskirts of cities—exactly the opposite, in fact, of the multicolored, multiform world imagined by a man who was described by a publicist of his times as "the Ariosto of utopians."

Although for most people Fourier remains "the one who invented phalansteries," the word crops up very rarely in the twelve great tomes of his complete works. Much is said there about the series of groups, or passional series, a collective term for the people who devote themselves to various specializations within a certain job or a certain passion; of the seristeries, or premises destined for use by the series; of the phalanx, which is the social unit—agrarian and industrial—formed by the series, and which is to make possible the combination of all 810 of the human characters and temperaments, and finally of the social order, based on the phalanxes, that will establish Harmony throughout the world.

Of the many contexts in which Fourier's visionary and meticulous spirit anticipated the works and days of Harmony, a place scarcely more than marginal is occupied by the description of the building, or group of buildings, lived in by the phalanx and called the *phalanstère*. Set amid a rural landscape, it brought together all the conveniences of city life and excluded all the nuisances execrated by our author to an almost obsessive degree: mud, filth, stinks, and noises.

And yet the emblematic success of the phalanstery—both as name and image—began at once, not just among unbelievers but even among his followers, with the title of the first Fourierist newspaper and the earliest community experiments. There must have been a reason for this immediate hold on the imagination.

The order proposed by Fourier was, in the first instance, a mental order, not abstract but phantasmal, a system of relationships between people and, even more, of relations within each individual person, concerning knowledge and inner clarity. The first things he asks of those who will listen to him are *doute absolu* and *écart absolu*—that is, that one should question and put aside everything that has been said and thought until now in terms of philosophy and above all of morality. Fourier has a good saying that it is not man who should be changed, but Civilization. And since the latter constitutes a large part of ourselves, what he is demanding is still an inner metamorphosis as a preliminary condition. We can understand how both his disciples and his adversaries, rather than racking their brains over this point, preferred to grasp at the more solid, stable, and external image that was offered them, that of the building. The history of the failures that Fourierism came up against in practice is all to be found in the folds of this doctrine, which is presented as irrefutably self-evident.

Even in our own century the rediscovery of Fourier by poets and writers (and psychoanalysts) has been accompanied by a rediscovery on the part of architects, as a precursor of town planning (another failed dream of happiness: Le Corbusier's *ville radieuse* is the reference most commonly made). But between the two rediscoveries there remains a hiatus that is hard to fill, consisting in the contradiction between two ways of *using* the utopia. We can either consider it for whatever there is in it that can be *achieved*, as the model for a new society that can grow on the fringes of the old one, later to eclipse it through the strength of new values; or we can view it for whatever in it appears *inflexible* to all conciliation, radically opposed not only to the world around us but also to the inner conditioning that governs our attribution of values, our ability to desire a different kind of life, and our very way of looking at the world: as a total way of looking that sets us inwardly free to free ourselves outwardly. We might say that Fourier is only today beginning to be read, since in his work we no longer attempt to separate the serious aspects from the fantastic or scandalous ones, as his embarrassed followers did, but consider the visionary aspects no less significant than the others, and the most serious aspects as imprinted with the same visionary spirit, and both of them the successful bearers of scandal.

This is only one of the many reversals in the history of our author's reputation. Although he spread abroad the picture of himself as an unheeded prophet waiting every day at noon for the patron who would finance his first phalanx, he was during his lifetime (at least for the last twelve years of it) at the head of an ample school of followers that was not lacking generous patrons, either, and he lived to see the first attempt—and failure—at a societal experiment. His school survived for several decades after his death, though amid bitter dissensions, and the experiments multiplied. In the years 1830–48 Fourierism extended overseas. For the influence it had on the revolutionary Russian intelligentsia we need only recall the Petrashevsky circle in Moscow, whose members (including Dostoyevsky) ended up in 1849 facing a firing squad and (after a last-minute pardon) exiled to Siberia. In the United States the experimental commune at Brook

Farm, founded in New England by the Reverend George Ripley as an application of Emerson's transcendentalist philosophy (and in which Hawthorne had a hand), was transformed into the North American phalanx as a result of the Fourierist propaganda of Albert Brisbane. Experiments and influence spread as far afield as Romania and Spain.

In spite of all this, as a practical project and a political movement Fourierism got nowhere, not only because the agricultural phalanxes came to grief and dissensions multiplied within the school, but also because the evils of the civilization denounced by the master grew to such proportions that it was no longer possible to hope to cure them with the good example of such tiny colonies.

At the same time as Fourier, his chief rival also declined into obsolescence. This was Saint-Simon, against whose school Fourier had not been sparing in his attacks. But in the oblivion they share, their two paths are radically divergent. If no one today reads Saint-Simon or refers to him, it is because we are living in the midst of his system, because the technocratic and productivistic "industrial society" he prophesied has triumphed. This has not been the panacea for social evils that he promised. Nor has it eliminated from the scene the much-execrated military power, has in fact joined forces with this power, and continues to be the implicit and unchallenged model toward which the historical future is tending, personified by the two colossi who now carve up the planet between them.

Compared with Saint-Simon, Fourier is the last word in outdatedness. Lucid as he was in his critique of the present, he understood nothing of what was then coming to the boil. Both of them spoke of the "new industrial world," but the Anglophile Saint-Simon (who in addition was a veteran of the American Revolution) had his eyes open on a world that was anything but utopian, whereas the Anglophobe Fourier gives us a kermess of happy farmers, and in his examples refers to nothing but horticulture and gardening, or to workshops scarcely above the level of cottage industry.

This macroscopic error of perspective (or unconscious repression, or deliberate determination to cancel the rejected perspective from his own field of vision) was not all that rendered Fourier impracticable. Eagerness to include the whole universe pervades his farraginous volumes, with their labyrinthine structure upon which complicated subdivisions proliferate a mass of prefaces, interludes, and conclusions indicated by a riot of terminology such as *prolégomenes, préambule, intermède, cislégomenes, extraduction, arrière-propos*, as well as a selection of *antienne, cis-médiante, trans-médiante, intrapause, cis-lude, ulter-pause, ultralogue, ultienne, postienne, postambule*, etc., etc., with lists and synoptic tables arranged according to a particular numbering system, so that the numbers alternate with special graphic signs that indicate the *pivot*, or center of the series (from which radiate the two wings and the two ailerons, ascending and descending), and the *ambigu*, or term of transition from one series to another, an arrangement that can also correspond to a musical scale, with chords in the major or the minor. But the eccentricities of form are in perfect keeping with the flow of the arguments, which burst

their banks in all directions, amid continual references
to a future work in which the basics will be found.

What therefore distinguishes this work from the
notebooks of so many would-be talented scribblers,
constructors of universal systems, which pour continually into the wastepaper baskets of publishers and
scholarly reviews—those works by misunderstood
philosophers and weekend cosmographers that in his
youth Raymond Queneau (a great reader of Fourier,
incidentally) proposed to take a census of by combing
the catalogues of the Bibliothèque Nationale?

More even than the vision of a society dedicated to
festivals and processions, in costumes garnished with
plumes and flounces, with the challenge of combat in
gastronomy and *galanterie*, a society that domesticated
zebras and ostriches, it was the cosmic prophecies that
bore the brunt of the derision of the wits: the aurora
borealis that would become permanent and turn the whole
world into a temperate zone; the sea that would acquire
the flavor of lemonade; the moon that, long since mur-
dered by the fetors of the earth, would be replaced by
five smaller moons; and animals useful to man—the
antilion, the antiwhale, the anticrocodile—that would
take the place of fearsome beasts.*

---

*In partial compensation for his lack of technological foresight,
Fourier can be seen as a Jules Verne who suggests, instead of om-
nipotent machines, the creation of new species of animals to help
man: the antilion is a perfect prefiguration of the automobile; the
antiwhale works as the engine of a steamship. But there are also
prophecies of even more unexpected technological inventions, such
as that of telecommunications via satellite (*Oeuvres complètes*, IV, p.
261).

Was Fourier a madman, then? Or a hoaxer who poked fun at his readers? Or a humorist appealing to a crafty reader? Or was it all a smokescreen to help him smuggle in the real content, the radical critique of society? Maybe none of these definitions is exact, and if Fourier shares something with the thinkers of his time, and before and after, it is precisely the ambition to extend his argument to fields as far as possible from their point of departure, to the natural sciences and to cosmology; this would be in keeping with the age-old systematic tradition that the specialization of disciplines has never entirely suffocated. "Is this not perhaps the habitual attitude of the philosopher who is absolutely determined to bend reality to the *system* he has discovered?" observes one of his most recent commentators, Emile Lehouck. "Fourier, who upsets the disposition of the plants, is no more ridiculous than the Hegel of the *Philosophy of Nature*, who claims to explain the animal and vegetable kingdoms by a series of theses, antitheses, and syntheses. . . . The most illustrious thinkers have had recourse to bizarre and highly artificial constructions to escape from the contradictions of their metaphysics or to reconcile scientific discoveries with religious beliefs. . . . Yet these philosophers are not treated as madmen, but studied with the greatest respect."

However that may be, our way of reading him was bound to change radically with changes in social outlook. From 1848 on, all projects for future society had to reckon with the fact that the industrial workers had entered the field as a "class" of their own. And the umpteenth contradiction in the story of Fourier is that the theorists of the new revolutionary perspective were not only the ones who buried his doctrines forever, but also the most sympathetic, congenial, and *modern* of his nineteenth-century readers.

Pitilessly sarcastic about other theorists of their time, Marx and Engels willingly took up the cudgels in behalf of their three precursors of a generation earlier: the "utopians" Saint-Simon, Owen, and Fourier. But for the last of the trio, apart from a solid historical understanding, and in defiance of his detractors such as Karl Grün or Eugen Dühring, they express an instinctive admiration on the *poetic* level. "Some of these novels—for example, the system of Fourier—are stamped with a truly poetic spirit; others, such as those of Owen and Cabet, are without the least grain of poetry." And having stigmatized the orthodox Fourierists as "doctrinaire bourgeois . . . at the antipodes" from their master himself, Marx and Engels point out the contrast between the "systematic form" and "real content" of the system, which remains the ultimate way of reading him (and not only him), a way that has now been developed and redefined very acutely by Roland Barthes as the contrast between *system* and *systematic*.

It was chiefly the temperament of Engels that established a congenial bond that extended to all the basic aspects of Fourier's work: the critique of society, of the family, of the economy (as the discoverer of the "plethoric crisis" of capitalism, because of which "superfluity becomes the source of poverty"), as well as his gifts as a satirist ("one of the greatest satirists of all time") and perhaps even as a mathematician. And as for his historical vision, Engels does not hesitate to declare that Fourier "handles dialectics with as much mastery as his contemporary Hegel. Faced with all that chitchat about the infinite perfectibility of man, with equal dialectical skill he stresses the fact that every phase of history has its ascending branch and also its descending one, and he applies this way of seeing things also to the future of humanity."

Marx, who was less keen than his friend to exalt Fourier's work *in toto*, also read it with amused familiarity, but points out its basic incompatibilities. In the *Grundrisse*, while quarreling with Adam Smith, who looked upon labor as sacrifice and nothing but, Marx at the other extreme taxes Fourier with ingenuousness and frivolity for having believed that labor could ever become a pleasure and a diversion. For Marx, emancipated labor—free creativity or participation in the socially productive process—will no longer be a sacrifice because man will fulfill himself as the *subject* of productivity, though this will involve no less effort.

Today we may realize that this raises the most dramatic question of our time. If socialism realistically accepts that suffering is still a necessary element in the process of production, what distinguishes exploited labor from emancipated labor will in the end boil down to a sublimation of the toil and suffering on the part of the workers. The conviction that one is realizing socialism as a philosophical model absolutely must precede any perceptible satisfaction. But for how long? And who can guarantee that this conviction is not also the result of some ideological manipulation that, in order to attain emancipation, the true revolution is not going to go on perpetrating forever? When we come to think about it, the utopian imagination, with a model that was immediately perceptible to the senses, also had a certain "realism" of its own; or, better, its own possibility of a swift comparison with reality. One could see at once whether the attempt to put it into practice corresponded to the model: if *le bonheur* was not an immediate result, then the experiment was a failure. And this did not mean that the model itself could not go on exerting its influence as an inflexible opponent to reality.

In opposition to eighteenth- and nineteenth-century thought, which looked to reason as a basis for morality, Fourier thought that the only solid ground on which to base a moral position was the principle of pleasure. In this sense the modern commentators who tend to consider him as a precursor of Freud have every right to do so, as long as they bear in mind that Freud did not think that any kind of human civilization was possible without repression and sublimation. What I mean is that the relationship between Fourier and Freud emerges as something not unlike his relationship with Marx. Fourier aims to construct a cognitive and practical system without sublimating anything or anyone, let alone repressing them. Or rather, it is "passions" accepted for what they are, that lead directly to a sublime result. With the organization of the Little Hordes—the most famous and surprising of Fourier's thoughts as an educationalist—children who have a taste for dirt become the benefactors of society in Harmony because the task of garbage collecting is for them as pleasing as a game. In hussar uniforms, the Little Hordes gallop around on ponies accompanied by the clamor of trumpets, bells, and drums, in a perpetual subversive carnival. (Their "antisublimation" extends even to language: the Little Hordes speak in *argot*.)

In Fourier's classification of the passions, along with the "five simple appetites of the senses" and the "four simple passions of the soul" (ambition, friendship, love, parenthood), it is chiefly the three "distributive" ones that he was proud of having discovered, *la cabaliste, la papillonne,* and *la composite*. These he describes with the greatest color and warmth, and they are in a position of privilege as basic mechanisms of the societal system.

The *cabaliste* (from *cabale*, "plot," and a key word in court diplomacy under the *ancien régime*) is the passion for intrigues and rivalries. The *composite* (otherwise referred to as "exalting" or "meshing") is the demand for pleasures that fulfill both the senses and the spirit by abandoning oneself to a blind enthusiasm. The *papillonne* ("butterfly," also known as "alternating") is the passion for change, novelty, and stimulus. The series or groups into which the social life of Harmony is arranged are chiefly based on these three passions—or better, on the *cabaliste* and the *papillonne*. Insofar as it is an irrational "letting go," he does not succeed in bringing the *composite* so clearly into focus. A day in Harmony involves hopping around continually from one group to another, in the fields or in the workshops (one never does more than two hours at a stretch at any one job), and the same thing is true at meals and festivals. Contrary to what the name might seem to imply, to rise to the heights of the *papillonne* required the most methodical and punctilious organization. Each "industrial group" was rather like a football team, and by passing from one group to another each "societary" took on roles and responsibilities that differed from one moment to the next. To make up these teams, to arrange the shifts to fit in with the timetables of other squads, and to put them into friendly competition so that each separate activity was like a match in one unending championship, required the stimulus of the *cabaliste*, the passion for strategy, for team games, for aggressiveness and the urge to conflict brought into play as a social force.

Next to the most illustrious classifiers of human passions—both in the church, from Saint Thomas to the Jesuits, and in philosophy, from Descartes to Spinoza—Fourier appears at one and the same time more simplistic and more inventive. But what strikes us about his system is his diagrammatical practicality applied to such debatable and elusive material. In any situation one can always to a certain degree put something in the pigeon hole that corresponds to a certain sense of smell or touch, of ambition or the pleasure there is in parenthood.

Let us not forget that the three "distributive" passions discovered by him were also called "mechanized," while one of them (the *composite*) was even called "meshing." Walter Benjamin, even in his rather negative assessment, was the first to stress an essential point that makes Fourier less foreign to the age of technology than he seems to be at first sight. His utopia "owes its most profound impulse to the advent of machinery. . . . This incredibly complicated organization appears to us as a mechanism. The cogwheels of passion . . . are rudimentary analogies of the machine in the psychological field."

Fourier's dream, described in the title of one of his chapters as "the alliance of the marvelous with arithmetic," we might today call "the alliance of Eros with cybernetics" without weakening the force of the contradiction, the irreconcilability that exists between dream and reality. The way we see it, Harmony is one vast controller of desires. The phalanx relies on a constantly active computer to make the calculations needed for the perfect sorting out of the various groups. Fourier worked for a lifetime in order to establish data that would bring about the happiness of the human race on punched cards.

The tradition of which we might call him the final outcome is that of La Mettrie, Helvétius, and Diderot—or, at any rate, he would have shared their execration of the *philosophes*, of the "inexact sciences," and of the whole culture of the century in which he was born. Fourier's anti–eighteenth-century rebellion spares nothing and no one. With all the rancor of a tradesman ruined by the curses and woes of the turn of the century,* he avenges himself on the real or supposed authors of his misfortunes, from mercantilism to Robespierre, from the continental blockade to Rousseau and Voltaire. When he intones against austere Republican virtues, against egalitarianism, against atheism, Fourier is a positive de Maistre. In the revolution and the Napoleonic Wars he saw nothing but massacres and failures.

As I sit writing these pages, the *Aufklärung* is not

---

*The hatred he bore toward tradesmen, together with his love of classification and a somewhat summary ethnic typology, led him to loathe the three mercantile peoples *par excellence*: the English (responsible for the "insular monopoly," and against whom he wrote a pamphlet), the Jews, and the Chinese (these last two peoples incurring further blame for being "patriarchal").

getting a very good press from intellectuals, and no one will accuse Fourier of being a reactionary because he was an enemy of the Enlightenment and of the Immortal Principles of 1789. But even if we considered it a rationalistic progressivism that had undergone no setbacks, it would still be hard to mistake Fourier's argument for that of a legitimist. Rather, one gets the impression that he is talking about something else, that on each and every occasion he is so far ahead of the debate of his times that he is only using the same words to say things that are completely different.

Thus, when he declares that to object to the throne or the altar is useless and damaging, we must bear in mind that the society he wishes to found upon inequality is expressed chiefly in terms of formal hierarchies, as well as in the distribution of four-twelfths of all profits to the capital investors. On account of this—apart from the parody honors paid to them as to a king at a costume party—the sovereigns of Harmony have all the characteristics of solid bourgeois who enjoy the benefits of a larger stock portfolio than others have. Otherwise they participate in the various series with various functions and duties, regardless of their royal dignity, and get up every morning at four o'clock to pick bergamots or bake *vol-au-vents* just like everyone else. As for the clergy, far from abolishing it Fourier would aim to increase it. It is composed of both priests and priestesses (also called "corybants" and "corybantesses") who direct the marriage rites, and in this "omnigamous" regime enjoy prerogatives that are far from ascetic.

In a word, it is precisely in his fantasies of throne and altar that this negator of the French Revolution shows himself to be a son of the revolution—or, rather, its remote descendant, just as if he were not writing under the Restoration or the July Monarchy, but in a world that had centuries ago forgotten the meaning of the old institutions. Similarly, this overturner of the rationalist eighteenth century reveals himself as a son of the eighteenth century in every crevice of his thought.

Certainly the culture of the eighteenth century that produced him is more complex than any label that could possibly be applied to it, and Fourier himself does not know whether to place it at the end of the line of the *lumières* (that is, of the Enlightenment) or of the *illuministes*, in the sense this word still retains in French, that of *illuminati* or occultists. These are two areas of the eighteenth-century map that are partly opposed and partly superimposed.

Typical of this sphere of ideology is the belief that human actions ought to collaborate in carrying out the divine purpose, which is perfect in itself but requires man's help to put it into effect. It is not for nothing that Fourier's preaching apparently started in the Masonic lodges of Lyon. In spite of this, he directs harsh reproaches at the Masons for not having profited from the opportunities opened up by the revolution, for the founding of a new religion. Certainly his theory of the "aromatic bodies" of the stars falls within the vast tradition of occultism, even if with applications that are typical of Fourier, such as the conviction that the dead in the other world cannot be happy unless the living are happy. If the living are unhappy, how in the name of justice could it be possible for the dead to be happy?

Fourier was in fact so *other*, so different from everyone else, that we can scarcely be surprised that the second half of his century and the first half of ours turned their backs on him. Poets and writers included: Baudelaire went through a phase of sympathy for Fourier that then turned to antipathy; Flaubert knew enough of his writings to make Bouvard and Pécuchet go through a Fourierian stage during their frustrating encyclopedic wanderings.

Stendhal's prediction remained isolated and unfulfilled. In September 1837, just a month before Fourier's death, Stendhal said—or put into the mouth of a Fourierist friend in *Mémoires d'un touriste*—"His status as a sublime dreamer will not be recognized for twenty years." This prophecy on the part of a contemporary as congenial as the man who saw beauty as the *promesse du bonheur*, who thought of aesthetic meaning as a utopia with which to challenge the present, hits the mark today, when the terms have been reversed and we can once more read the *promesse du bonheur* of Fourier's utopia and enjoy it as an aesthetic object. Only in this indirect way can we again put it forward as a promise of happiness, at a time when all promises of happiness seem to be suspended and indirect, as in an interplay of mirrors.

From there we come straight to the Second World War. André Breton, then a refugee in the United States, read a work of Fourier's and wrote a verse essay that is at one and the same time a diary of this experience, a journal of his American travels, and a bitterly disenchanted discourse on the state of the world. The *Ode à Charles Fourier*, published in 1945, remains one of the meatiest and most impassioned items in the bibliography of this utopian, in the form of a discussion with him against the background of a world situation that seems to negate all his prophecies.

In the postwar years one can say that there is no piece of work by Breton or initiative inspired by him that is lacking in echoes of Fourier. Breton's rediscovery was followed by the finding of the "censored" unpublished *Nouveau Monde amoureux*, the anastatic reprinting of the *Complete Works*, a renewed feeling of Fourier's modernity in a climate of protest and antirepressive thought, and finally, in 1970, a series of treatments of him by outstanding figures in French culture: Butor, Barthes, Klossowski, and Blanchot. (Queneau had gone exploring on his own as early as 1958–59, in the course of his encyclopedic "pataphysical" travels.)

At the time when Breton wrote the *Ode*, the manuscripts on the love life of Harmony were not yet known, for neither the author nor (still less) his disciples had dared to publish them (and Breton did not fail to reproach Fourier for his reticence on this point). *Le Nouveau Monde amoureux*, the volume that contains them, was published in 1967 in an edition that more philological care would have rendered even worthier than it is; since then it has been a text of central importance to the evaluation of Fourier.

If, within the austere climate of his political doctrines, the proposal put forward for polygamous and "omnigamous" unions did and will continue to cause scandal, the reader who approaches this text with preconceptions formed by its libertine reputation will instead find an element of unbending prudery in Fourier. He insists that girls and boys under the age of fifteen should be kept clear of all information on sexual matters. He has the Romantic cult of emotional purity, and in the sample book of the phalanx (in which every type of passion must find its adepts) he foresees couples so angelic as to love each other solely Platonically. He gets furious with women who, by yielding too soon and without any emotional preamble, catch a man unprepared, make a fool of him, and then proceed to treat him as impotent. This vindication of spiritual dignity for the male sexual "fiasco" inspires one of his most stirring pages directed against the "imperiousness of the Civilized."

It is true that the "angelic" couples preserve their chastity by establishing a network of carnal relationships with other persons of both sexes. All the same, it is Platonic love that Fourier gives preference to—so much so that it almost seems as if the whole roundabout of sexual relations provided for in his love affairs "in orchestra" or "amorous quadrilles" has no other purpose than to surround and exalt the rarest and most yearned-for joy of all, which is spiritual love.

In Harmony, the more the passions are satisfied the less they are left to their own devices. Nothing can ever be left to chance. To put the complicated organization of "omnigamy" into action, the theoretical argument is at a certain point transformed into a real and proper novel, or, we might say, a piece of theatre, since it is largely written in dialogue. This is *Fakma, or The Whirlwind of Cnidos*. Not that it shows Fourier at his best as a writer. Far from it, and he knew it himself, declaring: "I provide the theme, and let someone else add his prose.

It needs flowers of rhetoric and the dust of butterfly wings." But it tells us a lot about the literary roots of Fourier's world, set somewhere between the seventeenth-century "precious" style of Honoré d'Urfé's *Astrée* and the eighteenth-century satirical fictions inspired by *The Arabian Nights*. The visual repertoire of evasion has not really changed much since then. In the eyes of the modern reader, the adventures of the vast and stupendous Fakma will seem much like the erotic fantasies of the Barbarella cartoons.

However, the real surprise of *Le Nouveau Monde amoureux* is quite another: the explanation of the world of "amorous manias." Sexual perversions are the final test for Fourier's ethics, with their refusal to see "wrong" in any passion, whatever it may be. Methodical and imperturbable, the author succeeds in demonstrating that the passions always can and must do good to one's neighbor and never do him harm, because there is only wrong when a passion is opposed or repressed. Using the example of a Russian princess who delighted in torturing her serfs, but only because she was not free to follow her lesbian preferences, Fourier, with the least of effort, succeeds in removing the gigantic stumbling block put in his way by the parallel work of that other great compulsive writer and visionary, Sade. The sadistic component of Eros, destructive and blindly egotistical, is dissolved ("evaporated," says Barthes) in the perfect distributive mechanism of the societal system, in which every secret propensity can be understood and satisfied.

To describe Fourier in relation to Sade—seeing that in French critical thought today it appears that the whole of literature can be viewed only in relation to that extreme point—therefore becomes obligatory.* For Pierre Klossowski, Fourier's work, in which "the seriousness of perversion must be replaced by play," is to be considered without hesitation as "as unusual, as important, as frenzied as that of Sade." On the other hand, Maurice Blanchot, in a piece in which he casts a distinctly cold eye on our author, describes Fourier's as "a passion without desire . . . a measured passion, not erotic, which satisfaction succeeds in fulfilling and which therefore always reaches its objective. Which would be very insipid if behind every passion, as its unfailingly disguised power and truth, the sovereign passion of unity did not watch over its alternations, amounting to a system the complications of which are forever postponing its achievement." According to Blanchot, Fourier was animated by the "concern to reassure himself by reassuring us with the certainty of a happiness that has become a universe. . . . Measure—measured happiness—is such a measureless necessity that it not only forces the whole universe to change, but is not content with the universe and makes it one element of another, and so on almost endlessly, until we reach that tranquil night in which everything comes to a halt but nothing fades."

One could say that any tragic vision of the world is incompatible with this viewpoint which, though extremely sensitive to whatever is negative in his (and our)

---

*A more complete picture of the visionary worlds that came into being around the French Revolution should extend to a comparison with the third—or first in order of time—great compulsive writer and visionary: Restif de La Bretonne. He may be likened to Fourier for his bold exploration of human nature and his cosmological imagination, though he often yields to the hypocrisy of the false moralist.

civilization, is always capable of dissolving negativeness, evil, and vice simply by the strength of its regulative serenity. Even perversions, for all their exclusiveness and egotism, if publicly accepted and practiced with the help of the social organization, become a precious aid to general harmony. The distribution tables of passional tendencies, necessary to the proper functioning of the groups and series, have to start from the rarest and most bizarre tastes, both gastronomic (like those of the astronomer Lalande, who was said to eat live spiders) and erotic (like those of a Prussian officer who confined himself to scratching his beloved woman on the heels). The census of manias is essential to the discovery of which other characteristics accompany them, and then to the extension of the study of correlations to tendencies that become little by little more common. Fourier heralds the need for a "Kinsey Report" on a large scale, and one that will make it possible to establish the "horoscope" of each individual from birth, thus preventing crime and not allowing talent and genius to go to waste.

In love, as in gluttony, pleasure is a matter of the utmost precision. It was not for nothing that Fourier was a kinsman and friend of Brillat-Savarin, the author of *The Physiology of Taste*. His own gluttony is never generic: he always refers to a specific dish, and a particular way of cooking that dish.

Some of his examples of *bonheur* were inspired by the high-life habits of the rich. His violent quarrels with mercantile civilization censured not wealth, for it was a bearer of pleasure, but, rather, the inability to enjoy wealth. We should not forget that in his diagram of the passions, or "passional tree," the word *luxisme* is applied to the branch that spreads out into the five appetites of the senses; by *luxisme* he means the desire for "inner luxury" (or health) and "outer luxury" (or wealth), both being conditions needed for the full exercise of the senses. Far from trying to dissolve the connection between wealth and pleasure, Harmony strives to generalize both.

Some scholars have attributed to him a life style in conformity with his hedonistic theories, but it is not clear whether he had any direct experience of pleasure-loving ways. Of any sprees he might have enjoyed as a traveling salesman and guest in family-run pensions, no evidence is left to us. In *Le Nouveau Monde amoureux* he hints, as if speaking of a basic moral experience for him, at having by chance discovered in himself an "amorous mania"; the pleasure of being present at and sharing in the love play between two women. In the erotic phantasmagoria he constructed, lesbianism is surrounded by a particular kind of nimbus. Another passion that emerges from his pages, though unconfessed this time, is gerontophilia. With what fervor of dedication do we see young men girding up their loins for acts of "amorous charity" toward elderly matrons and "patriarchesses." Also, one of the most delightful of his gastronomic examples concerns the predilection for leathery old hens. . . .

But these constants of his fantasy world do not allow us any inferences about the man and his private life. Disciples and memorialists agree in describing him as an austere, cold, surly man, a character that corresponds well with the features we see in his portraits and the fanatical concentration to which the great mass of his written work bears witness. They say he never laughed, spoke little (his closest friend, Just Muiron, was deaf), lived alone in a modest apartment full of cats and flowering plants, and walked the streets with a surveyor's stick because he had a mania for measuring everything. Frank E. Manuel, an American historian who has tried to reconstruct the psychological portraits of the "Prophets of Paris," wonders whether "this inventor of the system of passionate attraction had ever experienced one."

The "perennially gay nature" to which Engels attributed Fourier's satirical genius was therefore one of those natures that find their good cheer only in the act of writing. While putting Fourier into his *Anthologie de l'humour noir*, Breton found his real antecedent—even temperamentally—in Swift, who with Sade and Lichtenberg precede him in the genealogy of "black humorists." A vein of latent misanthropy runs through the pages of this missionary of universal happiness. The echo of Molière is explicit in *Hiérarchie du cocuage*, Fourier's best effort as a "moralist," which is quite in the line of the great French seventeenth-century authors of "Characters."

One of the derogatory judgments made about him in the nineteenth century (that of Eugen Dühring, who called him a "social alchemist," thus provoking a heated defense from Engels), in today's changed intellectual attitude toward alchemy, which dispenses with the rudimentary dichotomy between charlatanism and science, strikes us as a happy metaphor. If alchemy was first and foremost a technique of knowledge and the inner transformation of man carried out by means of a ritual transformation of matter, Fourier's way—diverg-

ing from that of science, and based on a system of analogies hailing from the medieval tradition—is similar to
alchemical research; as such, it establishes a relationship
of affinity with the work of artists and poets, in their
manipulation of linguistic and mythical material in the
hope of managing by their means to "change life."

A lot is said nowadays about the *modernity* of Fourier, making him out to be a precursor of psychoanalysis
(of Freud, or of Reich, or of group therapy), comparing
him to Norman O. Brown (who refers to him often)
or to Marcuse (who on the contrary never mentions
him), or considering him as one of the classics of anti-
authoritarian and antirepressive teachings, or adopting
him as a tutelary deity (whether by the Paris students
of May 1968, or the hippie communes in California, or
the feminist revolution, or communal experiments in
free love). In my opinion, all the "operative" messages
that are attributed to him do nothing but subject him
to a kind of interpretation from which he had the good
luck to escape when he ceased to be read as a handbook
for the foundation of a new society, while continuing
to function as a test of our ability to think and "see" the
freedom of all and sundry, to give meaning and stringency to limitless satisfaction of our desires. One might
almost think that Fourier felt compelled to mingle social
organization and "astral copulations" in his pages to
prevent his words from being accepted as gospel. Every
time his argument runs the risk of being taken at face
value—lo and behold—his practical instructions for the
phalanx give way to vegetable or animal "hieroglyph-
ics" or the positioning of the "biniverses" and the
"triniverses," and the reader is obliged to remember that

what he has before him is a written text, the effectiveness of which does not lie in its "illusion of transparency."

It is no coincidence that by means of a text that is "bastard," "ambiguous," and "composite," as is that of Fourier (I give these adjectives the positive meaning they had for him, which they fully deserve), one finally gets to the point of defining the experiment that a literary discourse has made upon itself, for its own use, for the public use as well, and which it can pass on for the use and the *usefulness* of each and every other kind of discourse.

On Fourier, III:
Envoi: A Utopia of Fine Dust

Almanacco Bompiani 1974 (Milan), December 1973. The almanac, which was devoted to the subject "Utopia Revisited," began with this essay, then entitled "Which Utopia?"

When an attempt to put into practice some idea of society less monstrous than others is crushed by the military in some country or other, we always read the phrase "the end of a utopia." But, on the contrary, this characteristic of risk, of taking a bet, of hanging by a thread, of finding oneself daily confronted by an unexpected problem—in fact, everything that makes for the pathos of real revolutions lived day by day—is quite foreign to utopias (the written ones, that is). They come to us as mechanisms that function perfectly in every cogwheel, self-sufficient, self-regulating, and self-reproducing, innocent of any teething troubles at the start and of an end that is always possible.

Utopia defies time by setting itself up in a no-place, rejecting relationships with the "other" world, which is of necessity hostile. I admit that Fourier, for example, established a gradual process, an evolution within Harmony itself, and at first allowed for relations with "civilized" philistine neighbors, on, one might say, the level of cultural exchanges or informative tourism. But later he recommended isolation, and he, too, planned his "iron curtains." Utopia feels the need for compactness and permanence in opposing the world it rejects, a world that presents an equally refractory front.

This is already enough to qualify utopias as a product favored by periods in which practical action is the loser. It is no coincidence that there were two great ages for utopias: the time when there was a decline in hopes for a true rebirth of the Reformation (even though Thomas More's book came out a year before Luther nailed up his Theses), and the later time when the full flood of the French Revolution was subsiding.

We have to ask ourselves at once if the same thing holds good for our own time, with all the setbacks it has faced. The present interest in utopias would seem to confirm the parallel, but this is still a reflected interest, in critical and historical terms, and it remains to be seen what the creative equivalent of utopia is in our age. Rather than utopia in the classic sense, structured as a type of literature, we find utopian fields of energy spread here and there, above all by literature and art, and even in their most inflexible suggestions quite ready to be absorbed by habit—just think of what the most intransigent Surrealism aimed to do. We can follow a direct or an indirect offshoot of this among those of our youth, who are inspired by an artistic or playful vision of liberation, or at any rate one that is nonmoralistic.

But as a literary form utopia survives only as an antiutopia (Huxley, Orwell), as the vision of a hellish future where the best that can be seen is a condemnation.

On the other hand, we cannot fail to take account of the opposite, utopian-technological temptation, which tends ever more toward all-embracing models, even if the futurologist who aspires to being scientific has to confine himself to general tendencies and partial views.

However this may be, no one any longer thinks of describing a perfect city, or the hour-by-hour daily lives of its inhabitants. The massive weight and complexity of the world have hardened around us, and they leave no loopholes. The political imagination always needs an elsewhere, but a geographically determinate one. If there is to be imagination (however little it may still possess the "power" that was attributed to it by the generous slogans of May '68), then it must have the benefit of areas in flux, open to interpretations that leave some margin for the creativity of the interpreter, like the China of the years of the Cultural Revolution. But even there (and I am speaking of the China of statements made by Western left-wingers, not of the China that is in China and follows another logic, or a hundred different logical rules which we do not know) we are dealing not with utopia but with a utopian charge of energy that has constantly to accommodate new data that come in, and to digest information that is sometimes unwelcome.

The vision of a universal future has been diverted

from political thought, and confined to a minor kind of literature, science fiction, though here, too, it is a negative utopia that dominates, a journey into the infernal regions of the future. Thus this way of writing, which aimed to extend its arrangement of signs even to the arrangement of things, has been taken prisoner by another literary strategy, which is more immediately effective emotionally: a story of distant wanderings and adventure that is capable of giving us rapid glimpses of tomorrow but has no power to change our way of living here in this world.

Did utopia ever have this power? Certainly for Campanella it did, and maybe also for the outlandish Saint-Simonists of Enfantin. Actually to *see* a possible different world that is already made and in operation is to be filled with indignation against a world that is unjust and to reject the idea that it is the only possible one.

During the course of the centuries, criticism of the present moment has in the literary *topos* more often expressed itself in terms of the return of the golden age, of the mythical past (or at the very least in terms of Arcadia), and then of the Noble Savage, and, more sporadically, of the approved and symmetrical myth of the city of the future, where justice and happiness reign according to reason. This goes to show that in the face of what is unacceptable in the present, the tendency to regress is more common than the aspiration toward an *eschaton* that always demands a higher ideological investment and comes up against strong resistance (and I speak only of internal resistance). But one has to say that in any return to the golden age there is also a utopian element, just as in the utopias there is no lack of suggestions of a return to the past.

Is this escapism? I have always had reservations about the negative meaning that the word "escapism" has in the language of historical and literary criticism. For a prisoner, to escape has always been a good thing, and an individual escape can be a first necessary step toward a collective escape. This must also be true on the level of the words and images of fantasy. To escape from the prison of representations of the world that remind you of our slavery with every phrase they contain means to suggest another code, another syntax, another vocabulary, by means of which to give shape to the world of your desires. Certainly anyone who thinks that by doing this he has found freedom, and who is content with it, is the victim of a cruel misunderstanding, but no more than someone who is satisfied with a verbal and symbolic freedom, even if the language he uses exposes its flank less to the accusation of "escapism." In short, if no one can with credibility cast doubts on the superiority of "scientific" political thought over "utopian" thought, there still comes a moment when we have to ask ourselves whether that step ahead toward the scientific method has not had its losses as well—which is to say, whether along with all the paper scenarios for utopia we have not lost something invaluable. Utopia conceived of its aim, a regenerated world—and, indeed, *saw* it—in terms of its outward results: a city, a way of living together, a whole body of ways of behaving; whereas the scientific theory was to be conceived—and, indeed, stated—in terms of philosophical discourse, abstract and a lot harder to verify. The materialism of the visionaries has far more body to it than that of the philosophers.

For years I felt it was a serious lacuna that Marx refused to predict what socialist society would be like; it took me a long time to understand that this was a principle inherent in his method. One does not hand out recipes for the cooking of the future. A recipe always presupposes future kitchens; otherwise one does not write recipes, one just proceeds with cooking and that's that. When Marx was writing, and for some time afterward, the "Do Not Enter" sign on the road to utopian projects meant one should concentrate all one's thought and practice on criticizing, and formulating a strategy of attack against, the only society actually in existence, and this implied an austere and demanding discipline. But as soon as an alternative society came into being, and the experimental fluidity and effervescence of its beginnings (which could indeed be called utopian) was followed by official apologetics for the present as if the present were the most desirable of all futures, then a veto took effect—explicitly or implicitly—on efforts to imagine any model but the existing one.

In the last fifteen years or so there have been countless models claiming to represent the realization of a new society, and the phases within each model set themselves up as models themselves; this at least ensures us a varied sample of defects and errors to be avoided, and enjoins para-utopian activities to construct models with already tested pieces, collages made with fragments of models that are already historic. I am saying this not to reiterate an old complaint, but in order to trace the roots of a lust for prefiguration that we have been carrying with us for ages, and which was also stimulated by the fact that during the same years the urge to project human happiness, both in general and in particular, took control of capitalism (or at least paid visits out of office hours).

In our yesterday of the postwar years, the premises for revisiting utopia rose from the same grounds on which city planning was setting itself up as a pilot discipline that would give technical, aesthetic, and social form to the theatre of our lives. After all the setbacks that faith in rational projection and prediction has suffered since then, after so many good intentions have been blunted against the wall of the inertia of vested interests and conditioned behavior, after the networks of so many urban projects have seen their mesh torn asunder by fish that were just too big for them, and now that the outlook for capitalist culture revolves around an image of catastrophe, concentrating all its fantasies on it (the foreseeing, preventing, or administering of catastrophe), this is when we choose to revisit utopia. But why? And in what frame of mind?

Not, certainly, as with Leonardo's drawings, which head the family tree of all inventible or constructible machines, but, on the contrary, with autonomous logico-fantastic machines, and on account of their very inflexibility toward compromise with today or with the probable tomorrow. Is this one of the many escapes into the future, which knows it is that and nothing more? Or worse, an intellectual alibi, a refuge for beautiful spirits? There is no lack of diagnosticians of bad conscience among us, and they will not hesitate to give us their answer. All I am trying to do here is reconstruct a diary of my own relations with utopia, most of which are private, and to register both the high points and the low. The autonomous logico-fantastic machine is something I like insofar as (and if) it serves some real need: the need to enlarge the sphere of what we can imagine, and to introduce into our limited range of choices "absolute rejection" by means of a world thought out in all its details according to other values and other relationships. In a word, utopia not as a city that can be founded by us but that can found itself in us, build itself brick by brick in our ability to imagine it, to think it out to the ultimate degree; a city that claims to inhabit us, not to be inhabited, thus making us possible inhabitants of a third city, different from utopia and different from all the habitable or uninhabitable cities of today; a city born of the mutual impact of new conditionings, both inner and outer.

The side of utopia that has most to say to us is therefore the one that turns its back on any attempt to put it into practice. This holds good also for those nineteenth-century reformers who considered themselves not utopians, but inventors of projects that could be put into effect at once, such as Owen and Cabet, who set up new communities and took the risk, and met with inevitable failure.

It is always the *place* that gives utopia such trouble. Where should one put it? On the borders of an existing society, in order to convert that society by example? In that case it is only a step from the radicalism of reform to the compromise of reformism. In a new world, in virgin territories, on a desert island? (Let us not forget that utopianism was born after the voyage of Columbus.) But we know that a true no-man's-land does not exist: exporting a civilization is called "colonialism," even if we are convinced that we are founding something brand-new, and vigorous, and different from the culture of the metropolis. As for Fourier—who declared that he was waiting only for a patron to give a start to Harmony—when his followers tried to put his societal model into practice, he hastened to disassociate himself. He knew, or at least foresaw, that if his system departed from the written page, from the argument he preached, it would lose its force as absolute opposition to all that had ever been said and done.

Among Fourier's modern readers some have wondered whether his dream has not partly come true today in our "leisure" society, perhaps in institutions such as the Club Méditerranée, where free time is meticulously programmed. This suspicion should be enough to demolish his entire edifice, but it seems to me that he rides the blow. The comparison with today reveals the extent to which Fourier's idea of a radical organization of happiness is incompatible with the niggardly prospects of commercialized happiness.

Different, in my belief, is the argument to be made about the other monumental early-nineteenth-century prediction, that of Saint-Simon. The model of "industrial society," of technocratic power, put forward by Saint-Simon could be said to have won, and now guides top-level choices, whether American or Soviet (even though he did want to do away with the military, and in this respect the reality is lagging far behind the prophecy). The narrowing of the distance from reality is the trial by fire for a utopia: either it is left in ashes, like that of Saint-Simon, or it rises from them, like the phoenix.

Far better are the more visionary utopias of a Cyrano or a Restif de La Bretonne. Therefore, in the years around '68, I took it into my head to read Fourier, and to read him as one reads a poet, a novelist, or a moralist—that is, to lay one's hands on a system of moral fantasy. And what interested me was the almost unique case of an antirepressive morality based on exactitude, methodical rigor, and classification.

If I mention this experience of mine here it is because nothing much came of it, and I don't know if others have had the same reaction as I did to reading Fourier—that is, dissatisfaction. Something in my approach was not quite right. Poets or novelists or moralists (I speak of the real ones), once they have become yours, tend to stay with you; the utopian doesn't. Utopia has no consistency. You may participate in the spirit of it, and *believe* in it, but other than on the page it does not come with you into the world, and you yourself do not manage to follow it up. Once I have shut the book, Fourier does not follow me, and I have to go back and browse to find him there, to admire him in all his clarity and obstinacy. But I have realized that the moment I have paid him this debt of admiration, every step I take is a step away.

Certainly, in recent times, my need to come up with some tangible representation of future society has declined. This is not because of some vitalistic assertion of the unforeseeable, or because I am resigned to the worst, or because I have realized that philosophical abstraction is a better indication of what may be hoped for, but maybe simply because the best that I can still look for is something else, which must be sought in the folds, in the shadowy places, in the countless involuntary effects that the most calculated system creates without being aware that perhaps its truth lies right there. The utopia I am looking for today is less solid than gaseous: it is a utopia of fine dust, corpuscular, and in suspension.

Guide to
The Charterhouse of Parma
for the Use of New Readers

La Repubblica, September 8, 1982.

How many new readers will approach Stendhal's novel thinking of the new filmed version of *The Charterhouse of Parma* that is shortly to appear on television? Perhaps very few in comparison with the number of viewers, or maybe a great number when matched against the statistics for readers of books in Italy. But no statistics will be able to provide us with the most important datum: how many young people will be overwhelmed from the very first pages, and be suddenly convinced that the most wonderful novel in the world could only be this one, and recognize it as the novel they have always wanted to read and one that will be a touchstone for all the novels they read in future. I am speaking chiefly of the first chapters. As one reads on, one finds a different novel—in fact several novels, all different from one another, and this demands adjustments in the way we participate in events. However, the power of the opening continues to make itself felt.

This is what happened to me, as to so many in successive generations over the last century. (*The Charterhouse of Parma* was published in 1839, but we must bear in mind the forty years that elapsed before Stendhal was understood—a phenomenon he had predicted with extraordinary precision, even though of all his books this one had the greatest immediate success, and to launch it had the advantage of an enthusiastic article from Balzac that went on for seventy-two pages!)

We have no means of knowing whether this miracle will continue, or for how long. The reasons a book catches the imagination—its powers of seduction which are a different thing from its value in an absolute sense— are made up of a great number of imponderable elements. (So is its absolute value, supposing that such a concept has any meaning.) But one thing for sure: if I pick up *The Charterhouse of Parma* even today, as in all the rereadings I have made at different times and through all the changes in taste and outlook, then I feel the impetus of its music, that *allegro con brio* that captivates me. It is in those first chapters, set in Milan under Napoleon, in which history with its rumble of cannon goes hand in hand with the rhythm of individual life. And the atmosphere of pure adventure that one enters with the sixteen-year-old Fabrice on the sopping battlefield of Waterloo, among the *vivandiers'* wagons and the escaping horses, is the true novelistic spirit of adventure, made up of a mixture of peril and safety with a strong dose of candor. What is more, the corpses, with their staring eyes and rigid arms, are the first real corpses the literature of war ever used to explain what a war really is. And the atmosphere of woman's love that enters from the very first pages, composed of protective trepidation and jealous intrigue, already reveals the real subject of the novel, which is destined to stay with Fabrice right through to the end (an atmosphere that in the long run does not fail to be somewhat oppressive).

Is it the fact of belonging to a generation that lived through wars and political disasters in its youth that has made me a reader of *The Charterhouse of Parma* for life? But in my personal memories, so much less serene and liberated, it is dissonances and clamor that dominate, and not that music that carries one away. Perhaps the very opposite is true, and we think of ourselves as children of an epoch because we project Stendhal's adventures onto our own experience and transfigure it, as Don Quixote did.

I said that *The Charterhouse of Parma* is many novels rolled into one, and I dwelt on the beginning, a chronicle of history and of society, a picaresque adventure. Then one gets into the body of the novel—the world of the little court of Prince Ranuccio Ernesto IV (this apocryphal Parma can be historically identified with Modena, as is passionately claimed by such Modenese as Antonio Delfini, though Parmesans such as Gino Magnani remain attached to it as a sublimated personal myth).

At this point the novel becomes theatre, an enclosed space, the board for a game played by a limited number of characters, a gray motionless scene for a whole chain of emotions that do not coincide with one another: Count Mosca, a man of power who is slavishly in love with

Gina Sanseverina; Gina herself, a woman who gets whatever she wants, who sees only through the eyes of her nephew Fabrice del Dongo; Fabrice, who at first loves only himself, then has a few quick adventures as a garnishing, and finally concentrates all the forces gravitating on and around him by falling hopelessly in love with the angelic, solicitous Clélia.

All this takes place within the shabby world of political and worldly intrigues of the court, with the prince obsessed with fear because he has had two patriots hanged, and Rassi the public prosecutor, who is perhaps the first character in any novel to incarnate bureaucratic mediocrity with all the cruelty that can go with it. The conflict here, according to Stendhal's intentions, is between this image of the reactionary Europe of Metternich and the absoluteness of passions that spare themselves nothing, the ultimate refuge of the generous ideals of an age that has gone down in defeat.

The dramatic core is one of melodrama. The opera was the first key used by the music-loving Stendhal to get to understand Italy, but in *The Charterhouse of Parma* the climate (luckily) is not that of tragic opera but rather (as discovered by Paul Valéry) of operetta. Though tyranny is gloomy, it is at the same time timid and awkward (far worse had actually happened in Modena), while the passions are peremptory but have fairly simple mechanisms. Only one character, Count Mosca, has any real psychological complexity, composed of calculation but also desperation, of possessiveness but also a sense of the void.

But the "court-novel" aspect of the book does not end here. The transfiguration of the reactionary Italy of the Restoration is overlaid by the plot of a Renaissance story, one that Stendhal hunted down in libraries and in fact recounted in his *Italian Chronicles*. We are here concerned with the life of Alessandro Farnese, who was very much loved and protected by an aunt of his—a worldly, scheming woman—and had a glorious career in the church in spite of his libertine, adventurous youth (he had even killed a rival and ended up as a prisoner in the Castel Sant'Angelo), finally arriving at the point of becoming pope, by the name of Paul III. What has this bloody story of fourteenth-to-fifteenth-century Rome got to do with that of Fabrice in a society that was hypocritical and full of moral scruples? Abolutely nothing. Yet Stendhal's project started precisely there, with the idea of transposing Farnese's life into his own times, in the name of some continuity in Italy of the life force and passionate spontaneity that he never tired of believing in (though he also perceived other things in the Italians, and more subtle ones: distrust, anxiety, cautiousness).

Whatever the primary source of inspiration was, the beginning of the novel had such an impetus of its own that it could have gone ahead on its own, forgetting about the Renaissance chronicle. All the time, every so often Stendhal remembers it, and goes back to thinking of Farnese's life as a sort of guide. The most obvious consequence is that Fabrice, as soon as he has doffed his Napoleonic uniform, enters a seminary and takes vows. For the whole of the rest of the novel we have to imagine him dressed as a monsignor, which was certainly uncomfortable for him and is also so for us, because it takes a certain effort to put the two ideas together, and his situation as a churchman has very little effect on his conduct as a character—and none whatever on his spirit.

Some years before, another hero of Stendhal's, also youthful and inflamed with the glory of Napoleon, had decided to take the cloth in view of the fact that the Restoration had barred the way to a military career to anyone who was not a scion of a noble family. But in this antivocation of Julien Sorel's is the central theme of *Le Rouge et le noir*, yielding a situation far more dramatic and detailed than that of Fabrice del Dongo. Fabrice is no Julien Sorel: he is not given the same psychological complexity. Nor is he Alessandro Farnese, destined to become pope, and as such the emblematic hero of a story that can be taken either as a scandalous anticlerical revelation or as the edifying account of a redemption. And who is Fabrice? Apart from the vestments he wears and the things he gets involved with, Fabrice is someone who tries to read the signs of his destiny, according to the science taught to him by Blanès, the abbot–astrologer who was his real instructor. He questions himself about the future and the past (was he or was he not at Waterloo, which was *his* battle?), but his whole reality is in the present, moment by moment.

The Charterhouse of Parma as a whole, like Fabrice, overcomes the contradictions of its composite nature by means of incessant movement. And when Fabrice winds up in prison, a new novel starts within the novel. This is the prison story of the tower and his love for Clélia, which is again different from all the rest, and even more difficult to define.

There is no more anguished human situation than that of a prisoner, but Stendhal is so refractory toward anguish that, even if he has to show us isolation in a cell in a tower (after an arrest that has taken place in mysterious and disturbing circumstances), the states of mind that he expresses are always hopeful and extroverted. *"Comment! moi qui avait tant de peur de la prison, j'y suis, et je ne me souviens pas d'être triste!"* "I don't remember being sad!"; never was a rebuttal of Romantic self-pity ever uttered with more candor and sanity.

This Farnese tower, which never existed either in Parma or in Modena, has a particular shape. It is composed of two towers, the slenderer one being built on top of the broader one (more like a house on the ramparts surmounted by an aviary, in which a young girl—Clélia—appears among the birds). It is one of the enchanted places in the novel (Trompeo in this regard recalls Ariosto, and in other respects Tasso). Without doubt, it is a symbol, so much so that, as is the case with all true symbols, it is hard to decide what on earth it symbolizes. Isolation within oneself, that goes without saying; but also, and even more, getting outside oneself and communicating love, because never has Fabrice been so expansive and talkative as he is through the highly complicated and improbable systems of wireless telegraphy with which he manages to correspond from his cell, both with Clélia and with his ever-helpful aunt Gina.

The tower is the place where Fabrice's first romantic love is born—for the unattainable Clélia, his jailer's daughter—but it is also the gilded cage of his love for Gina, of which he is still a prisoner. So much so that when the tower first enters the picture (chapter XVIII), we have the story of a young Farnese thrown into prison because he became the lover of his stepmother. It is the mythical core of Stendhal's novels, "hypergamy," love of women of higher social status, or of older women (Julien and Madame de Rênal, Lucien and Madame de Chasteller, Fabrice and Gina Sanseverina).

The tower also represents height, and the ability to see a long way. The incredible view that Fabrice commands from up there includes the whole of the Alps, from Nice to Treviso, and the entire course of the Po from Monviso to Ferrara. But that is not all: he sees his own life as well, and the lives of others, and the network of intricate relationships that go to make up a destiny.

As from the tower his eyes embrace the whole of northern Italy, so from the summit of this novel written in 1839 the future history of Italy is already in view: Ranuccio Ernesto IV, prince of Parma, is an absolutist petty tyrant, but also a Carlo Alberto who foresees the next developments in the Risorgimento and nourishes the hope that he will one day be the constitutional king of Italy.

A historical and political reading of *The Charterhouse of Parma* has always been easy and virtually obligatory, starting with Balzac (who said this novel was like *The Prince* of a new Machiavelli!), and it has been equally easy to show that Stendhal's attempt to exalt the ideals of liberty and progress suffocated by the Restoration is extremely superficial. But Stendhal's very lightness of touch can give us a historical and political lesson, when he shows us how the ex-Jacobins or supporters of Bonaparte become (or remain) authoritative and zealous members of the legitimist establishment. That so many positions adopted, and so many actually risky actions that seemed to be motivated by the most absolute convictions, then turn out to have had very little behind them, is something we have seen again and again, in Milan and elsewhere, but the beauty of *The Charterhouse of Parma* is that this is stated without any fuss, as if it went without saying.

What makes *The Charterhouse of Parma* a great "Italian" novel is the feeling for politics as a calculated adjustment and a distribution of roles: on one side the prince who, while he persecutes the Jacobins, is concerned to establish a future understanding with them that will enable him to put himself at the head of the imminent movement of national unity; on the other Count Mosca, who ceases to be an officer in Napoleon's army and becomes a reactionary minister and leader of the extremist party (but is prepared to encourage the real extremists only to give proof of his moderation by abandoning them), and all this without his being in any way personally touched by it.

As the novel proceeds, we get further and further away from Stendhal's other image of Italy, as the country of generous sentiments and spontaneous living, that happy place that met the eyes of a young French officer on his arrival in Milan. In the *Vie d'Henri Brulard*, when he got to the moment of describing happiness, he broke off the story: *"On échoue toujours à parler de ce qu'on aime."*

This phrase provided the theme and the title for the last essay of Roland Barthes, which he was to have read to the Stendhal conference in Milan in March 1980; but while he was writing it he was involved in the car accident that cost him his life. In the pages that remain, Barthes observes that in his autobiographical works Stendhal mentions the happiness of his youthful days in

Italy several times, but never manages to make them felt.

And yet twenty years later, by a kind of *après-coup* that is still part of the contorted logic of love, Stendhal wrote about Italy in some triumphant pages, and these indeed fire a reader like myself (but I do not think I am the only one) with that jubilation, that radiance that the personal diary spoke of but did not manage to communicate. These are the admirable pages that make up the beginning of *The Charterhouse of Parma*. There is a sort of miraculous harmony between the mass of happiness and pleasure that burst upon Milan with the arrival of the French, and our joy as readers: the effect narrated coincides at last with the effect produced.

Stendhal's Knowledge of
the "Milky Way"

Paper read at the fourteenth International Stendhal Conference, Milan, March 1980

It was during his period in Milan that Henri Beyle, until then a more or less brilliant socialite, a dilettante of uncertain vocation and a versatile writer of uncertain success, worked out something that we cannot call his philosophy, since it tends in exactly the opposite direction from that of philosophy, and that we cannot call his theory as a novelist, since he defines it in terms of a polemic against novels, maybe unaware that he himself was shortly going to become a novelist—in fact, something that we can only call his method of knowing things.

This method of Stendhal's, based on individual experience in all its unrepeatable uniqueness, contrasts with philosophy, which tends toward generalization, universality, abstraction, and geometric design. But it also contrasts with the world of the novel, seen as a world of substantial and unambiguous forces, of continuous lines, of vectorial arrows pointing toward an end, for his method aims at knowledge of a reality that manifests itself in the form of small, localized, instantaneous events. I am attempting to define this cognitive process of Stendhal's as if it were independent of its object, but what Beyle actually wanted to know was a psychological object, the nature of the passions, and, indeed, of the passion *par excellence*: love. *De l'amour* was the treatise the still-anonymous author wrote in Milan to exploit the experience of his longest and unhappiest Milanese love affair, the one with Mathilde Dembowski. But we can certainly try to extract from *De l'amour* what in the philosophy of science is now called a "paradigm," and see if it holds good not just for the psychology of love but for all aspects of Stendhal's vision of the world.

In one of the prefaces of *De l'amour* we read:

Love is like the thing in the sky we call the Milky Way, a brilliant cluster made up of little stars, many of which are themselves nebulae. Books have noted four or five hundred of the little successive feelings that go to make up this passion, and only the crudest of them, often making mistakes and taking what is secondary for what is the main thing.

The passage goes on to criticize eighteenth-century novels, including *La Nouvelle Héloïse* and *Manon Lescaut*, just as on the page before he had refuted the philosophers' claim to describe love in terms of a geometrical figure, however complicated.

Let us, then, say that the reality on which Stendhal aims to base his knowledge is punctiform, discontinuous, unstable, a dust cloud of phenomena that are not homogeneous but isolated from one another and capable of being subdivided in turn into even more minute phenomena.

At the beginning of the treatise we get the impression that the author is approaching his subject in the classifying and cataloguing spirit that in those same years led Charles Fourier to draw up his meticulous synoptic tables of the passions with a view to their harmonious combinatorial satisfaction. But Stendhal's mind is very much opposed to a systematic order, and he continually avoids it even in this book, which ought to be his most ordered. His rigor is of another kind, and his argument is organized around a basic idea that he calls "crystallization." From there it radiates outward, exploring the field of meanings underlying the nomenclature of love, as it does with the neighboring semantic areas of *bonheur* and *beauté*.

It happens with *bonheur* as well that the more one tries to confine it within a concrete definition, the more it dissolves into a galaxy of instants separate from one another—exactly as with love. This is because (he says as early as chapter II) "the soul wearies of all that is uniform, even with perfect happiness." In a note he explains, "The very nuance of existence gives only a single instant of perfect happiness; but the frame of mind of a passionate man changes ten times a day." And yet this dust cloud of *bonheur* is something that can be measured and numbered according to precise units of measurement. In fact, in chapter XVII we read:

Albéric, at the theatre, meets a woman more beautiful than his mistress. Permit me a mathematical evaluation: let us say a woman whose features promise three units of happiness instead of two. (Let us suppose that perfect beauty gives a quantity of happiness expressible by the number four.) Need we be surprised that he prefers the features of his mistress, which promise him a hundred units of happiness?

We see that Stendhal's mathematics immediately become very complicated. On the one hand, the quantity of happiness is of objective size, proportional to the quantity of beauty; on the other, it is of subjective size, being projected by amorous passion onto a measureless scale. Not for nothing is this chapter, one of the most important in the treatise, entitled "Beauty Dethroned by Love."

Therefore, even in *beauté* there is an invisible line that divides every sign, and we can discern there an objective aspect (difficult to define) of the quantity of absolute beauty, and the subjective aspect of what is beautiful to us, comprising "every new beauty discovered in what one loves." The first definition of beauty given in the treatise, in chapter XI, is "a new capacity to give you pleasure." There then comes a page on the relativity of what beauty is, exemplified by the attitudes of two fictitious characters in the book: for Del Rosso the ideal of beauty is a woman who at every instant suggests a physical pleasure, while for Lisio Visconti she must incite the passion of love.

If we bear in mind that both Del Rosso and Lisio are personifications of two psychological tendencies of the author, things get even more complicated, because the process of division now concerns even the subject.

But here we touch on the theme of the multiplication of Stendhal's personality by means of pseudonyms. Even the ego can become a galaxy of egos: "the mask must be a series of masks and the pseudonym a systematic polyonymy," writes Jean Starobinski in an important essay on the subject.

But let us for now go no further into this territory, but consider the enamored subject as a single indivisible spirit, especially since at that point there is a note explaining the definition of beauty insofar as it is *my* beauty— that is, beauty for me—"promise of a character useful to my spirit . . . above the attraction of the senses." Here we witness the appearance of the word "promise," which in a note to chapter XVII characterizes the definition that was to become most famous: *"la beauté est la promesse du bonheur."*

Concerning this phrase, its antecedents, presuppositions, and echoes down as far as Baudelaire, there is a valuable article by Giansiro Ferrate ("Il valore e la forma," *Questo e Altro*, June 1964), which throws light on the central point about the theory of crystallization: the transformation of some negative peculiarity of the loved one into a pole of attraction. I should mention that the crystallization metaphor comes from the mines at Salzburg, where they throw in leafless boughs and gather them up again several months later all covered with crystals of rock salt glittering like diamonds. The branch as it was is still visible, but every knot and twig and prickle acts as a support for a transfigured beauty. Thus the lover's mind fixes every detail of the loved one in a sublime transfiguration. And here Stendhal dwells upon a very unusual example, which seems to have been of great importance to him, both on the plane of general thory and on that of personal experience: the *marque de petite vérole* on the face of a beloved woman. Still quoting from chapter XVII:

Even the little defects of her face, for example a smallpox scar, touch the heart of the man in love, and throw him into a profound reverie when he sees them in another woman. It is that he has felt a thousand emotions in the presence of that smallpox scar, that these emotions are for the most part delightful, that they are all of the greatest interest, and that, whatever they are, they all rekindle with incredible force at the sign of that mark, even when seen on the face of another woman.

It might be said that all Stendhal's arguments about beauty circle around the *marque de petite vérole*, almost as if only through this glimpse of the absolute ugliness of a scar could he arrive at the contemplation of absolute beauty. It could also be said that his whole case study of the passions revolves around the most negative situation, that of the failure or "fiasco" of a man's sexual powers, as if the entire treatise about love gravitated toward the chapter called "Des fiascos," and that the whole book was written for no other purpose than to get to that famous chapter, which the author did not then dare to publish, and which came out only posthumously.

Stendhal approaches the subject by citing Montaigne's essay mentioning the same questions, but whereas for Montaigne this is one example in a general meditation on the physical effects of the imagination and, conversely, on the "*indocile liberté*" of the parts of the body that do not obey the will—a treatment that is a precursor of Groddeck and modern investigations of the body—for Stendhal, who always proceeds by subdivision and not by generalization, it is a matter of untying a knot of psychological processes, self-love and sublimation, imagination and lack of spontaneity. The most yearned-for moment for him as a man constantly in love, the first intimacies with a new conquest, can become the moment of greatest anxiety; but it is precisely on this spiral of absolute negativeness, this plunge into darkness and nullity, that knowledge can be based.

Starting from this point, we might imagine a dialogue between Stendhal and Leopardi, a "Leopardian" dialogue in which the poet exhorts Stendhal to draw the most bitter conclusions about nature from the experience he has had of life. There could even be a historical basis to it, given that the two of them did in fact meet in Florence in 1832. But we can also imagine Stendhal's reaction—on the basis, for example, of the pages of *Rome, Naples, and Florence* devoted to the intellectual conversations in Milan of fifteen years before (1816), in which he shows the skeptical detachment of the man of the world and concludes that in the company of philosophers he always manages to get himself disliked, something that does not happen to him with beautiful women. So Stendhal would have swiftly extricated himself from the dialogue with Leopardi and followed his own path, that of a man who wishes to lose nothing either of pleasure or of pain, because the inexhaustible variety of situations that derive from them is enough to bestow interest on life.

If, therefore, we want to read *De l'amour* as a "discourse on method," we find it difficult to place this method among those operating at his time. But we might perhaps fit it into the "circumstantial paradigm" that a young Italian historian, Carlo Ginzburg, has recently attempted to discern in the human sciences during the final twenty years of the last century. One can trace a long history of this circumstantial knowledge, based on semiotics, on attention paid to the traces, the symptoms, the involuntary coincidences, that lend weight to marginal details, to unconsidered trifles, to what the consciousness habitually refuses to snap up. It is not out of place to put Stendhal into this context, with his punctiform knowledge that connects the zenith with the nadir, *amour-passion* with the *marque de petite vérole*, never excluding the possibility that the most obscure trace might be the most luminous mark of destiny.

Can we say that this method enunciated by the anonymous author of *De l'amour* will be followed by the Stendhal of the novels and the Henri Brulard of the autobiographical writings? For Henri Brulard we can definitely say yes: his intentions were by definition the opposite of those of the novelist. The novel (or at least the most obvious and widespread notion of it) tells stories with a well-defined design, in which well-defined characters follow out their own dominant passions with coherent determination; whereas Stendhal as an autobiographer tries to seize the essence of his own life, of his own individual uniqueness, by the accumulation of inessential facts, without any direction or form. Conducting such an exploration into a life ends up becoming exactly the opposite of what one means by narrating.

"Will I have the courage to write these confessions

in an intelligible manner?" we read at the beginning of the *Vie d'Henri Brulard*. "One has to narrate, and I write considerations on minimal events, but it is precisely on account of their microscopic dimensions that they need to be recounted very distinctly. What patience you will need, O reader!"

Memory itself is fragmentary by its very nature; more than once in the *Vie d'Henri Brulard*, memory is likened to a peeling fresco: "It is always like in the frescoes in the Camposanto in Pisa, where one makes out an arm perfectly well, but the piece beside it that showed the head has fallen off. I see a series of very clear images, but without any features except those they had with regard to me. Even more, I see these only through the memory of the effect produced on me." For this reason, "there is neither originality nor truth except in details."

As Giovanni Macchia writes in an essay devoted to this very obsession with detail: "The whole journey of existence is lined with a bedlam of little facts that seem superfluous, and that mark and reveal the rhythm of existence, such as the banal secrets of any one day, which we pay no attention to and even try to destroy. . . . That way of looking at everything at a human level, that refusal to pick and choose, to correct, to adulterate, gave birth to his most astonishing psychological observations, to his social insights."

But not only the past is fragmentary. In the present as well, what is glimpsed and involuntary may have a greater effect, like the half-open door through which he tells us in his journal he once spied on a young woman undressing, hoping to see now a thigh and now a breast. "A woman who, whole and entire in my bed, would not have moved me in the least, seen on the sly gives me enchanting sensations. In this situation she is natural, I am not worried about my role, and I give myself over entirely to sensation."

And it is often from the darkest and most unmentionable moments that the process of knowledge develops, not from the moment of full self-realization. At this point we must link up with the title chosen by Roland Barthes for his speech: *"On échoue toujours à parler de ce qu'on aime."* The journal ends at the moment of Stendhal's greatest happiness: his arrival in Milan in 1811. Henri Brulard starts by realizing his own happiness on the Janiculum when he is on the threshold of fifty, and at once he feels the need to start telling us about the unhappiness of his childhood in Grenoble.

The time has come for me to wonder if this sort of knowledge holds good for the novels as well—that is, to wonder how we can fit it in with the normal image we have of Stendhal, that of the novelist of the life force, of the will to self-assertion, of cold determination to pursue the heat of one's passions. Or, to put it differently: does the Stendhal who fascinated me in my youth still exist, or was he an illusion? I can answer the last question immediately: yes, he exists, he is there just as he was, and Julien on his rock is still gazing at the sparrowhawk in the sky, still identifying with its strength and its isolation. I realize, however, that this concentration of energy now interests me less, and I am more concerned with discovering what is beneath it—all the rest of it, which I cannot call the "hidden part of the iceberg" because it is not hidden at all, but in fact holds up and holds together all the remainder.

Certainly Stendhal's heroes are characterized by a straightforwardness of personality, a continuity of will power, a compactness of the ego in living out their inner conflicts, which appear to take us to the very antipodes of the existential notion I have tried to describe as punctiform, discontinuous, and a dust cloud of phenomena. Everything in Julien is determined by his conflict between timidity and will power, which drives him as by a categorical imperative to press Madame de Rênal's hand in the dark garden in those extraordinary pages of inner combat in which the real presence of erotic attraction ends up getting the better of both the presumed severity of the one and the presumed unawareness of the other. Fabrice is so joyously allergic to any form of anguish that even when locked up in the tower he is not touched by depression, and for him the prison becomes a means of incredibly complicated amorous communication, almost the condition on which he can make his love come true. Lucien in *Lucien Leuwen* is so taken up with his *amour-propre* that overcoming the mortification of a fall from a horse, or the misunderstanding of an imprudent phrase uttered to Madame de Chasteller, or the *gaucherie* of having raised his hand to his lips, determines all his future conduct. The journey of Stendhal's heroes is certainly never linear: given that the stage on which they act is so far from the Napoleonic battlefields of their dreams, in order to express their potential energies they have to put on masks as different as possible from their inner images of themselves. Julien and Fabrice don the priest's cassock and undertake a career in the church (I don't know how credible this is from a historical point of view). Lucien confines himself to buying a missal, but his is a double mask: that of an officer of the House of Orléans but nostalgic for the House of Bourbon.

This full-bodied self-awareness in living out one's own emotions is still more evident in the female characters—Madame de Rênal, Gina Sanseverina, and Madame de Chasteller—women always older than or socially superior to their young lovers, lucid and decisive of mind, knowing what they are about, and capable of supporting their lovers in their hesitations rather than becoming their victims. Perhaps they are projections of a mother image that the writer scarcely knew, and that in *Henri Brulard* he caught in the snapshot of the resolute young woman who sprang like a deer over her child's bed. Perhaps they are the projection of an archetype that he was searching for in ancient chronicles, such as that young stepmother who fell in love with a Prince Farnese, mentioned as the first prisoner in the tower, as if to make an emblematic, mythical core of the bond between Gina Sanseverina and Fabrice.

To this web of desires woven by the male and female characters we should add the will of the author, which is the real subject of the work; but each will is autonomous and can only propose things which the others are free to accept or reject. In a marginal note in the manuscript of *Lucien Leuwen* he wrote: "The best sporting dog can only put the game within range of the hunter's gun. If he doesn't shoot, the dog can do nothing. A novelist is like a dog to his hero."

On one of these paths followed by dog and hunter in Stendhal's most mature novel, *Lucien Leuwen*, we witness the emergence of a depiction of love that is truly like a Milky Way, dense with feelings and sensations and situations that pursue one another, superimpose and cancel one another, according to the program announced in *De l'amour*. This occurs principally at the ball during which for the first time Lucien and Madame de Chasteller have a chance to talk and get to know each other. The ball begins in chapter XV and ends in chapter XIX, with a series of tiny incidents, exchanges of conversation that are nothing remarkable, and degrees of shyness, haughtiness, hesitation, love, suspicion, shame, and contempt, on the part of both the young officer and the lady.

What strikes us about these pages is the profusion of psychological details, the variety of the switches of emotion, the hesitations of the heart. The reference to Proust, destined to be the ultimate stage along this road, only underlines the extent to which everything here is brought off with the utmost economy of description, and with a straightforwardness that allows the attention always to be concentrated on the story's essential knot of relationships.

That look he gives to provincial, legitimist, aristocratic society in the days of the July Monarchy is the cold scrutiny of a zoologist examining the morphological species of a minuscule fauna, as he says in those very pages, in a phrase put into the mouth of Lucien: "I ought to study them as one studies natural history. Cuvier told us, there in the Jardin des Plantes, that studying the worms, insects, and most appalling sea crabs methodically, being careful to take note of their differences and similarities, is a sure way of curing the repulsion that they inspire."

In Stendhal's novels the settings—or at any rate certain settings, such as the receptions and the drawing rooms—serve not so much to establish atmosphere as to locate positions precisely. Places are defined by the movements of the characters, by their positions at the moment when they produce certain emotions and certain conflicts; reciprocally, every conflict is defined by having been produced in that given place and at that given time. Yet Stendhal the autobiographer has the curious need to pin down places not by describing them but by sketching them out on rough maps, on which, apart from rudimentary features of the decor, we find where various people were at the time, so that the pages of the *Vie d'Henri Brulard* read like a kind of atlas. What is the meaning of this topographical obsession? Is it haste, letting descriptions go in order to work them up later on the basis of mere jottings? Not just that, I believe. Given that he is concerned with the uniqueness of every event, the map is useful for pinning down the space in which an event takes place, just as the narrative serves to fix it in time.

The actual places described in the novels are more outdoors than in-, such as the alpine landscapes of the Franche-Comté in *Le Rouge et le noir*, and those of Brianza seen from the bell tower of the Abbot Blanès in *The Charterhouse of Parma*. But of all Stendhal's landscapes, I would give the palm to the plain and unpoetic description of Nancy, as it appears in chapter IV of *Lucien Leuwen*, in all its utilitarian squalor of the early industrial era. It is a landscape that heralds a drama in the conscience of the protagonist, caught as he is between middle-class dullness and aspirations toward an aristocracy that is a shadow of its former self; it is objective negativeness, ready, in the case of this young lancer, to crystallize into glittering gems of beauty, once enhanced by the transports of love and life. The poetic power of Stendhal's view of things is not only that of enthusiasm and euphoria, but also that of a cold revulsion for a totally unattractive world that he feels compelled to accept as the only possible reality: the suburb of Nancy, where Lucien is sent to put down one of the first workers' uprisings, and the parading of mounted soldiers through the dingy streets in the faint morning light.

These social upheavals are conveyed by Stendhal according to the way their capillary vibrations affect the behavior of individuals. Why does Italy have a unique place in his affections? We continually hear him repeat that Paris is the kingdom of vanity, as opposed to Italy, the land of sincere and disinterested emotions. But we must not forget that in his personal geography there is another pole: England, a civilization that he is constantly tempted to identify himself with.

In a passage in *Souvenirs d'égotisme* he chooses between England and Italy and comes down heavily on the side of Italy, precisely because it was what today we would call "underdeveloped," whereas the English way of life, which forced workers to toil for eighteen hours a day, seems to him "ridiculous." "The exorbitant and oppressive labor of the English worker avenges us for Waterloo. . . . The poor Italian in his rags is far closer to happiness. He has time to make love, and for eighty or a hundred days a year abandons himself to a religion that is all the more amusing to him for being a little frightening."

Stendhal's notion is one of a certain rhythm of life that has time for everything, and above all for wasting time. His point of departure is his rejection of provincial pettiness, and his rancor toward his father and toward Grenoble; he sought out the big city. For him Milan was a big city where the discreet pleasures of the *ancien régime* as well as the fervors of his Napoleonic youth still survived, even if many aspects of that Italy of bigotry and poverty were not exactly made to please him.

London was also an ideal city, but there the things that gratified his snobbish tastes were paid for by the hardships of advanced industrialization. In his personal geography, Paris was a point equidistant between London and Milan. It had the priests in power as well as the law of profit. Hence Stendhal's unremitting centrifugal thrust. His is a geography of escapism. I ought also to include Germany, since that was where he found the name to sign his novels with, and therefore an identity more important to him than all of his other masks. But I would say that Germany for him was merely nostalgia for the Napoleonic epic, a memory that tended to fade away on him.

The *Souvenirs d'égotisme*, an autobiographical fragment concerned with a time when he was in Paris but, as it were, suspended between Milan and London, is therefore the text containing the whole map of Stendhal's world. We could call this book Stendhal's best novel *manqué*. Perhaps the novel failed to come into being because its author did not have a literary model to convince him that what he wanted to write could ever become a novel, but it was also because only in this form could he succeed with a story of shortcomings and actions that fell short of target. In the *Souvenirs d'égotisme* the overriding theme is his absence from Milan, which he had left after his famous unsuccessful love affair. In a Paris seen by him as a place of exile, every happening ends in a fiasco: sexual fiascos with prostitutes, spiritual fiascos in his relations with society and in intellectual matters (for example, in his visits to the philosopher he admired most, Destutt de Tracy). And then comes his trip to London, where the chronicle of failures culminates in the extraordinary story of a failed duel, and his search for an arrogant English captain whom Stendhal had not thought of challenging at the right moment, and whom he looked for over and over again in all the taverns down by the docks.

There is one single oasis of happiness in this history of failures. In one of the most wretched slums of London is a house run by three prostitutes, which, instead of being the sinister trap that he had anticipated, turns out to be a place as miniature and pretty as a doll's house. The girls are impoverished youngsters who welcome the three boisterous French tourists with grace, dignity, and discretion. Here at last is a picture of *bonheur*, poor and fragile as it may be, and very distant from the aspirations of our egotist!

Should we therefore conclude that the real Stendhal is a negative Stendhal, to be sought only in his disappointments, setbacks, and losses? That is not so. The thing that Stendhal always aims to assert is the existential tension that arises from measuring one's own individuality (and one's own limitations) against the individuality and limitations of one's surroundings. Simply because existence is dominated by entropy, by dissolution into instants and impulses like corpuscles without forms of their own or links with others, he thinks that the individual realizes himself according to a principle of conservation of energy, or, rather, of the continual reproduction of charges of energy. This is near to understanding that entropy will win out in the end, and that of the universe with all its galaxies nothing will be left but a whirlwind of atoms in space.

Montale's Rock

La Repubblica, December 15, 1981; written on the death of Eugenio Montale.

To write about a poet on the front page of a daily newspaper entails a certain risk. One has to make a "public" statement, underline a vision of the world and history, and the moral teaching implicit in his poetry. Everything one says is true, but then one realizes that it could be true also of another poet, that the unmistakable accent of those lines has been left out of the discussion. Let us, therefore, try to keep as close as possible to the essence of Montale's poetry in explaining why today the funeral of this poet who was so little inclined toward anything official, and so far from representing the image of "national seer," is nonetheless an event in which the whole country feels involved. This is all the more singular considering that the great declared faiths of the Italy of his time never numbered him among their adepts; indeed, he never spared his sarcasm toward any "cleric either red or black."

The first thing I would like to say is that Montale's lines are unmistakable on account of the precision and uniqueness of verbal expression, the rhythm, and the image evoked:

> . . . il lampo che candisce
> alberi e muri e li sorprende in quella
> eternità d'istante.

> . . . the flash that crystallizes
> trees and walls surprises them in that
> eternity of an instant.

I am not speaking of richness and versatility of verbal technique, a gift that other Italian poets have had to a supreme degree, and which often goes along with a copious and overblown style, a thing as remote as possible from Montale. Montale never wastes a stroke, but comes out with the unique expression at the right moment and isolates it in all its uniqueness.

> . . . Turbati
> discendevamo tra i vepri.
> Nei miei paesi a quell'ora
> cominciano a fischiare le lepri.

> . . . Troubled
> we went down into the thickets.
> In my parts, at that hour of night,
> the hares begin to sing.

I will come straight to the point: in an age of generic and abstract words, words good for all purposes, words good only for not thinking and not saying anything, a plague of language that spreads from the public to the private sector, Montale was the poet of exactitude, of deliberate choice of vocabulary, of terminological precision used to pin down the uniqueness of an experience.

> *S'accese su pomi cotogni,*
> *un punto, una cocciniglia,*
> *si udì inalberarsi alla striglia*
> *il poney, e poi vinse il sogno.*

> There kindled on the quince trees
> a spot, a shell-scale,
> we heard the pony rear up under the currycomb,
> and then the dream took over.

But all this precision to say what? Montale speaks to us of a spinning world driven by a wind of destruction, with no solid ground to stand on, where we have no help but that of an individual morality hanging on the edge of the abyss. It is the world of the First and Second World Wars, and perhaps even of the Third. Or perhaps the First remains out of the picture (beneath the already rather faded photos in the cinémathèque of our minds run the spare, minimal lines of Ungaretti), and it is the precariousness of the world as seen by young people after that war that forms the background to *Ossi di seppia*, as the mood of *Occasioni* is one of waiting for a new catastrophe, and the theme of *La bufera* is the acting out of this, and the ashes it left. *La bufera* is the best Italian book to come out of the Second World War,

and it is talking about that theme even when it is talking
about something else. Everything is implicit there, even
our anxieties of afterward, right up to those of today:
the atomic catastrophe:

> . . . e un'ombroso Lucifero scenderà su una proda
> del Tamigi, del Hudson, della Senna
> scuotendo l'ali di bitume semi-mozze dalla fatica,
> a dirti: è l'ora.

> . . . and a gloomy Lucifer will alight on a bank
> of the Thames, of the Hudson, of the Seine
> shaking bitumen wings half stunted with fatigue,
> and tell you: the hour has come.

and the horror of concentration camps past and future
(in "Il sogno del prigioniero").

But it is not the direct descriptions or declared al-
legories that I want to place in the foreground. Our
historical condition is seen as a cosmic condition, and
even the most minute natural presences in the poet's
everyday observation appear as vortices. It is the rhythm
of the verse, the prosody, the syntax, that contain this
movement in themselves, from the beginning to the end
of his three great books.

> I turbini sollevano la polvere
> sui tetti, a mulinelli, e sugli spiazzi
> deserti, ove i cavalli incappucciati
> annusano la terra, fermi innanzi
> ai vetri luccicanti degli alberghi.

> The wind whips up the dust
> onto the roofs, in eddies, and on empty

squares, where horses with lowered heads
sniff the ground, stock-still in front
of the glittering windows of hotels.

I spoke of an individual morality to resist the historical or cosmic catastrophe that from one moment to the next might erase the ephemeral traces of the human race; but I have also to say that in Montale, however far he is from joining in any chorus or any impetus toward solidarity, we always find a feeling of the interdependence of each of us with other people's lives. *"Occorrono troppe vite per farne una"* ("Too many lives are needed to make just one") is the memorable ending to a poem in *Occasioni* in which the shadow of a kestrel in flight gives the sense of the destruction and re-creation that imbue every form of biological and historical continuity. But the help that can come from nature or from men, if it is not to remain purely illusory, must connect with a tiny rivulet that rises *"dove solo/morde l'arsura e la desolazione"* ("where only/drought and desolation grip"). It is only by swimming up rivers until they become hair-thin that the eel finds a safe place to procreate. It is only *"a filo di pietà"* ("by the hairbreadth of mercy") that the porcupines on Monte Amiata can find anything to drink.

This difficult heroism dug in one's very gut, and in the aridity and precariousness of existence, this anti-heroic heroism, is the answer that Montale gave to the problems of poetry in his generation: how to write verse after (and against) D'Annunzio (and after Carducci, and after Pascoli, or at least a certain image of Pascoli). It is the problem that Ungaretti resolved with the flash of the word in all its purity, and Saba by regaining an inner sincerity that included pathos, affection, and sensuality—human features that the man who was Montale rejected, or thought could not be said.

There is no message of consolation or encouragement in Montale unless we accept the awareness of an inhospitable and stinting universe. It is along this arduous path that his message continues that of Leopardi, even if their voices sound very different. In the same way, Montale's atheism is more problematical than Leopardi's, shot through with continual leanings toward something supernatural that is at once corroded by his basic skepticism. If Leopardi dissolves away the consolations of the philosophy of the Enlightenment, the suggestions of consolation put forward by Montale are those of our contemporary irrationalisms, which he evaluates one by one and drops with a shrug, constantly reducing the surface of the rock under his feet, the rock to which he clings with the determination of a castaway.

One of his themes, which over the years became more frequent, is the way in which the dead are present in us, the uniqueness of every person whom we cannot resign ourselves to losing: "*il gesto d'una/vita che non è altra ma se stessa*" ("the gesture of a/life that is not another, but itself"). These are lines from a poem in memory of his mother, in which there are birds that have returned, a gently sloping landscape, and the dead: the repertoire of the positive images in his poetry. At this moment we can scarcely give his memory a better frame than this:

Ora che il coro delle coturnici
ti blandisce nel sonno eterno, rotta
felice schiera in fuga verso i clivi
vendemmiati del Mesco . . .

Now that the birdsong of the quails
soothes you in sleep eternal, scattered
happy swarm in flight toward the harvested
slopes of Mesco . . .

And go on reading "inside" his books. This is a
sure guarantee of his survival. For however many times
we read them and reread them, his poems seize us as
soon as we open the book, and we can never exhaust
them.

The Pen in the
First Person

For the Drawings of
Saul Steinberg

Introduction to Saul Steinberg, *Still Life and Architecture*
(New York: Pace Gallery, 1982). Originally published in
Derrière le Miroir (Paris), May 1977.

The first to consider the instruments and actions of
his own work as its true subject was a thirteenth-century
poet. Guido Cavalcanti wrote a sonnet in which his pens
speak in the first person, along with the instruments
used for cutting and sharpening them. They introduce
themselves in the opening lines:

> *Noi siàn le triste penne isbigottite,*
> *le cesoiuzze e'l coltellin dolente. . . .*

> We are the sad, dismayed pens,
> the scissors and the sorrowing knife. . . .

This essay was translated by William Weaver.

The poet ("the hand that moved us") is too desperate to do anything but sigh, and his writing tools address the reader directly (perhaps the reader is a woman, the one to whom the previous sonnets and the present sighs are directed, or else a third person, an impartial witness), asking for sympathy.

The sonnet speaks of sorrows in almost every verse, and yet its music, its effect, is an *allegro con brio* of extraordinary lightness.

With these verses Guido Cavalcanti opens modern poetry. He opens it, and he closes it. After him, poets prefer to forget that while they write they are writing and not doing something else. Through more than three hundred sonnets, Petrarch pretends to believe he is walking in the open countryside, overwhelmed by suffering and anguish, whereas he is actually seated comfortably in his study, his cat on his lap, as he contentedly polishes his verses.

We have to wait until Mallarmé for the poet to realize that the place where his poem happens is *"sur le vide papier que sa blancheur défend"* ("on the empty paper protected by its whiteness"). With Mallarmé there are no doubts that written words are written words and that the night's darkness is simply the black of the inkwell. This awareness, however, remains implicit; more than another fifty years must pass before it becomes evident.

The pen that Cavalcanti dropped is picked up by Steinberg. It is the pen as subject of graphic action. Every line presupposes a pen drawing it, and every pen presupposes a hand holding it. What lies beyond the hand is a debated question: the "I" who draws is identified with a drawn "I," not the drawing's subject but its object. Or, rather, it is the universe of drawing that draws itself, explores, tests, and redefines itself each time. (The physical universe proceeds in the same fashion, I believe.)

The drawn world has an aggressiveness of its own: it invades the desk, captures anything alien to it, joins all lines to its own line, overflows the page. . . . No, it is the outside world that enters and becomes part of the page. The pen, the hand, the artist, the desk, the cat—everything is engulfed by the drawing as if by a whirlpool, all the papers on the desk, letters, envelopes, postcards, rubber stamps, postage stamps, dollar bills with the truncated pyramid, the eye over it, and the Latin motto. . . . No, it is the substance of the graphic sign that is revealed as the true substance of the world, the flourish or arabesque or thread of dense, feverish, neurotic handwriting that replaces any other possible world. . . .

The world is transformed into line, a single line, broken, twisted, discontinuous. Man, too. And this man transformed into line is, in the end, master of the world, though he cannot escape his condition as prisoner, because, after many scrolls and curlicues, the line tends to close in on itself and entrap the man-line. But he is surely his own master, because he can construct or dismantle himself, segment by segment, and as a final way out he can commit suicide with two crisscrossed strokes of the pen, to discover that crossed-out death is made of the same substance as drawing-life, a movement of the pen on the page. Or else we can say that he always retains the supreme freedom of guiding the line in the least expected direction so that the drawing is no longer able to be closed. To draw a cube observing the rules of perspective, and then allow one corner to go off in a direction where it will never join up with the other corners: this incongruous corner contains the real proof of the existence of the "I," the *ergo sum*.

This consubstantiality of the drawn world and the "I" is only relative, however, because within it many universes open up, parallel and incompatible with one another. In one dimension, linear, threadlike figures move; in another, minutely decorated figures. A world without thickness is detached from a world that is all volume; a continent where everything is suggested by outlines and one where everything is shaded do not seem to have any meeting place. And so the universes are multiplied by the number of instruments and techniques and styles that can be used to give form to figures and signs.

But perhaps, deep down, the styles know they are not self-sufficient; perhaps each of them knows it exists only in contrast with every other possible style. The geometry-book cubes dream of the thickness of matter that has lived and suffered as "artist's cubes" have. And these, in their turn, dream of the diaphanous impassiveness of geometric diagrams. Abstract motifs dream of a figurative bed on which to consummate their loves: do you think a pattern of concentric circles drawn with a compass cannot be gripped by frenzied, amorous longing for a freehand spiral?

Steinberg's irresistible vocation—or, let's say, the historic mission to which he has been called—is to move in a space of limitless dimensions of the drawn and the drawable, to establish communication between the most contradictory stylistic universes, to make elements belonging to divergent figurative cultures or conventions of perception coexist within the horizon of the same page. A row of houses on the street, each of a different period and style, if it is to be depicted or even looked at, requires the employment of different graphic techniques. Just as the people who pass by on the sidewalk carry, each of them, the style of drawing that can portray their essence, a lighter or heavier pressure of the pen on the paper, the thickness of the ink, or the expanse of white that encloses their secret.

The countless and multiform ways of using pens and pencils and brushes are to be found on Steinberg's page, including the countless and multiform ways in which pens and pencils and brushes can portray pens and pencils and brushes. Until the moment comes when *the* pens make their entrance into the picture, and *the* pencils and *the* brushes in their presence as physical objects, an absolutely modest presence, but absolutely sure of being, of being *there*. Here, then, are Cavalcanti's *dismayed pens*, which return to testify in the first person the transfiguration of the artist in the practice of his art.

"Sometimes I think and imagine that among men there exists a single art and science, and that this is drawing or painting, and that all the others derive from it." This is Michelangelo speaking, in his *Roman Dialogues*, reported by a Portuguese artist of his times, Francisco de Holanda. "Certainly, in fact, if you soberly consider everything that is done in this life, you will realize that each of us, unaware, is painting this world, whether by creating and producing new forms in figures, or by wearing varied garments, whether by constructing and occupying space with buildings and painted houses, or by tilling the fields, adding colors and signs, working the earth, by sailing the seas, fighting and dividing legions, and finally by deaths and funerals, as also by all other operations, achievements, and actions."

These words of Michelangelo upset the relation between world and art. Here the world is not seen as an object portrayable by art and art as a portrayal of the world; a new horizon opens in which the living world is seen as a work of art and art proper is seen as art in the second degree or simply as part of the overall work. Everything man does is depiction, visual creation, spectacle. The world, marked by man's presence in its every part, is no longer nature: it is produced by our hands. A new anthropology is announced whereby every activity and production of man counts as visual communication in its linguistic and aesthetic aspects.

But is man the only one who tends to create forms and figures? Doesn't every animal have the same tendency, and every plant and inanimate thing, and thus the whole world, the universe? We could say, then, that man is an instrument the world employs to renew its own image constantly. The forms created by man, being always somehow imperfect and bound to change, guarantee that the world's appearance as we see it is not definitive, but a phase, working toward a future form.

So much for the world. And art? Art will be a reflection on forms, a hypothesis of visual formalizations of a virtual world, a criticism of the permanent world's fair in which we are involved, playing the triple role of exhibitors, exhibits, and audience.

These definitions all apply to the art of Steinberg. On the one hand, his drawing crosses the frontier between self and the world and invades space so that the draftsman finds himself caught in his drawing and the visitor to the exhibition is caught in the picture exhibited. On the other hand, a continuous "travel diary" assails with implacable irony the depicting world and the depicted world; every visual opportunity is carried to its extreme, paradoxical consequences; every contradiction of the plastic materials of our daily experience is exacerbated to the point of absurdity.

The past is added to the present in our cities like a collage of detailed engravings of objects overladen with ornaments in an old catalogue; they are enthroned over a sketch, done with the tip of the pen, of a street full of traffic. And the only image we can form of the future is marked by the visual mortgages that city planners and comic strips, cubo-futuro-constructivism and science fiction have deposited on it, which give a face to our anguish at what lies in store for us.

Line as the trace of movement, as delight in movement, as paradox of movement. Galileo Galilei, who deserves to be as famous for his happy invention of imaginative metaphors as for his strict scientific thinking, among the many metaphors with which he enlivens the discussions of the earth's movement around the sun in the *Dialogue Concerning the Two Chief World Systems*, uses one in which he speaks of a ship, a pen, and a line.

A ship leaves Venice bound for Alexandretta: imagine on the ship a pen that traces the course in a constant line that stretches across the eastern Mediterranean. (The reader can imagine a pen the size of the ship's rudder, drawing its line on a sea of paper; or else a very long strip of paper that crosses the Mediterranean and unrolls on the deck of the moving ship under a little pen that leaves its slender wake of ink.) This line will be a perfect arc of a circle, even if "sometimes more curved, sometimes less, as the vessel had gone more or less fluctuating": minimum inflections compared with the length of the line, just as the inflections would even be less perceptible if a hand holding the pen moved it this way and that during the voyage.

"And if a painter then, at our sailing from the port, had begun to draw on a paper with that pen, and had continued the drawing until Alexandretta, he would have been able to make by its motion a drawing of figures, perfectly surrounded on several sides with detailed landscapes, buildings, living creatures, and other things, though all the real, true, and essential movement traced out by the nib of that pen would have been no other than a very long but simple line. . . ."

The *true* line, corresponding to the movement of the ship, does not remain on the paper, because the grand movement of the ship is common also to the paper and the pen, while the small movements of the painter's hand leave their sign: those drawn during the voyage in the same way as if the ship were motionless. Galileo uses this example to demonstrate that, being on earth, we are not aware of earth's movement around the sun, because everything on earth shares in that same motion.

With this, the demonstration ends. But the image of the invisible line that the pen draws in absolute space, moving with the ship (or with earth)—a line whose signs left on the paper are only slight deviations and accidents—continues to enchant Galileo's imagination; he abandons himself to a kind of digression or caprice on the movements of the pen. He assigns this to another character in the dialogue, the Aristotelian Simplicio, who, unable to follow the strict logic of his Copernican interlocutors, can allow himself to pursue an image merely for the pleasure it affords him:

I have nothing else to say, and I was well-nigh transported with that delineation, thinking how those strokes drawn so many ways, hither, thither, upward, downward, forward, backward, and interwoven with thousands of turnings, are not essentially or really other than small pieces of one sole line drawn all one way, and with no other alteration than the shift of the straight line sometimes a shade to the right and to the left, and the movement of the tip of the pen, now faster and now slower, but with the minimum unevenness. And I consider how in the same way one would write a letter, and how these more fanciful writers, to show the lightness of their hand, without lifting their pen from the page, in a single line draw with a thousand turns a charming interweaving, if they were in a boat sailing rapidly, they would convert all the movement of the pen, which in essence is a single line drawn all toward the same direction and very slightly inflected or departing from perfect straightness, into a curlicue. . . .

The metaphysics of the absolute line and the inexhaustible acrobatics of the graphic gesture: thus Galileo heralds the sidereal comet Steinberg, who traces his orbit across the sky of paper.

In Memory
of Roland Barthes

La Repubblica, April 9, 1980.

One of the first details known about the road accident that took place on February 25 at the intersection of Rue des Ecoles and Rue Saint-Jacques was that Roland Barthes had been disfigured so that no one there—only two steps away from the Collège de France—was able to recognize him. The ambulance that took him to the Salpêtrière hospital considered him as "name unknown" (he had no documents on him), and as such he remained for hours unidentified in the ward.

In his last book, which I had read a few weeks before (*La Chambre claire: Note sur la photographie*), I had been struck above all by the wonderful pages about the experience of being photographed, on the discomfort of seeing one's own face become an object, and on the relationship between the image and oneself. So it was that in my concern for his fate one of my first thoughts was to remember what I had so recently read, and the frail and anguished link with his own features that had been suddenly torn as one tears up a photograph.

But on March 28, in his coffin, his face was not in the least disfigured. It was him as I had so often met him in the streets of the Quartier with a cigarette dangling from the corner of his mouth, in the manner of those who were young before the war (the historical aspect of the image, one of the many themes of *Chambre claire*, extends to the self-image that each of us offers in the course of his life); but it was fixed forever, and the pages from chapter five, which I went back and reread at once, now spoke to me of that, and only of that, of how the fixing of an image is death, and of the inner resistance one has to being photographed, and also of being resigned to it. "One might think that, in terror, the Photographer would have to fight enormously to prevent the Photograph from being Death. But I, already an object, I do not fight." An attitude that now seemed to reverberate in all that one managed to hear about him during the month he spent in the Salpêtrière, unable to speak.

(The real danger at once turned out to be not the fractures to the head but to the ribs. And then his worried friends immediately thought of another quotation: the one about the rib amputated in youth because of pneumonia and kept in a drawer until he decided to throw it away, in *Barthes par lui-même*.)

These journeys into memory are not coincidental. All of his work, I now realize, consists in forcing the impersonality of the mechanisms of language and knowledge to take into account the physical nature of the living, mortal subject. The critical discussion about him—which has already begun—will be between supporters of the one or the other Barthes: the one who subordinated everything to the rigor of a method, and the one whose only sure criterion was pleasure (the pleasure of the intelligence and the intelligence of pleasure). The truth is that these two Barthes are really one, and it is in the presence of these two aspects together— continuous and variously dosed—that we find the secret of the fascination that his mind exerted over many of us, which Umberto Eco explained very well here in *La Repubblica* on March 28.

That gray morning of the 28th, I was wandering around the desolate streets behind the hospital looking for the "amphitheatre" from which I had learned that Barthes's body would start on the journey to the country cemetery where his mother lay buried. There I met Greimas, who had also arrived early, and he told me about how he had first met Barthes in 1948 in Alexandria and had made him read Saussure and rewrite *Michelet*. For Greimas, the inflexible master of methodological rigor, there was no doubt whatever: the real Barthes was the Barthes of the semiological analyses, such as the *Système de la mode*, carried out as they are with discipline and precision. But the main point on which he disagreed with the necrologists of the newspapers concerned their attempts to bring definitions (such as "writer" or "philosopher") to bear on a man who eluded all classifications, because all that he had done in his life was done out of love.

The day before, François Wahl had called to tell me

the time of that private, almost secret ceremony, and had spoken of the *"cercle amoureux"* of young men and women that had gathered around the death of Barthes, a circle that was as if jealous and possessive of a grief that could tolerate no display other than silence. The stunned and speechless group whom I joined was mostly made up of youngsters. Among them were a few famous people, and I did recognize the bald pate of Foucault. The plaque on the building did not mention the university name "Amphitheatre," but called it the "Salle de Reconnaissance," so I understood that it must be the morgue. From behind white sheets hung all around the hall, a coffin would emerge from time to time, carried on the shoulders of bearers as far as the hearse and followed by a family of modest people, stumpy old women, each bunch identical with those of the funeral before, as if in some repetitive illustration of the uniform power of death. For us who were there for Barthes, waiting silent and motionless in the courtyard as if following the implicit command to reduce the signs of a funeral ceremony to a minimum, everything that met the eye in that courtyard enlarged its function as a sign: on every detail of that shabby rectangle I felt the acute gaze that had been engaged in discovering revealing glimmers in the photographs of *Chambre claire*.

And so now that I reread that book I find it all tends toward that journey, that courtyard, that gray morning. Because it was from a flash of recognition among the photographs of his recently dead mother that Barthes started on his meditations, as he tells us at length in the second part of the book: an impossible search for the presence of his mother, found at last in a photo of her as a child, an image that was "lost, distant, that did not resemble her, the photograph of a child I never knew," and one that is not reproduced in the book, so that we can never know the value that it took on for him.

A book on death, then? As his previous one (*Fragments d'un discours amoureux*) had been on love? Yes, but this is also a book on love, as is shown by a passage on the difficulty of avoiding the "weight" of one's own image, and the "meaning" to give to one's own face: "It is not indifference that removes the weight from the image—nothing more than an 'objective' automatic photograph can make you into a criminal individual under the eye of the police—but it is love, supreme love."

It was not the first time that Barthes had spoken about being photographed. In his book on Japan (*L'Empire des signes*), one of his lesser-known books though rich in the subtlest observations, he sees photos of himself published in Japanese newspapers and makes the extraordinary discovery that there is something indefinably Japanese about his look, which is explained by the habitual way of retouching photos in those parts, in which the pupils are made round and dark. This argument about the deliberate acts that superimpose themselves on our features—history, belonging to a certain culture, but above all the deliberateness with which someone else uses our image as an instrument—comes up again in *Chambre claire* in a passage on the power of *truquages subtils* in reproduction. A photo in which he had thought he recognized his grief at a recent death he found again on the cover of a satirical book directed against him; on that cover his face had become inexpressive and sinister.

My reading of this book and the death of the author have come too close on each other's heels for me to be able to separate them. But I must succeed in doing so in order to give an idea of what the book is: a progressive approximation to a definition of that particular kind of knowledge opened up by photography, an "anthropologically new object."

The reproductions in the book are chosen according to this way of thinking, which we might call "phenomenological." Speaking of the interest a photograph arouses in us, Barthes distinguishes one level, that of *studium*, or cultural participation in the information or the emotion the image conveys, and another, that of *punctum*, or the surprising, involuntary, and transfixing element that certain images communicate—certain images or, rather, certain details of images. The reading Barthes makes of the works of photographers, famous or anonymous, is always unexpected. It is very often physical details (hands, fingernails) or particulars of dress that he picks on to reveal their singularity.

As opposed to the recent theories of photography as a cultural convention, an artifice, a nonreality, Barthes stresses the "chemical" basis of the operation, the fact of a photograph's being a sign made by light rays emanating from something that exists, that is actually there. (This is the fundamental difference between photography and language, which is capable of speaking about things that are not. In the photograph we are looking at something that has been and is not there any more.

This is what Barthes calls the *"temps écrasé"* of photography.)

A book typical of Barthes, with its more speculative moments in which it seems that by dint of multiplying the meshes of his terminological network he will never extricate himself again, and the sudden illuminations like self-evident flashes that arrive as surprising and definitive gifts, *La Chambre claire* from the very first pages contains a statement of the method that has always been his: he refuses to define a "photographic universal" and decides to take into consideration only those photographs "that I was sure existed for me." "In this basically conventional debate between subjectivity and science, I arrived at this bizarre notion: why could there not be, in some way, a new science for every object. A *Mathesis singularis* (and no longer *universalis*)?"

This science of the uniqueness of every object that Roland Barthes continually approached with the instruments of scientific generalization, and at the same time with poetic sensitivity aimed at defining what is singular and unrepeatable (this aesthetic gnosiology or eudaemonism of understanding), is the great thing that he— I do not say *taught* us, because one can neither teach nor learn this—but showed us is possible. Or, at least, that it is possible to seek it.

The Bestiary
of Marianne Moore

La Repubblica, May 19, 1981.

I am sorry to say that I have never seen a mockingbird or heard one sing, but I am always glad when I meet one in the pages of American writers and poets, where this bird often appears as a garrulous and mysterious *spiritus loci*. I find mockingbirds in two of Marianne Moore's poems, one of which is of the kind I admire most in the work of this always admirable poet: that is, a snapshot of nature observed in a way that acquires a totally implicit moral meaning, as in an emblem.

The poem starts with three mockingbirds still too young to fly, waiting on a branch for their mother to come and feed them. In short lines and immediate images, Marianne Moore shows us these fledgling birds who are already as big as their mother but almost featherless, "feebly solemn," with their awkward movements and insatiable greed. The exactness of description Marianne Moore manages to get into her lines, with their complex metrical lightness and elaborate alliteration (for example, "toward the trim trio on the tree-stem"), succeeds in conveying a mass of information arranged around a perfectly precise subject—in this case the biological question of camouflage both visual (the plumage, which is grayish-black on the outside but has white stripes beneath the wings and tail) and above all sonic (with the various kinds of song that mingle with those of other birds).

When they are fed, the three young birds spread their wings and tails and become visible. Their mother realizes the danger of this, but though her voice has become harsh, as happens after hatching a brood, she manages to recover the musical warblings of a past season. Her voice

> comes back to one from
> the remote
>   unenergetic sun-
>   lit air before
> the brood was here. . . .

as if to ignore the presence of the nest and the nervous tension it implies for her. If there is a link between these events, it is not made explicit. There is just one adjective—"astute," said of the mother bird—that gives us a clue. And, in fact, a cat has seen them and is climbing up the tree. The youngsters, who do not know how to fly, shift along the branch; at that moment the mother flies at the cat and attacks it with her bayonet of a beak.

This ending combines two themes that Marianne Moore is particularly fond of. One is the contrast between the lightning instinct of the bird (the poem is called "Bird-Witted") and the way the cat behaves on the basis of a prudent, well-thought-out plan:

> the
> intellectual cautious-
> ly creeping cat.

Then the other theme is the courage and above all the uneconomical self-sacrifice of the mother, because saving her family meant exposing herself to even greater efforts ("by hope rewarded").

This is one of her shortest and simplest poems, which means that to understand it properly in all its implications might take a whole evening, even if one had a good book on ornithology at hand (and with a facing-page translation that would give one a start). But of the many ways of enjoying poetry this is one of the best, though not the only one.

The other poem with a mockingbird in it, "Virginia Britannia," is of the fuller, more complex, and more ramified type, in which I get a little lost. The subject matter is drawn not just from moral reflection and the observation of nature, but from a great number of books of widely differing kinds. In a mosaic of data and quotations Marianne Moore gives us a historical and biological description of Virginia, presenting us with the most various types of plant life and human destiny (the mockingbird is an image of this multiplicity). Dominant here as well is the sense of the pitilessness of life, both biological and human:

Like strangler figs choking
a banyan, not an explorer, no imperialist,
not one of us, in taking what we
pleased—in colonizing as the
saying is—has been a synonym for mercy.

If this is the background, we cannot be surprised at Marianne Moore's predilection for the theme of armor or the shield. Among the animals in her bestiary is an abundance of those equipped with shells or armor of some sort, such as the pangolin or scaly anteater "made graceful by adversities, con-/versities." (I imagine that "conversities" is a word coined for the occasion. Could it mean that the adversities are converted into ways of overcoming themselves?) But although she exalts them as models of exactitude, it seems that the poet does not wish to propose them as a model for humanity: man is the animal who manages to exceed his limitations by a process of unprogrammed creativity, simply because he is without any natural defenses.

I say "it seems" because with Marianne Moore things are never that simple. The mathematical exactitude of nature (for example, the birds' nests built "in parabolic concentric curves") and evolution's fondness for difficult and costly solutions are praised by Marianne Moore in comparison with the inaccurate calculations of human greed ("The Iconosphere").

What is certain (see "Armor's Undermining Modesty") is that if this poet is always fascinated by armored animals, because the image corresponds to some inescapable existential problem of hers, the solution she provides to the problem is clean contrary to the spectacular, warlike armor of which zoology gives us a great variety of examples (like illustrations of the Knights of the Round Table, which, as Marianne Moore points out, do not correspond to the historical truth: the knights must have gone around dressed like Roman soldiers).

The true armor must be moral. This is the point made in a fine essay by Randall Jarrell, who in his discussion of "Armor's Undermining Modesty" makes a remark that we may agree with even when applied to Marianne Moore's poetry in general: "I do not understand everything, but what I understand I like, and what I don't understand I like almost better."

The most eloquent poem on this subject ("His Shield") opens with a list of spiny creatures—hedgehog, porcupine, sea urchin, rhinoceros with horned snout. But for defense the poet's preference goes to the salamander skin. This was worn by the mythical Prester John, who reigned over a land of fabulous riches, yet "his shield was his humility" because "the power of relinquishing / what one would keep; that is freedom."

Her final word of advice in this poem is, believe it or not, "be dull": as depressing a moral as has ever been expressed. More depressing than repressive, even if a good dose of repression is not lacking in our poet. A thing of importance to her is what can "countenance continence." Maybe she identifies with "impassioned Handel" who "never was known to have fallen in love." In another of her famous poems, "The Jerboa," she speaks of the desert rat, admiring its ability to live on little and contrasting this with the excess of wealth in the Roman Empire.

Marianne Moore never speaks of herself or her state

of mind, but the prickly morality that constantly emerges from her lines gives us some idea of the life of this Missouri spinster, who lived much of her life with her mother (and her brother, an army chaplain) and at the same time was part of the most sophisticated literary avant-garde. What I mean is the inner struggle to forge psychological armor around her fragility, and a cheerful serenity based on a way of looking at things that was always both acute and on the alert. In photographs of her we can recognize a tough, mordacious old lady, all eyes (like her mockingbirds), and always winged with a broad-brimmed hat.

For some years she was a librarian at the New York Public Library, and, in common with all other writer-librarians, she was an omnivorous and encyclopedic reader. Her lines play host to a collage of quotations from books of all sorts, from zoology to heraldry, local history or biography, geographical magazines, explorers' memoirs, or treatises on economy in the use of steel.

In "Poetry," which is one of her statements on poetics, she replies to Tolstoy, who saw poetry in everything except "business documents and school-books," that anyone truly interested in poetry demands on the one hand "the raw material" and on the other "that which is . . . genuine."

Few poets can match Marianne Moore in combining on the same level both erudite bibliomania and the direct, instantaneous observation of a photographer of nature. Animals are the element common to these two opposing slopes in her territory. The imaginary animals of medieval bestiaries, the peculiarities of domestic fauna or exotic animals—all are equally interesting to her. In

"Sea Unicorns and Land Unicorns," or in "The Buffalo," the gamut runs from the mythical emblem to the zoological documentary. In "The Plumed Basilisk" and in "Elephants" it happens the other way around. I do not know Marianne Moore's translation of *The Fables of La Fontaine*, but I think they might be illuminating with regard to this matter. Anyway, what is important is the progression from animal life to moral life, as in Montale's poem "L'anguilla." (T. S. Eliot's bestiary is quite another thing. His delightfully rhymed forms are entirely at the service of theological allegory.)

In "The Frigate Pelican," "the unconfiding frigate-bird" teaches us the relationship with natural forces, whereas the other birds "blow back, allowing the wind to reverse their direction"; in the midst of this gliding of wings come the words *Festina lente*. And Marianne Moore follows this Latin motto, as it were in an attempt at translation, with a question: "Be gay / civilly?"

The snail, on the other hand, gives us a memorable lesson in poetic style: "contractability," modesty without adornment, holding to "the principle that is hid"; while even the absence of feet becomes "a method of conclusion." (I can't help recalling Francis Ponge's *Escargots*. He was another great zoo-moralist, though in comparison his work seems less concise.)

Animals help Marianne Moore to express her own antiromantic moral stance (man gazes at the moon, while the frigate bird is wary to stay clear of the python), which is antimoralizing (talking about snakes, she says: "The passion for setting people right is in itself an afflictive disease / Distaste which takes no credit to itself is best"). It is also antisophisticated ("Principally throat,

sophistication as it al- / ways has been—at the antipodes
from the init- / ial great truths"), antieconomical (Randall Jarrell says that she is moved only by useless labors
and difficulties faced for the sheer love of difficulty, like
the intricate shell of the nautilus), and antipompous because of its fierce renunciation and *amor fati*.

> as
> the sea in a chasm, struggling to be
> free and unable to be,
> in its surrendering
> finds its continuing

so the imprisoned bird tells us by his song that

> satisfaction is a lowly
> thing, how pure a thing is joy.

Her ideal (as in the poem "Propriety," with its
monosyllabic drumming) is a rightness and appropri-
ateness of words, rhythms, and images: a note in Brahms
and in the throat of a bird, the pecking of a woodpecker
as it goes "spiraling a tree— / up up up like mercury."

Man, the Sky, and
the Elephant

Preface to an Italian translation of Pliny's *Natural History*
(Turin: Einaudi, 1982).

In Pliny the Elder's *Natural History*, for the sheer
pleasure of reading, I would advise concentrating on
three books: the two that contain the main lines of his
philosophy, which are the second (on cosmography) and
the seventh (on man), and—as an example of his jumping back and forth between erudition and fantasy—the
eighth (on the animals of the earth). We can of course
find extraordinary pages everywhere. For example, in
the books on geography (III and VI), on aquatic zoology,
entomology, and comparative anatomy (IX and XI),
botany, agronomy, and pharmacology (XII and XXXII),
or on metals, precious stones, and the fine arts (XXXIII
and XXXVII).

Pliny has, I think, always been used chiefly for reference, both to find out what the ancients knew or thought they knew on any particular subject, and to pick up oddities and eccentricities. From this point of view one cannot neglect book I, the summary of the whole work, the interesting thing about which is the wealth of unexpected juxtapositions: "Fish that have a pebble in their heads; Fish that hide in winter; Fish that feel the influence of the stars; Extraordinary prices paid for certain fish." Or "Concerning the rose: 12 varieties, 32 drugs; 3 varieties of lily: 21 drugs; a plant born from one of its own tears; 3 varieties of narcissus: 16 drugs; a plant one dyes the seeds of so that it produces colored flowers; Saffron: 20 drugs; Where the best flowers grow; Which flowers were known at the time of the Trojan War; clothing that rivals flowers." Or yet again: "The nature of metals; Concerning gold; The amount of gold possessed by the ancients; The equestrian order and the right to wear gold rings; How many times has the equestrian order changed names?"

But Pliny is also a writer who deserves to be read at length for the calm movement of his prose, animated as it is by admiration for everything that exists and respect for the infinite variety of things.

We might perhaps distinguish a poetical-philosophical Pliny, with his feeling for the universe and his love of knowledge and mystery, from the Pliny who was a neurotic collector of data, an obsessive compiler who seems to think only of not wasting a single jotting in his mastodonic notebook. (In using written sources he was omnivorous and eclectic, but not without a critical sense. There were some things he accepted at face value, others that he simply recorded, and still others that he rejected as obvious fantasies. It is just that his method of evaluation appears to be very unstable and unpredictable.) But once we have recognized these two faces of Pliny, we have to admit immediately that he is always one and the same man, exactly as the world he aims to describe in all its variety of form is one and the same world. To achieve this aim, he did not hesitate to plunge into the endless number of existing forms, multiplied by the endless number of existing ideas about these forms, because forms and ideas had for him equal right to be part of natural history and to be examined by anyone looking into them for an indication of a higher "reason" that he was convinced they must contain.

The world is the eternal and uncreated sky, whose spherical, rotating face covers all terrestrial things (II. 2), but it is difficult to distinguish the world from God, who for Pliny (and the Stoic culture to which he belonged) is one God, not to be identified with any single portion or aspect of him, or with the crowd of characters on Olympus, though perhaps with the sun, the soul or mind or spirit of the sky (II. 13). At the same time, the sky is made of stars as eternal as he is; the stars weave the sky and yet are part of the celestial fabric: *aeterna caelestibus est natura intexentibus mundum intextuque concretis* (II. 30). But it is also air (both below and above the moon) that looks empty and diffuses the spirit of life here below, and produces clouds, thunder, hail, lightning, and storms (II. 102).

When we speak of Pliny, we never know to what extent we should attribute the ideas he expresses to the author himself. He is in fact scrupulous about inserting as little of himself as possible and sticking to what his sources tell him. This conforms to his impersonal concept of knowledge, which excludes individual originality. To try to understand what his sense of nature really is, and how much of it consists of the arcane majesty of principles and how much of the materiality of the elements, we have to cling to what is undeniably his own: the expressive substance of his prose. Look, for example, at the pages concerning the moon, where the tone of heartfelt gratitude for this "supreme heavenly body, the most familiar to those who live on earth, the remedy of darkness" ("*novissimum sidus, terris familiarissimum et in tenebrarum remedium*" [II. 41]), and for all that it teaches us with the rhythm of its phases and eclipses, joins with the agile functionality of the sentences to express this mechanism with crystal clarity. It is in the pages on astronomy in book II that Pliny shows himself to be something more than the compiler with an imaginative flair that he is usually taken for, and reveals himself as a writer possessing what was destined to be the chief quality of all great scientific prose: that of expounding the most complex subject with perfect clarity, while deriving from it a sense of harmony and beauty.

He does this without ever leaning toward abstract speculation. Pliny always sticks to the facts (what he considers to be facts or what others have considered to be such). He does not hold with an infinite number of worlds because the nature of this world is already hard enough to understand, and infinity would scarcely simplify the problem (II. 4). Nor does he believe in the music of the spheres, either as a din out of earshot or as inexpressible harmony, because "for us who are in

it, the world glides around both day and night in silence"
(II. 6).

Having stripped God of the anthropomorphic characteristics attributed by mythology to the immortals of
Olympus, Pliny is forced by the rules of logic to bring
God closer to man by means of the limits necessarily
imposed on His powers. In fact, God is less free than
man in one case, because He could not kill Himself even
if He wanted to. Nor does He have any power over the
past, over the irreversibility of time (II. 27). Like Kant's
God, He cannot come into conflict with the indepen-
dence of reason (He cannot prevent two plus two from
equaling four), but to define Him in these terms would
lead us astray from the natural immanence of His
identification with the forces of nature ("*per quae declar-
atur haut dubie naturae potentia idque quod deum vocemus* [II.
27]).

The lyrical or lyrical-philosophical tones dominant
in the earlier chapters of book II correspond to a vision
of universal harmony that does not take long to fall to
pieces. A considerable part of that book is devoted to
celestial prodigies. Pliny's science oscillates between the
intent to recognize an order in nature and the recording
of what is extraordinary or unique: and the second aspect
of it always wins out. Nature is eternal and sacred and
harmonious, but it leaves a wide margin for the emergence of inexplicable prodigious phenomena. What general conclusion ought we to draw from this? That we
are concerned with a monstrous order entirely composed of exceptions to the rule? Or else a set of rules so
complex it eludes our understanding? In either case, for

every fact an explanation must exist, even if for the time being this explanation is unknown to us: "All things of explanation that is uncertain and hidden in the majesty of nature" (II. 101), and, a little farther on, "*Adeo causa non deest*" (II. 115), "it is not the causes that are lacking"—a cause can always be found. Pliny's rationalism exalts the logic of cause and effect and at the same time minimizes it, for even if you find the explanation for facts, that is no reason for the facts to cease to be marvelous.

This last maxim concludes a chapter on the mysterious origin of the winds: the folds of mountains, the hollows of valleys that hurl back blasts of wind after the manner of an echo, a grotto in Dalmatia where one need only drop a light object to unleash a storm at sea, a rock in Cyrenaica that only has to be touched to raise a sandstorm. Pliny gives us many of these catalogues of strange facts unrelated to one another: on the effects of lightning on man, with its cold wounds (among plants, lightning spares only the laurel; among animals, the eagle, according to II. 146), on extraordinary rains (of milk, blood, meat, of iron or sponges of iron, of wool or bricks, according to II. 147).

And yet Pliny clears the ground of a lot of old-wives' tales, such as comets as omens (for example, he refutes the belief that a comet appearing between the pudenda of a constellation—was there anything the ancients did not see in the skies?—foretells an era of moral laxity: "*obscenis autem moribus in verendis partibus signorum*" [II. 93]). Still, each prodigy presents itself to him as a problem of nature, insofar as it is the reverse side of the norm. Pliny holds out against superstitions but cannot always recognize them, especially in book VII, where he deals with human nature. Even concerning easily observable facts he records the most abstruse beliefs. Typical is the chapter on menstruation (VII. 63–66), but it must be said that Pliny's views all accord with the most ancient religious taboos regarding menstrual blood. There is a whole network of traditional analogies and values that does not clash with Pliny's rationalism, almost as if the latter were based on the same foundations. Thus he is sometimes inclined to construct analogical explanations of the poetic or psychological type: "The corpses of men float face upward, those of women face down, as if nature wished to respect the modesty of dead women" (VII. 77).

On rare occasions Pliny reports facts vouched for by his own personal experience: "On guard duty at night in front of the trenches I have seen star-shaped lights shining on the soldiers' spears" (II. 101); "during the reign of Claudius we saw a centaur which he had had brought from Egypt, preserved in honey" (VII. 35); "I myself in Africa once saw a citizen of Tisdrus changed from a woman to a man on her wedding day" (VII. 36).

But for a tireless seeker such as he, a protomartyr of experimental science, destined to die asphyxiated by the fumes during the eruption of Vesuvius, direct observations occupy a minimal place in his work, and are on exactly the same level of importance as information read in books—and the more ancient these were, the more authoritative. All the same, to forestall criticism, he declares: "However, for most of these facts I would not vouch, preferring to go back to the sources to whom I turn in all doubtful cases, without ceasing to follow the Greeks, who are the most precise in their observations, as well as the most ancient" (VII. 8).

After this preamble Pliny feels free to launch into his famous review of the "prodigious and incredible" characteristics of certain foreign peoples, a passage that was to be so popular in the Middle Ages and even later, and to transform geography into a fairground of living phenomena. There are echoes of it in later accounts of *real* travels, such as those of Marco Polo. That the unknown lands on the fringes of the world should contain beings on the fringes of humanity should be no cause for wonder: the Arimaspi with a single eye in the middle of their foreheads, who contest the gold mines with the gryphons; the inhabitants of the forest of Abarimon, who run extremely swiftly on feet that point backward; the androgynous people of Nasamona, who assume alternate sexes during intercourse; the Tibii, who have two pupils in one eye and the image of a horse in the other. But the great Barnum presents his most spectacular acts in India, where one can find a people of mountain hunters who have the heads of dogs, and a race of jumping people with one leg only, who when they want to rest in the shade lie down and raise their single foot above their heads as a parasol. There is also a nomadic people with legs like snakes, and there are the Astomoi, who have no mouths and live by sniffing odors. Mixed in with these are pieces of information we now know to be true, such as the description of the Indian fakirs (whom he calls "gymnosophist philosophers"), or else things such as still provide us with those mysterious events we read about in the newspapers (where he talks about immense footprints, he could be referring to the

Yeti or Abominable Snowman of the Himalayas). Then there are legends destined to continue down through the centuries, such as that of the curing power of kings (King Pyrrhus, who cured disorders of the spleen by touching the patient with his big toe).

What emerges from all this is a dramatic notion of human nature as something precarious and insecure. The form and the destiny of man hang by a thread. Quite a number of pages are devoted to the unpredictability of childbirth, with the exceptional cases and the dangers and difficulties. This, too, is a frontier zone, for everyone who exists might very well not exist, or might be different, and it is *there* that it is all decided.

In pregnant women everything—for example, the manner of walking—has an influence on childbirth. If they eat oversalted food they will give birth to a child without nails; if they cannot hold their breath they will have more trouble in delivering; during childbirth even a yawn can be fatal, as a sneeze during coitus can cause a miscarriage. Compassion and shame come over one who considers how precarious is the origin of the proudest of living beings: often the smell of a lately extinguished lamp is enough to cause a miscarriage. And to think that from such a frail beginning a tyrant or a butcher may be born! You who trust in your physical strength, who embrace the gifts of fortune and consider yourself not their ward but their son, you who have a domineering spirit, you who consider yourself a god as soon as success swells your breast, think how little could have destroyed you! [VII. 42–44]

One can understand why Pliny was so popular in the Christian Middle Ages: "to weigh life in a just balance one must always remember human fragility."

The human race is a zone of living things that should

be defined by tracing its confines. Pliny therefore records the extreme limits reached by man in every field, and book VII becomes a kind of *Guinness Book of World Records*. They are chiefly quantitative records, such as strength in carrying weights, speed at running, acuteness of hearing or of memory, and so on, down to the size and extent of conquered territories. But there are also purely moral records—in virtue, generosity, and goodness. Nor is there a lack of curiosities—Antonia, wife of Drusus, who never spat; or the poet Pomponius, who never belched (VII. 80); or the highest price ever paid for a slave (the grammarian Daphnis cost seven hundred thousand sesterces, according to VII. 128).

Only about one aspect of human life does Pliny not feel inclined to quote records or attempt measurements or comparisons: happiness. It is impossible to say who is happy and who is not, since this depends on subjective and debatable criteria. (*"Felicitas cui praecipua fuerit homini, non est humani iudicii, cum prosperitatem ipsam alius alio modo et suopte ingenio quisque determinet"* [VII. 130]). If one is to look truth straight in the face, no man can be called happy, and here Pliny's anthropological survey reviews a whole rank of illustrious destinies (drawn mostly from Roman history) to show that the men most favored by fortune had to suffer unhappiness and mischance.

In the natural history of man it is impossible to include the variable that is destiny. This is the message of the pages Pliny devotes to the vicissitudes of fortune, to the unpredictability of the length of life, to the uselessness of astrology, and to sickness and death. The separation between the two forms of knowledge that astrology lumped together—the objectivity of calculable and predictable phenomena and the sense of individual existence as having an uncertain future—a separation that modern science takes for granted, can be found in these pages, but as a question not yet finally decided, so that exhaustive documentation is called for. In producing these examples Pliny seems to flounder a bit. Every event that has occurred, every biography, every anecdote can go to show that, if looked at from the point of view of someone living, life is not subject to either qualitative or quantitative judgment, and cannot be measured or compared with other lives. Its value is interior, all the more so because hopes and fears of another life are illusory. Pliny shares the opinion that after death begins a nonexistence equivalent to and symmetrical with that which came before birth.

This is why Pliny's attention is focused on the things of this world, the territories of the globe, heavenly bodies, animals, plants, and stones. The soul, to which any sort of survival is denied, can only enjoy being alive in the present, if it withdraws into itself. "*Etenim si dulce vivere est, cui potest essere vixisse? At quanto facilius certiusque sibi quemque credere, specimen securitas antegenitali sumere experimento!*": "To mold one's own peace of mind on the experience of before birth!" (VII. 190). In other words, we must project ourselves into our own absence, the only certain thing before we came into this world or after death. Hence the pleasure of recognizing the infinite variety of what is other than us, all of which the *Natural History* parades before our eyes.

If man is defined by his limitations, should he not also be defined by the points at which he excels? In book VII Pliny feels bound to include the praise of man's virtues and the celebration of his triumphs. Turning to Roman history as the exemplar of every virtue, he gives way to the temptation to reach a pompous conclusion in praise of the Empire by finding the zenith of human perfection in the person of Caesar Augustus. In my opinion, however, the characteristic note in his treatment is not this, but the hesitant, limitative, and disenchanted note, which best suits his temperament.

Here we can discern the questions that arose when anthropology was becoming a science. Should anthropology attempt to escape from a "humanistic" point of view to attain the objectivity of a science of nature? Do the men of book VII matter more, the more they are "other" and different from us, and perhaps most if they are no longer or not yet men at all? And is it really possible that man can emerge from his own subjectivity to the point of taking himself as an object of scientific knowledge? The moral that echoes back and forth in Pliny suggests caution and reservation: no science can illuminate us concerning happiness or fortune, the distribution of good and bad, or the values of existence. Each individual, when he dies, takes his secrets with him.

On this cheerless note Pliny might well have ended his dissertation, but he prefers to add a list of discoveries and inventions, both historical and legendary. Anticipating those modern anthropologists who maintain that there is continuity between biological evolution and technological evolution, from Paleolithic tools to electronics, Pliny implicitly admits that what man has added to nature becomes part of human nature. To demonstrate that man's true nature is his culture is only a step away. But Pliny, who has no time for generalizations, looks for what is specifically human in inventions and customs that might be considered universal. According to Pliny (or his sources) there are three cultural matters on which all peoples have reached a tacit agreement ("*gentium consensus tacitus*" [VI. 210]). These are the alphabet (both Greek and Latin), the shaving of men's beards, and the measurement of time by means of a sundial.

This triad could scarcely be more bizarre, given the incongruity between the three terms—alphabet, barber, and sundial—or, for that matter, more debatable. The fact is that not all peoples have similar ways of writing, nor is it true that everyone shaves; and as for the hours of the day, Pliny himself launches into a brief history of the various ways of subdividing time. But here we wish to stress not the "Eurocentric" viewpoint, which is not peculiar to Pliny or to his own age, but, rather, the direction he is taking. For the attempt to put a finger on the elements that are constantly repeated in the most diverse cultures, in order to define what is specifically human, was destined to become one of the principles of modern ethnology. And having established this point of *gentium consensus tacitus*, Pliny can conclude his treatise on the human race and pass on to other animate creatures.

Book VIII, which makes a general survey of the animals of the world, begins with the elephant, to which the longest chapter is devoted. Why is priority given to the elephant? Because it is the largest of the animals, certainly (Pliny's treatment proceeds according to an order of importance that often coincides with physical size), but also and above all because, spiritually, it is the animal "closest to man"! *"Maximum est elephas proximumque humanis sensibus"* is the opening of book VIII. In fact, the elephant—he explains immediately afterward—recognizes the language of his homeland, obeys orders, remembers what he learns, knows the passion of love and the ambition of glory, practices virtues "rare even among men," such as probity, prudence, and equity, and has a religious veneration for the sun, the moon, and the stars. Not one word (apart from that single superlative, *maximum*) does Pliny spend on describing this animal (which is, however, accurately portrayed in Roman mosaics of the time). He simply relates the legendary curiosities that he had found in books. The rites and customs of elephant society are represented as those of a people with a culture different from ours, but nonetheless worthy of respect and understanding.

In the *Natural History* man is lost in the middle of the multiform world, the prisoner of his own imperfection; yet, on the one hand, he has the relief of knowing that even God is limited in His powers ("*Inperfectae vero in homine naturae praecipus solacia, ne deum quidem posse omnia*" [II. 27]), while, on the other hand, his next-door neighbor is the elephant, who can serve him as a model on the spiritual plane. Between these two vast presences, both imposing and benign, man certainly appears cut down to size, but not crushed.

After the elephant, as in a childhood visit to the zoo, the review of the world's animals passes on to the lion, the panther, the tiger, the camel, the giraffe, the rhinoceros, and the crocodile. Then, following an order of decreasing dimensions, he goes on to the hyena, the chameleon, the porcupine, the animals that live in burrows, and even snails and lizards. The domestic animals are all lumped together at the end of book VIII.

Pliny's main source is Aristotle's *Historia animalium*, but he also goes to more credulous or fanciful authors for legends that the Stagirite rejected, or reported only to confute them. This is the case both with information about the better-known animals and with the mention of imaginary animals, the catalogue of which is interwoven with that of the real ones. Thus, while speaking of elephants, he makes a digression informing us about dragons, their natural enemies; in connection with wolves (though criticizing the credulity of the Greeks), he records the legends of the werewolf. It is in this branch of zoology that we find the amphisbaena, the basilisk, the catoblepa, the crocoti, the corocoti, the leukocroti, the leontophont, and the manticore, all destined to pass from these pages into the bestiaries of the Middle Ages.

The natural history of man is extended into that of animals throughout book VIII, and this not only because the knowledge recorded is to a large extent concerned with the rearing of domestic animals and the hunting of wild ones, as well as the practical use man makes of the one and the other, but also because what Pliny is doing is taking us on a guided tour of the human imagination. An animal, whether real or imaginary, has a place of honor in the sphere of the imagination. As soon as it is named it takes on a dreamlike power, becoming an allegory, a symbol, an emblem.

It is for this reason that I recommend to the reader who is wandering through these pages to pause not only at the most "philosophical" books (II and VII), but also at VIII, as the most representative of an idea of nature that is expressed at length in all the thirty-seven books of the work: nature as external to man, but not to be separated from what is most intrinsic to his mind—the alphabet of dreams, the code book of the imagination, without which there is neither thought nor reason.

Cyrano on the Moon

La Repubblica, December 24, 1982.

At the time when Galileo was clashing with the Holy Office, a Parisian supporter of his proposed an interesting heliocentric model of the universe: it was made like an onion that, "protected by a hundred thin layers that surround it, preserves the precious germ from which ten million other onions will have to derive their essence. . . . The embryo, in the onion, is the little sun of this little world, which warms and nourishes the vegetative salt of the entire mass."

With those millions of onions we pass from the solar system to the system of infinite worlds propounded by Giordano Bruno. All these celestial bodies, in fact, "which one sees or does not see, suspended in the blue of the universe, are only the foam of suns that are being cleansed. For how could these great fires subsist if they were not fed by some other matter that nourishes them?"

This foaming process is not so very different from the way we now explain the condensation of the planets out of the primordial nebulus, and the stellar masses that contract and expand: "every day the sun discharges and purges itself of the leftovers of the matter that fuels its fire. But when it has totally consumed all the matter that it is composed of, it will expand on every side to seek new nourishment, and will spread to all the worlds it has already created, and especially to those nearest to it. Then that great fire, recasting all these bodies, will launch them, as before, in all directions, and, having been purified little by little, will begin to act as a sun to these other planets which it will generate by hurling them out of its own sphere."

As for the motion of the earth, it is the rays of the sun that, "striking it with their rotation, make it spin as we make a globe spin by striking it with a hand"; or else it is the vapors of the earth itself that, "struck by the cold of the polar regions, fall upon it, and not being able to strike it other than sideways, make it turn around in this manner."

This imaginative cosmographer was Savinien de Cyrano (1619–55), better known as Cyrano de Bergerac, and the work I have quoted from is *The Other World, or States and Empires of the Moon*. A forerunner of the science-fiction writer, Cyrano nourished his fantasies on the scientific knowledge of his time and the traditions of magic during the Renaissance, and in so doing he hit on things that we are only able to appreciate three centuries later for what they were: for example, the movements of astronauts without gravity (accomplished by means of little bottles of dew that is then attracted by the sun), multistage rockets, and "sounding books" (one winds up the mechanism, places a needle on the chapter one wants, and listens to the sounds emitted by a kind of mouth).

His poetic imagination derives from cosmic feelings that lead him to evoke the sentiments of Lucretian atomism. Thus he extols the unity of all things, living or inanimate, and even Empedocles's four elements are reduced to one only, with the atoms sometimes more rarefied, sometimes less so. "You marvel at how this matter, mixed together at random, at the mercy of chance, could have created a man, seeing that so many things were needed for the construction of his being, but you do not know that this matter, while it was on the way to forming a man, has a hundred million times stopped to form now a stone, now lead metal, now some coral, now a flower, now a comet, on account of the too many or too few figures needed to plan a man." This combination of elemental figures determing the variety of living forms connects Epicurean science with the genetics of DNA.

Ways of going to the moon provide a sample of Cyrano's inventiveness. The patriarch Enoch binds two vases under his armpits, filled with the smoke from a sacrifice that must ascend to heaven; the prophet Elijah makes the same journey by getting into an iron ship and hurling a magnetic ball into the air. As for Cyrano himself, having rubbed an ointment made of ox marrow on the bruises sustained in previous attempts, he feels himself rising toward the satellite because the moon tends to suck up the marrow of animals.

Among other things, the moon contains paradise, which is improperly called "earthly," and Cyrano lands right on the Tree of Life, getting his face smeared with one of the famous apples. As for the serpent, after original sin God relegated it to within the body of man: it is the intestine, a serpent coiled upon itself, an insatiable animal that dominates man, causes him to obey its wishes, and rends him with its invisible teeth.

This explanation is given by the prophet Elijah to Cyrano, who is unable to resist a salacious variation on the theme. The serpent is also the thing that emerges from the loins of man and stretches toward woman, there to spurt out its poison and cause a swelling which lasts nine months. But these jokes of Cyrano's are not in the least pleasing to Elijah, and after one impertinence even greater than the rest, he chases him out of Eden. Which shows that in this entirely jocular book, some jokes are supposed to be taken as the truth and others are said only in fun, even if it is not easy to tell them apart.

After his expulsion from Eden, Cyrano visits the cities of the moon. Some are mobile, with houses on wheels that can change their site according to the season of the year, whereas others are sedentary, screwed to the ground into which they can sink in winter to escape inclement weather. As a guide he has a character who has been on earth a number of times in various centuries: the "demon of Socrates" of whom Plutarch wrote. This knowledgeable spirit explains why the moon men not only abstain from eating meat, but have particular regard for vegetables as well. They only eat cabbages that have died a natural death, because to decapitate a cabbage is to murder it. There is nothing to tell us, in fact, that since the Fall men have been any dearer to God than cabbages are, or that the latter are not endowed with sensitivity and beauty and are made more in the image of God. "If, therefore, our souls are no longer portraits of him, we no more resemble him in our hands, feet, mouths, foreheads, and ears than cabbages do in their leaves, flowerets, stalks, cores, and heads." As for intelligence, although he admits that cabbages do not have an immortal soul, he suggests they may have a share in a universal intellect, and if nothing of their hidden knowledge has come through to us, maybe it is only because we are not up to the task of receiving the messages they send us.

Intellectual and poetical qualities are combined in Cyrano in a way that makes him literally an extraordinary writer, whether in seventeenth-century France or in absolute terms. Intellectually he is a "libertine," a polemicist involved in a brawl that was at that time sending the old world-view up in smoke. He took sides with Gassendi's "sensism" and the astronomy of Copernicus, but he was nourished above all by the "natural philosophy" of sixteenth-century Italy: Cardano, Bruno, and Campanella. (As for Descartes, in the *Journey to the States of the Sun*, which forms a sequel to the journey to the moon, Cyrano made contact with him in an Empyrean reminiscence of Tommaso Campanella, and went to him with a fraternal embrace.)

From a literary point of view he is a Baroque writer.

His "letter" contain *tours de force*, such as his "Description of a Cypress," of which one could well say that the style and the object described become one and the same thing. Above all he is a *writer* through and through, less interested in expounding a theory or defending a thesis than in setting in motion a merry-go-round of inventions equivalent on the level of imagination and language to what the "new philosophy" and the new science were doing on the level of thought. In his *Other World* it is not the coherence of ideas that matters, but the delight and the freedom with which he makes use of all the intellectual stimuli that please him. This is the beginning of the *conte philosophique*—not a "story" with a thesis to demonstrate, but one in which ideas appear and disappear and tease one another in turn, for the pleasure of one who has enough familiarity with them to be able to be playful with them even when he takes them seriously.

Cyrano's journey to the moon could in some ways be said to herald *Gulliver's Travels*. On the Moon, as in Brobdingnag, the visitor finds himself among beings far larger than he is, who put him on show as a strange little animal. In the same way, the series of misadventures and meetings with characters of paradoxical wisdom are a foretaste of the wanderings of Voltaire's *Candide*. But Cyrano's literary fame came late. This book was published posthumously, mutilated by the censorship of timorous friends, and only saw the light in its entirety in our own century. Meanwhile, he had already been rediscovered in the Romantic age. First Charles Nodier, then (and above all) Théophile Gautier, on the basis of a widespread tradition, drew the outlines of the poet-swordsman and joker, which the excellent Rostand then transformed into his highly successful verse drama.

But in fact Savinien de Cyrano was neither a nobleman nor a Gascon, but a middle-class Parisian. The title "de Bergerac" he added himself, from the name of a property belonging to his lawyer father. As for his famous nose, it is likely that he really had it, for in this book we find a eulogy of noses worthy of consideration; though such a eulogy belongs to a genre common enough in the Baroque period, it is unlikely to have been written by someone with a tiny snub nose. (The inhabitants of the moon tell the time by using a natural sundial composed of their long noses, which project their shadows onto the "dial" of their teeth.)

But it is not only noses that are flaunted. Though an aristocratic moon man goes about naked, he wears a belt with a phallus-shaped bronze object hanging from it.

"This custom seems to me very extraordinary," I said to my young host, "because as a sign of nobility in our world it is customary to wear a sword." But he, without getting ruffled, exclaimed: "My little man, what fanatics the great men of your world are, to make a show of an instrument that indicates an executioner, made solely to destroy us, the sworn enemy of all that live, and on the other hand to hide a member without which we would be in the situation of that which is not, the Prometheus of every animal, and the tireless redresser of the shortcomings of nature! Luckless is that country in which the symbols of procreation are the objects of shame, while the agents of destruction are honored! And yet you call that member your pudendum, or shameful part, as if there were anything more glorious than creating life, or anything more atrocious than taking it away."

This shows that Rostand's bellicose swordsman was in fact an adept at "making love, not war," although still sharing a procreative urge that in our contraceptive age we cannot avoid thinking of as obsolete.

By Way of
an Autobiography

Grand Bazaar (Milan), September–October 1980.

You ask me for a biographical note—something
that always embarrasses me. Biographical data, even
those recorded in the public registers, are the most private things one has, and to declare them openly is rather
like facing a psychoanalyst. At least I imagine so: I have
never had myself psychoanalyzed.

I will start by saying that I was born under the sign
of Libra, so that in my charac   equilibrium and un-
balance mutually correct each other's excesses. I was
born when my parents were about to come home after
years spent in the Caribbean; hence the geographical
instability that makes me forever long for somewhere
else.

My parents' knowledge was all concentrated on the

vegetable kingdom, its marvels and its virtues. Attracted by another kind of vegetation, that of the written word, I turned my back on what they might have taught me; but wisdom in what is human also remained foreign to me.

I grew up from infancy to youth in a town on the Riviera, huddled in its microclimate. Both the sea contained in its gulf and the massive mountains seemed to me protective and reassuring. I was separated from Italy by a narrow strip of coast road, and from the world by a nearby frontier. To leave that shell was for me to repeat the trauma of birth, but I only realize that now.

Having grown up in times of dictatorship, and being overtaken by total war when of military age, I still have the notion that to live in peace and freedom is a frail kind of good fortune that might be taken from me in an instant.

Given this incentive, politics took up perhaps too great a part of the preoccupations of my youth. I mean too great for me, for what contribution I might have made, since things that seem distant from politics count far more as influences on the history (even political) of countries and of people.

As soon as the war was over, I felt the call of the big city more strongly than that of my provincial roots. I found myself hesitating for a while between Turin and Milan. My choice of Turin certainly had its own reasons and was not without consequences. Now I have forgotten both reasons and consequences, but for years I told myself that if I had chosen Milan, everything would have been quite different.

I set my hand to the art of writing early on. Publishing was easy for me, and I at once found favor and understanding. But it was a long time before I realized and convinced myself that this was anything but mere chance.

Working in a publishing house, I spent more time with the books of others than with my own. I do not regret it: everything that is useful to the whole business of living together in a civilized way is energy well spent. From Turin, a city that is serious but sad, it often happened that I would slip down to Rome. (Incidentally, the only Italians I have ever heard speak of Rome in other than negative terms are the Turinese.) And so Rome is probably the Italian city where I have lived longest, without ever asking myself why.

The ideal place for me is the one in which it is most natural to live as a foreigner. Therefore, Paris is the city where I found my wife, set up home, and raised a daughter. My wife is a foreigner, too, and when the three of us are together, we talk in three different languages. Everything can change, but not the language that we carry inside us, like a world more exclusive and final than one's mother's womb.

I realize that in this autobiography I have dwelt chiefly on the subject of birth, and talked about the later stages as of a continuation of my first seeing the light; and now I tend to go even further back, to the prenatal world. This is the risk run by every autobiography felt as an exploration of origins, like that of Tristram Shandy, who dwells on his antecedents and, when he gets to the point of having to begin to recount his life, finds nothing more to say.